Alexis Jean Fournier

In the Mainstream

In the Mainstream: The Art of Alexis Jean Fournier (1865-1948)

Rena Neumann Coen

N S NORTH STAR PRESS St. Cloud, MN

ACKNOWLEDGEMENTS

Many people have helped to make this book possible through their generous sharing of information, warm hospitality on research trips, help with introductions to Fournier collectors, and, in general, for unfailing support and encouragement throughout the process of research and writing.

I must first thank Allan Bartlett, Director of The Beard Art Gallery, Inc. of Minneapolis, who first suggested that I organize an exhibition of Alexis Jean Fournier's paintings and write a book about the artist. This book is, in no small part, a result of his unflagging enthusiasm for Fournier's work and his dedication to the task of making the artist better known to the public.

Others in the Twin Cities of Minneapolis and St. Paul who helped in various ways and to whom I am much indebted are Richard Beard Thomson, Chairman of the Beard Art Gallery, Inc.; Gerald Czulewicz of Antiques Americana; Jeffrey Hess, Historical Consultant; Tom O'Sullivan, Curator of the Minnesota Historical Society; Teresa Trembath of Teresa Berg Trembath, Inc.; and Wesley and Leon Kramer of Kramer Gallery, Inc.

In South Bend, Indiana I am grateful for the valuable help of Judy Oberhausen, Curator of the Art Center, Inc. of South Bend; Harold Zisla, Chairman of the Art Department of the University of Indiana in South Bend, and Doreen Zisla. In East Aurora, N.Y. Robert Rust, Director of the Roycrofters, Kitty Turgeon and Edward Godfrey were most helpful, as were Dr. Edna M. Lindemann, Director of the Burchfield Center, Western New York Forum for American Art at State University College at Buffalo, and Michael L. James of Buffalo, New York.

Alexis Jean Fournier's stepson, Edwin Lawrence and his wife, Doris Lawrence were gracious hosts in St. Petersburg, Florida. They made "Alex" a real person to me, a convivial and charming man who always took his art seriously, but never himself. He was a person I would have liked to have known.

Dr. Brucia Witthoft of Massachusetts State College at Framingham carefully read an early stage of the manuscript and made several excellent suggestions for its improvement. Professor William H. Gerdts, Chairman of the Graduate Art History Program, the City University of New York, also offered perceptive and cogent advice for the improvement of the manuscript. To both of these scholars I am deeply grateful for their generous gift of time and expert knowledge.

To all the Fournier collectors who helped so much I owe a special thanks for showing me their paintings, bearing with my many questions, aiding in the process of having their paintings photographed, and for courtesy and kindness every step of the way.

Last but not least, Jody Derosier helped immeasurably at a critical stage of putting this book together. To her and all the others, thank you.

Rena Neumann Coen
February, 1985

International Standard Book Number: 0-87839-041-3

 Printed in the United States of America. Published by North Star Press, P.O. Box 451, St. Cloud, Minnesota 56302.

Dedicated to
Ed

Contents

List of Plates

Unless otherwise noted, the works listed are by Alexis Jean Fournier. In the measurements, height precedes width.

In the Mainstream

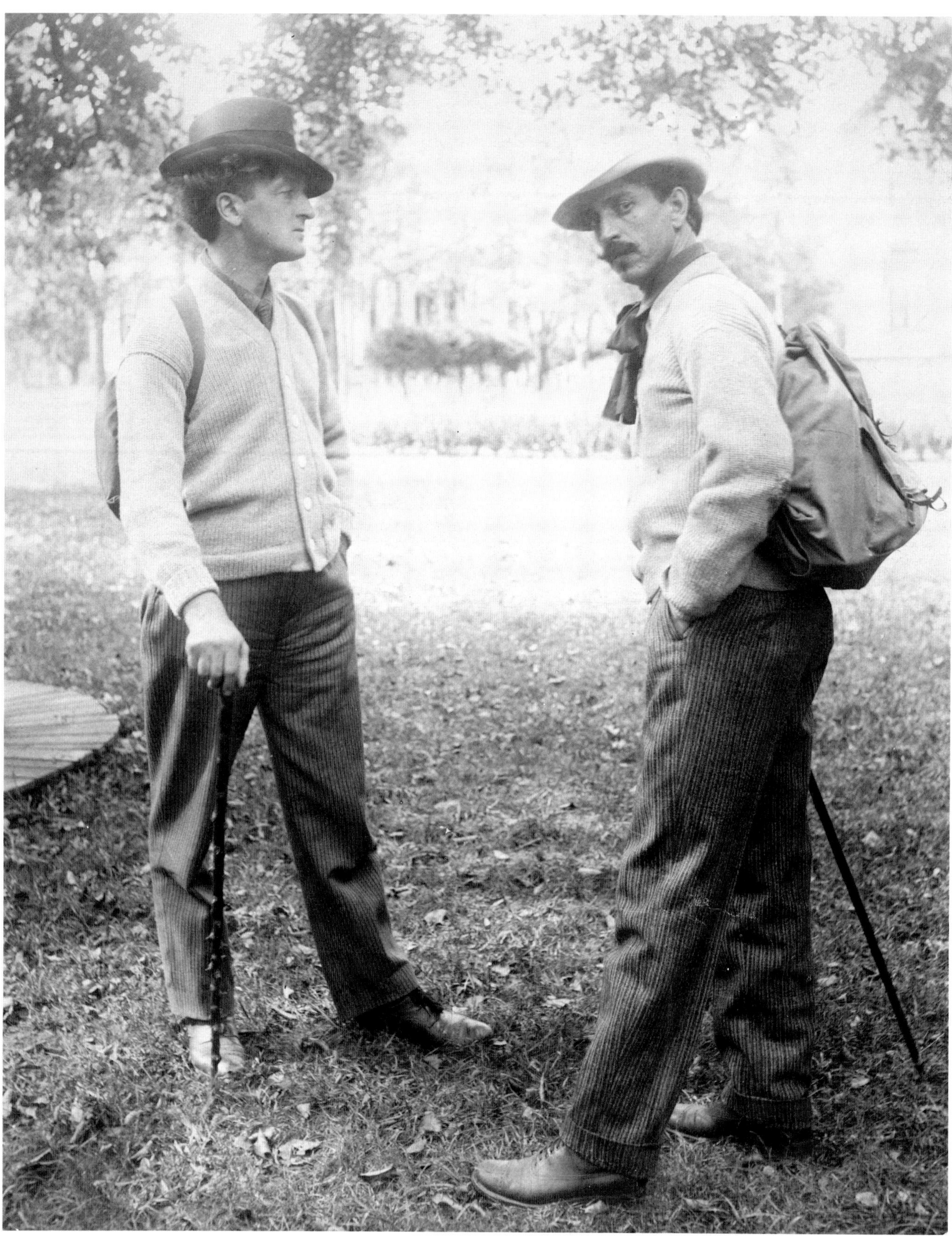

Chapter 1 October Vagabonds

At sun-up on October 1, 1908, two friends set out on a walking trip from the western New York village of East Aurora to New York City some 300 miles away. It was an adventure entirely in keeping with the personalities and interests of the two men who started out that day, for both of them were lovers of nature who had made careers of celebrating the out-of-doors, one with the pen and the other with the paintbrush (Fig. 1). One of them was Richard Le Gallienne, English journalist, poet, novelist, bon vivant and professional guest, a man of style, wit, charm and a way with words. The other was Alexis Jean Fournier, also charming, witty, in love with life and possessed of a considerable talent as a landscape painter. Le Gallienne and Fournier undertook their walking tour through New York State eager to observe nature in her many moods and to record them each in his own medium. "There's music in the singing of a reed, if men had ears," said Le Gallienne, quoting Lord Byron, and the two men were prepared to give ear to that music. They were also, characteristically, expecting to enjoy themselves, while listening to nature's song, breathing the clear autumn air, entertaining each other with talk and banter and reveling in the sense of freedom such a tour provided.

Like the dying summer itself, which the two hikers were seeking to prolong as far as possible, the accomplishments of both men represented a waning season of style and taste, a look backward toward a tradition that was quickly vanishing before the onslaught of the avant-gard trends that were beginning to make themselves felt in American artistic circles. In the small volume called *October Vagabonds*, in which Le Gallienne later described his walking tour with Fournier, he wrote, perhaps more symbolically than he was aware, that "summer was beginning to pack up, the great stage carpenter was about to change the scene, and the great theatre was full of echoes and sighs and sounds of farewell."[1] These farewells applied not only to the end of a season but also to the artistic styles of both men, styles which clung to lingering nineteenth century attitudes in a new century ill disposed to receive them. Nevertheless, those values and styles *did* survive, submerged for a while, like nature's own seasons, but never extinguished. Yielding briefly to the machine oriented art and to the many abstract and non-representational styles of the modern era, the figural, nature-based art that Fournier practiced, would rise again in the 1970's and 80's to proclaim once more the primacy of nature over the machine and the compelling force of the artist's communion with the outdoor world.

The walking tour of the October vagabonds was never completed. Proving as elusive as Le Gallienne's life-long quest for fame and fortune, their goal fell short of completion at the village of Towanda, not far from Scranton, Pennsylvania. There Le Gallienne fell ill (though in his book he imputed that illness to his companion). On the advice of a physician, the two friends reluctantly abandoned their walk and completed their journey in a railroad train—"shot into New York like a package through a tube" as Le Gallienne ruefully put it.[2] Though the machine had temporarily triumphed over nature, the two men resolved to try once more the following year, to start again where they had left off on the bank of the Susquehanna, watching "great fishes gliding through the dreamy water, and the mud turtle with her trail of little ones moving from rock to rock."[3] Though Le Gallienne soon recovered, other interests and events intervened and he and Fournier never resumed their walk through the natural beauty of New York state.

Le Gallienne's book is more than just a charming reminiscence. For us its significance lies not only in the vivid and loving description of New York State's western woods, hills and meadows, but also in the writer's account of his first encounter with the artist, whom he calls "Colin." For though Le Gallienne was British, he was enamored of America and spent much of his life there. His portrayal of "Colin" encapsulates America's attitude toward the artist, that beau ideal of the romantic genius, too absorbed in his own creative dream to care much about the "real" world of business and commerce. If a foreign, especially French, appearance flavored the dress and features of the artist, so much the better, for it was consonant with the essentially un-American activity of seeking art before practical success.

Encountering, one morning, a stranger seated calmly in the writer's own accustomed place in the woods near his home, Le Gallienne describes him as an incongruous apparition in the American woodland. "How on earth," he asks, "did this picturesque waif from the Quartier Latin come to stray so far away from the Boul' Miche! For the little boyish figure of a man that sat sketching in my place was the Frenchiest looking Frenchman you ever saw—with his dark, smoke-dried skin, his long, straight, blue-black hair, his fine, rather ferocious brown eyes, his long, delicate French nose, his bristling black moustache and short, string-shaped imperial. He wore on his head a soft white felt hat, somewhat of the shape affected by circus clowns. His coat was of green velveteen corduroy and he wore knickerbockers of an eloquent plaid."[4] Consciously or not, Le Gallienne was portraying the stereotypical nineteenth century American image of the artist-hero, picturesque, elegant and exotic.

Le Gallienne's sympathetic description of his artist friend is consistent also with the assumption, which then prevailed in American society, that what the artist produces is less significant than his personal role as society's mentor in the appreciation of the finer, more spiritual aspects of life. While the rest of the world tends to the necessary business of getting and spending, pre-occupied with the frequently sordid requirements for survival, the artist, all sensitivity and soul, represents the impulse toward culture and civilization. In such matters the artist serves as society's alter ego, for his life, even if unsuccessful in the business sense (perhaps especially if unsuccessful), proves that his goals are different from those of ordinary people, focused as they are on purer and higher objectives. "Not how is the idea expressed in stone or on canvas is the question," wrote the New England philosopher, Thoreau, "but how far it has obtained form and expression in the life of the artist."[5]

Thoreau was, in fact, voicing the Transcendentalist view that art, and even more the artist's life, could lead one to a clearer understanding of the beauties of nature and of nature's God. The artist, inspired by a special communion with God and nature, translated his own unique vision into the visible, tangible forms that could be comprehended by ordinary mortals. Of course the artist might have to use material techniques to express his vision of the natural world, but his imagination and intellect were more important than his technical skills. His role was to provide an intellectual and imaginative channel, conveying beauty and appreciation of nature directly from the Divine Spirit to the human observer. Though that Spirit held nature superior to art, it nevertheless valued art as the highest tribute man could pay to nature's God. Through the vocation of the artist, and especially it would seem, the landscape painter, others too could become sensitive to nature and thereby reach a more complete unity with the Supreme Being. However, the artist's life, if lived according to natural laws, was far more valuable than his acquisition of technical mastery in schools or academies. The artist's talent, wrote Elizabeth Palmer Peabody, was a treasure conferred directly by God, as a consequence of which "the Artist must himself become the masterpiece which the Creator of Man had in His idea when he breathed into him a living soul."[6]

If there seemed to be a contradiction between the image of the artist as an exotic, vaguely foreign hero and the artist as a natural man, the conflict could be resolved by the assumption that though the artist was indeed a divinely inspired interpreter of nature, he was, because of his genius, different from ordinary mortals and exempt from ordinary rules. Therefore he could be excused and even admired for his unconventional appearance and unbusiness-like vocation. Nevertheless, it was constantly emphasized by these New England writers that, though the *results* of the artist's work were limited according to his technical skills, the significance of his artistic soul was not. When Le Gallienne described his first encounter with the artist in the woods, in "a paradise of every sauntering vine and splendid, saucy weed,"[7] it was not the painting taking shape on the easel that aroused his admiration so much as the totality of the artist's emotional response to the scene in front of him. "Here was a man whose soul was evidently—color. There was a look on his face as if he could just eat those oranges and purples and soft greens; and there was a sort of passionate assurance in the way in which he handled his brushes, and delicately plunged them here and there in his colour box, that spoke a master. So intent was he upon his work that, when I came up behind him, he seemed unaware of my presence; though his oblivion was actually the conscious indifference of a landscape painter, accustomed to the ambling cow and the awe-struck peasant looking over his shoulder as he worked."[8]

The walking tour of the October vagabonds is also significant in that it embodied America's reverence for its own land, a reverence voiced particularly clearly in the nineteenth century. Indeed, this veneration of the American wilderness endowed the rural scene with a quasi-religious significance, stimulated, but by no means confined to, New England Transcendentalism. "The groves were God's first temples," sang William Cullen Bryant in *A Forest Hymn*.[9] Even after Emerson, Thoreau and Bryant had passed from the scene, the idea persisted that the American wilderness was not only unique, but that it represented a moral good as well. Far from the corrupting influence of decadent European societies, and removed also from the vices of America's own urban centers, rural America offered a safe, redemptive haven for those prepared to live in simple harmony with nature and nature's God. Ultimately deriving from the Puritan dream of the new world as a "City Upon a Hill," and stimulated by the eighteenth century Rousseauian vision of a natural paradise, this identification of wild, or at least rural, surroundings with simple virtue and personal morality persisted well into the twentieth century. In recounting the exhilaration of the two friends at the start of their walk, Le Gallienne wrote of the sense of freedom, the "romantic expectancy . . . (the) sense of our being entirely on our own resources, vagrants shifting for ourselves, independent of civilization."[10] He contrasted their present joy with the prospect of their urban destination, "today, breathing . . . God's fresh air, living the lives of natural men in a natural world, and tomorrow—Broadway, the horrible crowds, the hustle, the dirt, the smells, the uproar." "Let us," he persuaded his friend, "enter New York not by way of some sordid and clangorous depot, but through the spacious corridors of the Highlands and the lordly gates of the Hudson!"[11] Thus, on that October morning, three quarters of a century ago, the two vagabonds set out on their journey through nature—for art.

NOTES TO CHAPTER 1: October Vagabonds

1. Richard Le Gallienne, *October Vagabonds*, New York, 1910, p. 11.
2. Ibid., p. 196.
3. Ibid., p. 199.
4. Ibid., pp. 22-23. It is possible that Le Gallienne and Fournier met long before that chance encounter in the woods near East Aurora. Le Gallienne was in Minneapolis to deliver a series of lectures between November, 1900 and February, 1901. Fournier was in Europe at the time, but Le Gallienne returned for a shorter visit in October, 1902, and the two men may have met at that time.
5. Henry David Thoreau, *The Writings of Henry David Thoreau, Journal*, edited by Bradford Torrey, Boston and New York, 1906, I, (journal entry for July 11, 1840), p. 167.
6. Elizabeth Palmer Peabody, "Allston the Painter," *American Monthly Magazine* (May, 1836), p. 446.
7. *October Vagabonds*, p. 21.
8. Ibid., pp. 23-24.
9. William Cullen Bryant, "A Forest Hymn," *Poems*, New York, 1836, p. 39.
10. *October Vagabonds*, p. 51.
11. Ibid., pp. 39-40.

Chapter 2 Artistic Beginnings

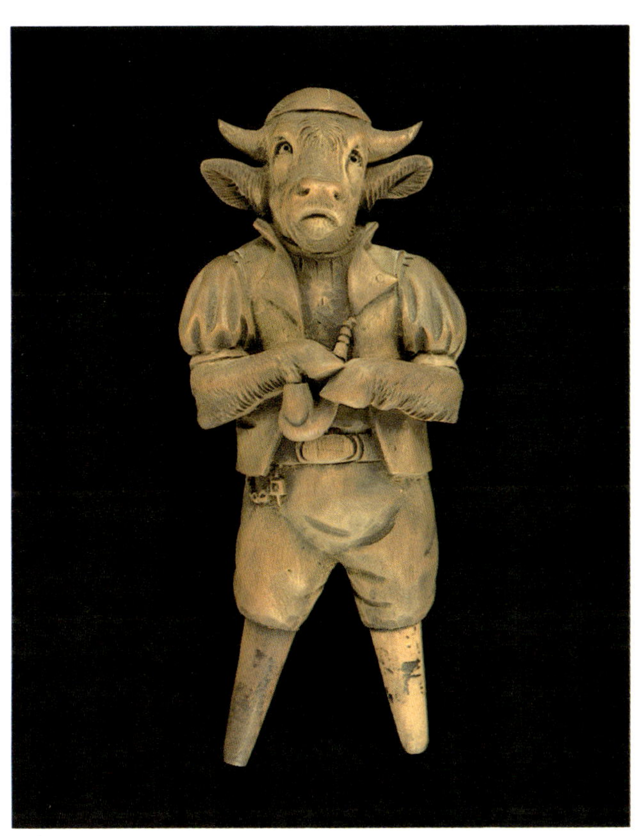

Fig. 1. Wood Carving of Bull with Pipe in Man's Clothing.

The October walking tour with Richard Le Gallienne, though characteristic of Fournier's passion for the out-of-doors, was not otherwise an event of major significance in his life. It does, however, provide an intellectual framework for it, setting the stage for an analysis of his art, an art deeply and reverently observant of nature and thus firmly rooted in the mainstream of the American landscape tradition.

Alexis Jean Fournier's origins were not, however, in the northeastern United States where that tradition was born and reached its maturity. He came into the world on the frontier, in a small house on the western edge of St. Paul, Minnesota on July 4, 1865. The day of Alexis Fournier's birth was an anniversary date in a pivotal year in our national history. The date was, of course, the eighty-ninth commemoration of the United States' Declaration of Independence as a free and sovereign nation. That nation had just fought a divisive and bitter Civil War whose victory had reaffirmed the unity and indivisibility of the federal republic. On July 4, 1865, less than three months had passed since the assassination of President Lincoln. The nation was embarked on a slow and painful recovery from the wounds of war and the even slower process of reconstruction. The United States stood at the threshold of an unprecedented advance in technical and industrial development which would in a few years place it among the richest and most productive in the world. The frontier was rapidly expanding as land hungry pioneers pushed their settlements ever westward, bringing in their wake the destruction of Indian tribal life. Jingoism was rampant and "manifest destiny" was the slogan of the day. The railroads were extending their networks until they covered the nation, and on May 10, 1869 Leland Stanford would drive a golden spike with a silver hammer at the meeting of two rail lines, one from the east and one from the west, at Promontory, Utah, thus cementing the identity of the United States as a single federation of states in a republic that stretched from the Atlantic to the Pacific Ocean.

The state of Minnesota was similarly at the beginning of a new era in its history. Its statehood was just eight years old and even its territorial experience extended back barely two generations prior to its admission to the union in 1857. Minnesota too was recovering from the war between the States for it had sent its own regiments into some of the bloodiest battles of the Civil War. After the war Minnesota, like the nation at large, entered a period of expansion, aided immeasurably by the completion of a railroad system that had by 1872 laid two thousand miles of track within its borders. A few years later James J. Hill, one of the pioneer entrepreneurs of the state, initiated his take-over of the bankrupt St. Paul and Pacific Railroad, later known as the Great Northern Railway. By 1893 he had pushed its track westward 1800 miles all the way to Seattle. Hill also had interests in the expanding lumber industry that played an important role in the economic development of Minnesota. Through the capital which it brought into the state, lumbering was influential in financing the flour milling industry, and by the end of the nineteenth century the Twin Cities of Minneapolis and St. Paul had become the flour milling center of the nation.

At the time of his birth, Alexis Fournier's parents, Isaie and Annie Marie Mathilde Fournier were recent arrivals in St. Paul, having come by ox cart from the village of Longueuil near Montreal, Canada. Isaie was a millwright, equipped with just the right skills for the growing pioneer cities of Minneapolis and St. Paul. His talents would be put to use in the building of the huge Pillsbury mill, which, when it was completed in 1893, was the largest flour mill in the world.

According to family tradition, Alexis Jean Joseph Fournier was welcomed into the world by Old Bets, a Dakota Indian woman from Chief Shakopee's village on the Minnesota River. She was a colorful character, well known in pioneer St. Paul where she functioned as a combination midwife and fortune teller. It is said, that on seeing the new born infant she immediately pronounced him destined for greatness—"his eye say so." But not all the local Indians were as friendly as Old Bets. An old woman entered the Fournier's house and stole a brightly colored shawl. In the shawl, however, was Alexis, age one month. Fortunately, his mother discovered his absence in time and rescued him.[1] Possibly, seeking a safer location the Fourniers left St. Paul in a covered wagon in January, 1866.[2] They headed for Fond-du-Lac, Wisconsin, where three of Isaie's brothers, and his parents too, had settled.

Soon after his arrival in Fond-du-Lac Alexis acquired in rapid succession two brothers, Henry and Frederick. Then when he was only three years old his mother died. Isaie later remarried and a fourth son, Edward, was born of this marriage.

Records of the Fournier family in Fond-du-Lac are confusing because the Fournier brothers there called themselves by the surname, Prefontaine. On one of his later trips to France, Alexis searched out the Fournier family seat near Bordeaux where he confirmed that the original family name was Fournier de Prefontaine.[3] Indeed, Isaie was the son of Alexis Prefontaine and his wife, Marie (Patenaude) Prefontaine, who arrived in Wisconsin from Canada in 1862 and are buried in St. Charles Cemetery in Fond-du-Lac. The reason for Isaie's change of name from Prefontaine to Fournier is unknown, though it may have had something to do with disputed property claims in Fond-du-Lac.

Little is known of Alexis' early childhood. In 1877, at the age of twelve, he was sent to school at a religious academy in Milwaukee, Wisconsin, where he learned some German in addition to the French and English already at his command. He had his earliest experiences in art at that academy for the priests there encouraged him to carve wooden images and crucifixes for the church altar. Though painting, and not sculpture would eventually become his chosen medium, the skills Alexis learned at the academy never left him and later in life he would carve wooden figures to entertain himself and his friends. These figures were quite different in purpose and spirit, however, from the religious objects he had carved as a boy, for a sardonic humor, typical of the artist, is evident in them. They generally represented mythological animals, such as the god, Pan, for example, or a bull dressed up in an artist's loose jacket and pants with a pipe in his paw and a watch fob dangling from his buckled belt (Fig. 1).

Alexis left the academy after less than two years because his family could no longer afford his tuition, but he stayed on in Milwaukee for a while, supporting himself by selling newspapers and working as an office boy. He later said that he had lived briefly in the hull of an old, abandoned ship which in the wintertime was frozen fast to its moorings.[4] At the same time he was taking his first lessons in art from a scene painter, whom he never named.[5]

The year 1879 was an important one in Fournier's young career. After a visit to Winona where his family was then living, he returned to Minneapolis and was employed briefly at "sign writing and decorative painting."[6] Later that year he was in Chicago, doing some scene painting for the McVicker Theatre with a Russian scene painter named Mazzanovitch.[7] He also worked in Chicago on the decoration of the Potter Palmer mansion under the supervision of A. F. Jacassey, a fresco painter.[8] One morning, while finishing a sketch for the frescoes for the Palmer residence, Fournier was startled to find Mrs. Palmer herself watching him work, and delighted when she commented approvingly on his sketches.[9] Throughout his life, the artist seems to have easily attracted influential patrons, and Mrs. Palmer may have been the first to encourage him. The work at the Potter Palmer home completed, Fournier returned to Minneapolis which was to be his home for the next decade and a half.

It is entirely typical of young artists in nineteenth century America that Fournier began his career as a sign painter. This was a tradition that went back to the painters of the early republic, and even beyond to the artists of colonial America. Such work offered an opportunity to earn a living with the brush before establishing a reputation in the fraternity of "fine artists." In any event, by 1883 Fournier was earning the then respectable wage of $2.50 a day at the Ball Sign Works of Minneapolis. He chafed at this uncongenial work, however, for as a later admirer put it, "it afforded no opportunity for the development of his taste nor the expression of his ideas and feelings."[10] Drawing kitchen stoves for newspaper advertisements, which also occupied him briefly at this time, was not much of an improvement. Scene painting, to which he soon progressed, was much better for it enabled him to paint, in however broad a form, the landscapes which he preferred to all other subjects throughout his life. Moreover, it left him time for independent sketching and painting and for roaming the countryside in search of subjects for his brush. His growing skill in landscape painting allowed him, in the words of the same critic, "to introduce into his (stage painting) work dashes of realism and truth foreign to scenic art."[11]

Though it is not known just how extensively Fournier was involved in painting stage scenery, we do know that on one occasion, around the middle of the 1880's, Fournier took a sketch of Fort Snelling to a Mr. Conklin, manager of the Grand Opera House of Minneapolis, hoping to obtain a commission for a stage set based upon it. This happened to coincide with the engagement at the Opera House of Joseph Jefferson, a well known actor of that time who was also an artist himself. The actor saw the sketch and commented favorably on it, remarking to Mr. Conklin that Fournier had a good eye for color and had captured nature.[12] Both observations were to be characteristic of Fournier's future work.

Scene painting was important not only because it was a common employment for many young American artists, but also because it was directly connected to that popular art form of the American nineteenth century, the painted panorama. The first panorama was introduced to the United States by the English artist, William Winstanley, in 1795. Interest in this art form was further stimulated by John Vanderlyn's panorama of the Royal Palace at Versailles which was displayed in a structure specially built for it in New York City in 1819. The panorama became extremely popular in the frontier communities of the midwest where these large scale paintings of historic events or broad landscape vistas particularly stirred the public imagination. Though many of the panorama painters were obscure artists whose names have been forgotten with their panoramas, others are well known to students of American art. David Gilmour Blythe, for example, the Pittsburgh artist who started his career on the Ohio frontier, completed such a project. Another who contemplated a panorama and made sketches and drawings for it was Seth Eastman, painter of the Indians and Commandant of Fort Snelling in the Minnesota Territory during the 1840's. Still others were Henry Lewis and John Banvard, both of whom painted panoramas of the upper Mississippi River Valley and the old Northwest.

The panorama was, in fact, a popular "show," a form of public entertainment that was the nineteenth century equivalent of the twentieth century motion picture. It consisted of one large picture or a number of related panels, painted on canvas, or even mattress ticking, that was unwound, section by section, from two vertical rollers at either end. Often a musical rendition or spoken commentary accompanied the emerging scenes, and sometimes juggling feats and acrobatic acts added to the entertainment. The admission fees provided income for the artist, while for their audiences, the panoramas, with their broad landscapes and quasinarrative subjects, provided a source of information, sometimes accurate and often entertaining, about the western frontier.

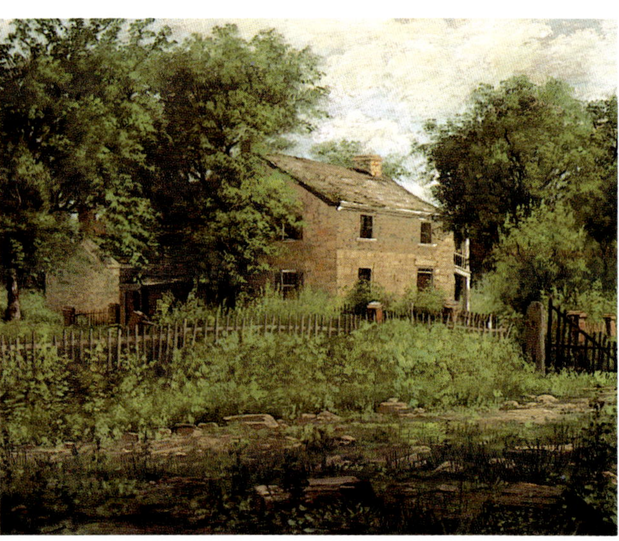

Fig. 3. Old Home of General Sibley at Mendota.

During the 1880's Fournier executed a number of local landscapes and paintings of old Minnesota homesteads that he may possibly have intended to incorporate into a large scale panorama. Such early paintings as *Farnhams' Mill* (Fig. 2) and *Old Home of General Sibley at Mendota* (Fig. 3) have the attention to precise detail and emphasis on local setting that are characteristic of the panoramist's art. Other early paintings, such as a *View of St. Paul Looking West*, have the lack of a central focus that was also common in the continuous scenes of the panorama. Though it is true that panorama enthusiasm had already reached its peak by the

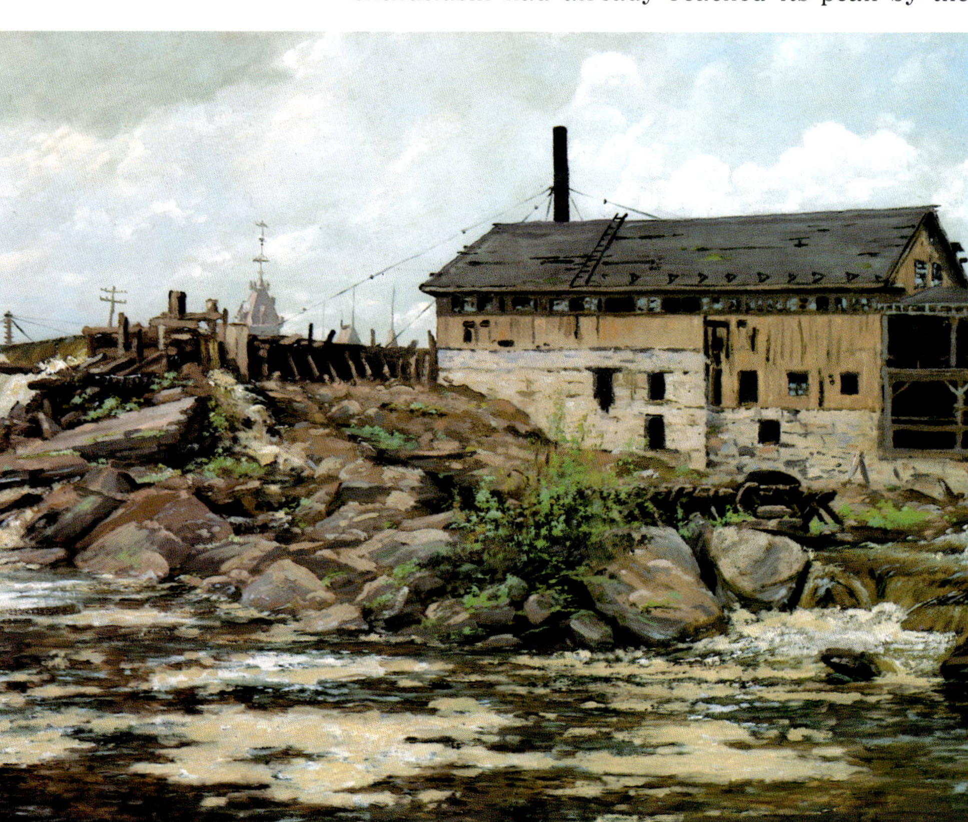

Fig. 2. Farnham's Mill.

mid-nineteenth century, melodrama in painting no less than on the stage seems to have been the temper of the times, and the panorama persisted in the frontier communities until the end of the century. Milwaukee was, in fact, a center for the revival of panorama painting in the late 1870's and 1880's, just at the time that Fournier was living there. He might also have been familiar with the work of Henry Lewis whose large panorama of the Mississippi River was translated into a series of prints that were later published in Germany. Lewis' panorama, after a colorful history, was eventually lost in the jungles of Southeast Asia, but the small oils that served as sketches for the project, remained behind in Minnesota.[13] In any event, Fournier did paint a large "mural" (actually a panorama) of the Indian Cliff Dwellers of the Southwest for the World's Columbian Exposition in Chicago in 1893.

The Indian Cliff Dwellers panorama had its origin two years earlier when H. Jay Smith, Superintendent of the Minneapolis Exposition Building and art director for its annual exhibitions, organized an exploring expedition to the Cliff Dwellers region of Colorado and New Mexico. He took along a photographer, a taxidermist, and Alexis Fournier as the official artist of the party. The explorers spent six months at the Cliff Dwellers site and returned with a large collection of Indian artifacts which were exhibited, along with Fournier's drawings, at the 1892 Minneapolis Industrial Exposition. Unfortunately, the original paintings and drawings have not survived, although the engravings made after them can be seen in the Catalogue of the Exposition of that year.

The Cliff Dwellers drawings were later elaborated by the artist in color and exhibited as a large mural in the Chicago Columbian Exposition in 1893. The mural was, of course, a panorama, the only example Fournier is known to have completed in this genre. The artist went to Chicago in the spring of 1893 to supervise its construction and installation, and later he was engaged to interpret the scenes for the thousands who flocked to the exhibit. Such a spoken commentary was entirely in keeping with the tradition of earlier panoramas. This event not only allowed Fournier to number himself among the panorama painters, but more significantly it paid him enough to consumate his long cherished dream of going to France to further his studies in art under some of the acknowledged masters there. Of this more in the next chapter.

By 1886 Fournier was achieving a modest success as a landscape painter, but he felt that he needed some professional instruction. He was only twenty-one years old, certain of his vocation, but mostly self-taught and aware that he still had much to learn. Fortunately, a suitable instructor arrived in Minneapolis in April, 1886, in the person of Douglas Volk, a Boston artist who had been invited by the members of the three year old Minneapolis Society of Fine Arts to be the director of the newly established Minneapolis School of Art (today called the Minneapolis College of Art and Design). The first home of the school was an old frame house at 1201 Hennepin Avenue; but two years later it moved to a modest one story building at 719 Hennepin Avenue which was erected on a lot given to the Society by Thomas Barlow Walker, an early patron of the arts, and of Fournier, in Minneapolis.

Though it was later claimed that Fournier had been a student of Volk's at the Minneapolis School of Art, he does not seem to have actually enrolled in the school, for the records of the first classes do not include his name.[14] He apparently did attend Volk's classes for a brief period in the spring of 1886, and then arranged for private instruction with him. In fact, Volk had much to teach the young Fournier. Fournier was still a provincial, self-taught artist with a dry, literal style and a frequently harsh color palette, as seen in *Minneapolis* of 1886.[15] By contrast, Douglas Volk, though only nine years older, was a sophisticated man of the world, much travelled and well trained as an academic painter. He had been born in Pittsfield, Massachusetts in 1856, the son of the American sculptor, Leonard Volk. At the age of fourteen he was taken to Rome by his parents. There he became interested in painting and enrolled in the St. Luke's Academy. By 1873 he was in Paris, studying with the French academician, Jean Léon Gérôme. On returning to the United States, Volk became an instructor at the Cooper Institute in New York, and while there he received the invitation to come to Minneapolis. He and Fournier became good friends and later shared a studio on Hennepin Avenue until Volk returned to the east in 1893.

On April 26, 1887 Alexis Fournier married Emma Fricke of Pine Island, Minnesota. He signed his name on the marriage certificate as A. Joseph

Fournier, using his first initial and third given name, one by which he was occasionally called later in his life. Two children were born of this marriage, Grace, later Mrs. Horace Cottom of Los Angeles who was born in 1888, and Paul, born about a year later, who would become a photographer in Buffalo, N.Y.

During the early 1880's the Minneapolis City Directories had listed Alexis Fournier as a "sign writer" of 282 S.E. Union Street, but by 1888 he is called an "artist." Though he still resided at the same address on S.E. Union Street, he had acquired the additional amenity of a studio above a tailor's shop at 412 Nicollet Avenue. It made the unknown tailor one of Fournier's earliest patrons. He liked the artist's paintings and Fournier liked the tailor's suits. A trade was arranged satisfactory to both parties and the tailor even agreed to exhibit Fournier's paintings in his shop window. In the studio on the second floor of the building, Fournier devoted himself to landscape painting and there he began to attract a number of patrons better known than the tailor on the ground floor.

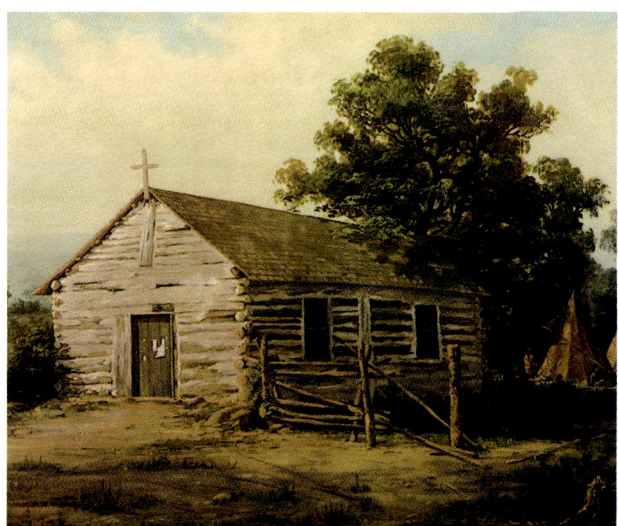

Fig. 4. The Chapel of St. Paul.

One of them was James J. Hill, St. Paul's railroad and lumber baron. Hill purchased a number of Fournier paintings to hang in the granite mansion he was building, between 1888 and 1891, on St. Paul's fashionable Summit Avenue. Fournier's artistic work was brought to Hill's attention by an enterprising Minnesota photographer named Edward Bromley. Bromley had antiquarian inclinations and had made a hobby of collecting photographs of old St. Paul. One of these was of St. Paul's first Catholic church, a humble log cabin built in 1841 by Lucien Galtier, Minnesota's pioneer priest. It was "so poor," Father Galtier later wrote, "that it would remind one of the stable in Bethlehem."[16] The log cabin church had been razed in 1855 but Bromley had found a photographic negative of it in the course of his incessant rummaging and he asked Hill to commission a painting based on the photograph. Hill agreed but asked, "Who would you get to paint it?" "I replied," said Bromley, that "Alexis Fournier would probably be pleased to do it." "How much do you think he would charge for one about three feet long?" "'Oh, says I, 'a hundred dollars for the picture and frame.'" "Go ahead" says Hill, "here's a check for the hundred."[17] The result of this commission was *The Chapel of St. Paul* (Fig. 4) which Hill later gave to the Minnesota Historical Society. This early patronage by one of Minnesota's most influential men was, of course, significant in the developing career of the young artist.

Though Fournier was as yet only in his early twenties, the years between 1886 and 1889 witnessed a remarkable progress in his development as a landscape painter. The dry, linear style and melodramatic colors of such early pictures as *Minneapolis* gave way to a broader, brushier style in which light began to define form. *Mill Pond at Minneapolis* (Fig. 5), *Lowry Hill* (Fig. 6) and *St. Anthony Hill* (Fig. 7) all painted in 1888, are, by comparison, subdued, revealing more subtle color

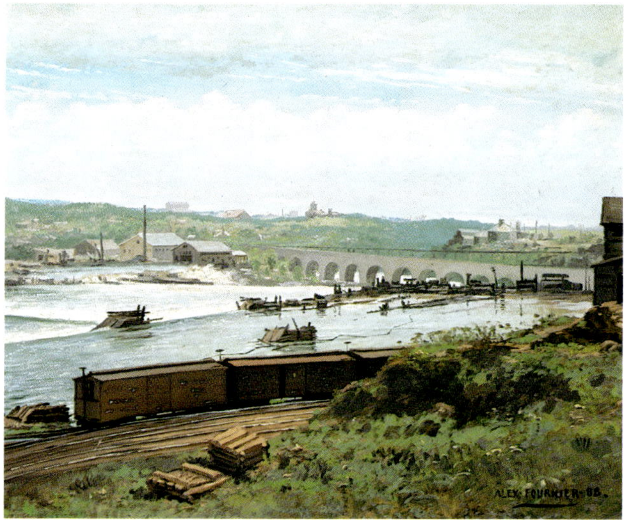

Fig. 5. Mill Pond at Minneapolis.

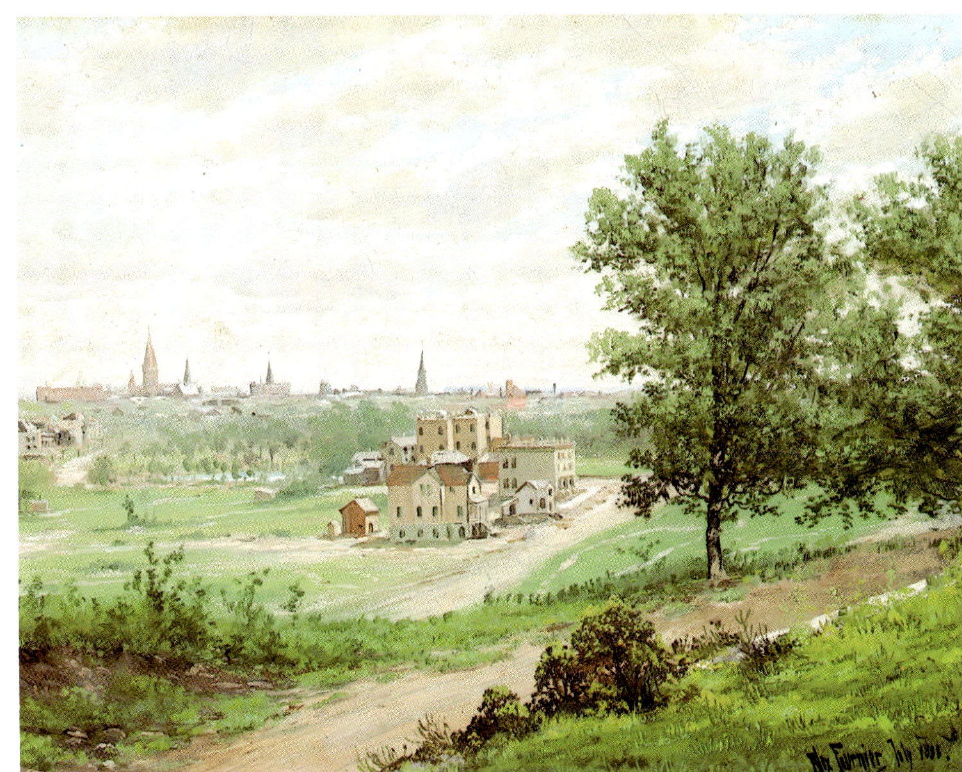

Fig. 6. Lowry Hill.

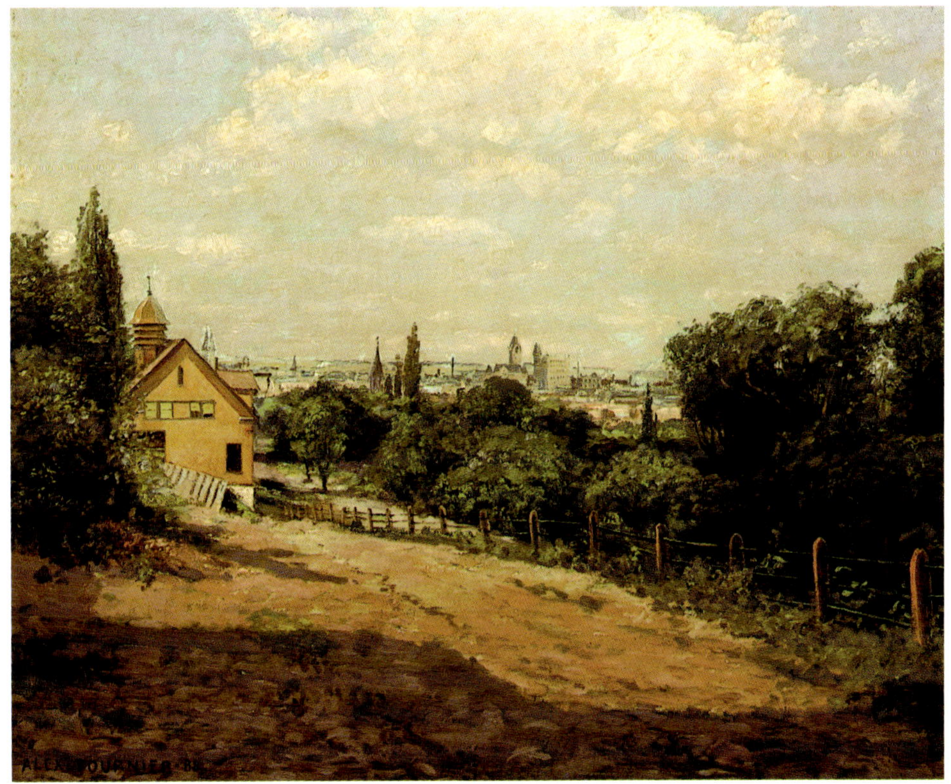

Fig. 7. View from St. Anthony Hill.

tones and a less fussy technique. *Mill Pond at Minneapolis* depicts the local scene with a robust realism that recalls the work of the French painter, Gustave Courbet, of a generation or two earlier. It is unlikely that Fournier was familiar with Courbet's work at this time, but in many of the paintings of the late 1880's he possessed a pragmatism and cool objectivity in approaching his subject that the French master would undoubtedly have appreciated.

In *Mill Pond* we see the tracks and recently completed stone arched bridge of James J. Hill's St. Paul, Minneapolis and Manitoba Railroad Company. Beyond it is the old steel truss that used to carry traffic across the Mississippi River. The tall building just showing to the left is the old "Exposition Building" where Fournier was already beginning to exhibit his work in local shows. It combined Romanesque, Classical and other modes in a fascinating eclectic mixture entirely in keeping with the taste for revival styles typical of nineteenth century American architecture. The Grand Army of the Republic had held conventions there and on June 7, 1892 the Republican National Convention met in its spacious hall to renominate Benjamin Harrison in his unsuccessful bid for reelection as President of the United States. To the right of the picture are the polygonal buildings which were the original gas tanks of the Minneapolis Gas Company, and just breaking the horizon to their left are the original buildings of the University of Minnesota.

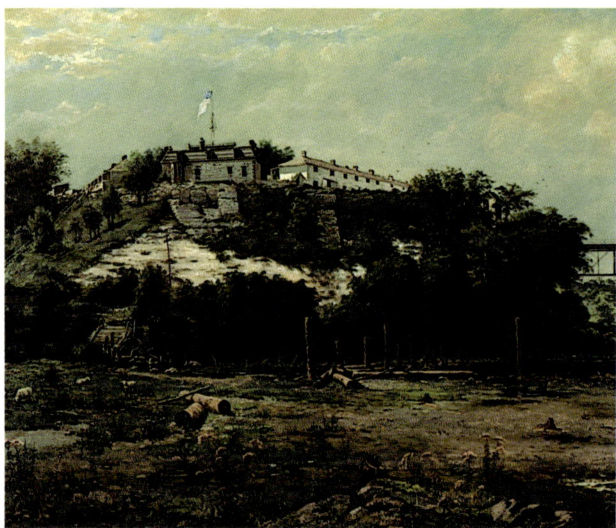

Fig. 8. View of Fort Snelling.

Lowry Hill and *St. Anthony Hill* are companion views of Minneapolis both painted in July, 1888. They reflect a feeling of transience, a moment in the city's history between provincial backwater and modern industrial center. In both paintings the view is from a height overlooking the city, the distant buildings veiled by a light mist of atmosphere, but the near ones shown with a crisp lucidity characteristic of Fournier's urban scenes at this time.

1888 is also the year in which Fournier painted the large *View of Fort Snelling* (Fig. 8). The fort had often caught the attention of both local and visiting artists for, situated as it is, high above the confluence of two scenic rivers, it possessed both historic and pictorial importance. Earlier artists such as John Casper Wild, Seth Eastman and even the primitive painter Edward K. Thomas, had tended to romanticize the subject and to offer "picturesque" views of the fort on its commanding promontory.

Fournier, however, offers us a far different, essentially "genre" or every-day-like view which avoids the dramatic overtones of the romantics and concentrates instead on the "here and now" of the realist painter. For one thing, the artist's vantage point is below the fort instead of at a distance overlooking it. This has the effect of putting the observer in a more immediate relationship with the subject, drawing him inside the picture instead of keeping him at a distance. The low vantage point also has the effect of filling up more of the canvas, thus avoiding the vast and lustrous skies of the romantics. The light is a natural one, that of an ordinary day rather than the stagey glow of a dramatic moment. The untidy shore scattered with debris and the remains of a wooden bridge, the shallow riverbed and the grazing sheep, all emphasize the genre quality of Fournier's work at this stage in his development and his focus on the ordinary, immediately recognizable scene.

The level of technical skill exhibited in this painting is quite astonishing, considering the rather naive work of only a year or two before. More significantly, the clarity and definition of particular objects in the painting do not leave the viewer emotionally detached as can happen in the presence of mere technical virtuosity. And the panoramic quality of the painting has been achieved without any loss of focus of the composition. This is one of Fournier's most powerful works. At the

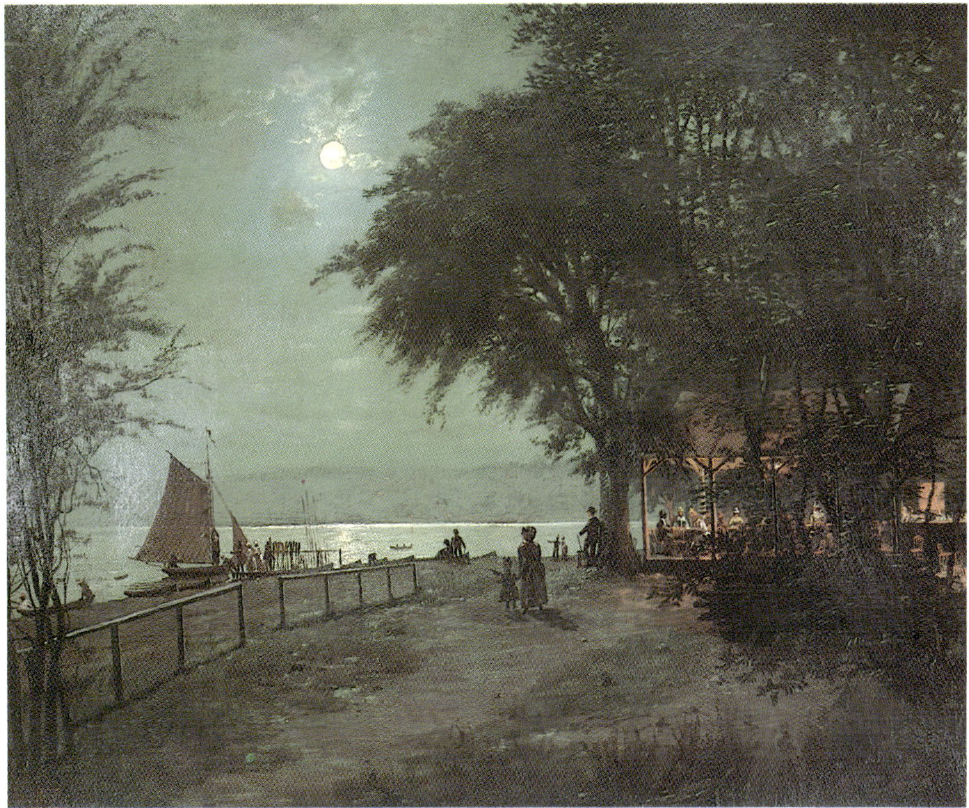

Fig. 9. Lake Harriet by Moonlight.

time of its production he was only twenty-three years old.

The *View of Fort Snelling* recalls George Inness' early work, particularly his *Lackawanna Valley* of 1855 which defines with similar clarity a transient moment between rural America and the industrial nation it was about to become. *Lackawanna Valley* is also panoramic without being dramatic, and genre in quality rather than picturesque. It is interesting that Fournier's urban scenes, like Inness' *Lackawanna Valley*, are early works and (excluding Fournier's Venetian pictures) exceptions in his oeuvre of peaceful country landscapes. Moreover, again like Inness, when Fournier later abandoned his city views in favor of completely pastoral scenes, he endowed the later pictures with a richer, more painterly quality, a more poetic tone, and an emotional warmth inspired by the canvases of the French Barbizon masters.

A year later, in 1889, Fournier painted *Lake Harriet by Moonlight* (Fig. 9), a picture comparable in quality to his *View of Fort Snelling* but totally different in character and technique. Here he has begun to explore the dramatic possibilities of light and its potential for endowing nature with an air of mystery and romance. But the Lake Harriet picture is still essentially a genre painting. In spite of its moonlit subject it is quite different from other nocturnal scenes painted by Fournier's older contemporaries such as George Inness or even

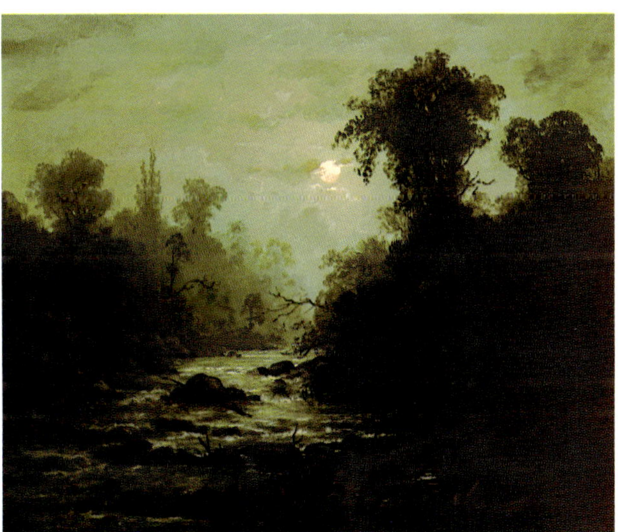

Fig. 10. The Glen by Moonlight.

Albert Pinkham Ryder. These two artists created moonlit subjects whose mood was intensely introspective, achieving a vision so personal that one almost feels an intruder in the private dream world of the painter. And though Fournier, like Inness and Ryder, was later to distill the inner reality of his personal vision and express it on canvas, the *Lake Harriet by Moonlight* is still a straightforward image of the artist's external world. The cool light of the moon, reflected from the surface of the lake contrasts with the warm glow of the lamplight in the lakeside pavilion, but it does so without the emotional and poetic overtones such a scene usually invites. Ordinary people sit at the pavilion tables or stroll along the lakeside path, enjoying a cool breeze on a summer's night. It is

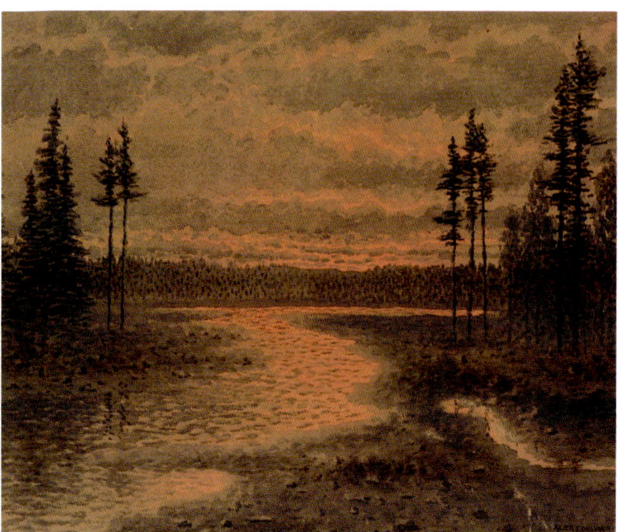

Fig. 11. Untitled: Twilight Scene.

all quite peaceful and undramatic. Still, an undated painting of about the same period, *The Glen by Moonlight* (Fig. 10), does suggest that the artist was awakening to the possibility of acting as the poetic interpreter of nature and not just as its prose translator. This painting, however, is so close to John W. Casilear's *Moonlight on the Glen* that the inspiration for it may have come from elsewhere than Fournier's own sensibilities.[18]

A few watercolors of this period also reveal a growing awareness of this aspect of the artist's role. One of them (Fig. 11), an untitled twilight scene, painted in 1889, studies the light effects of a fiery sunset sky whose final gleams are reflected in the water below. Silhouetted against this backdrop, and, in their careful symmetry retaining

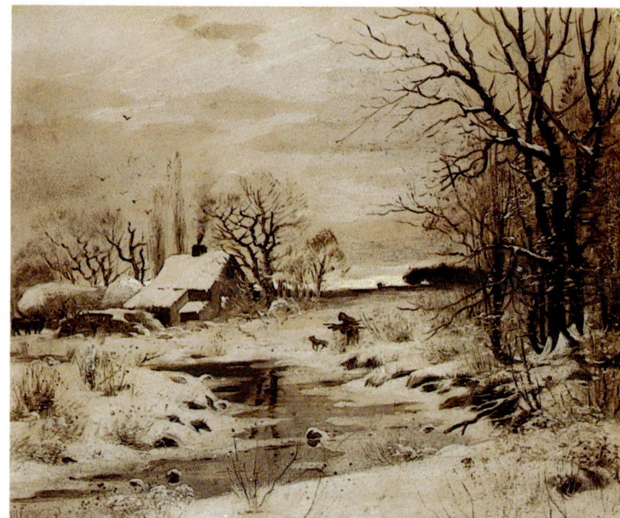

Fig. 12. My Cottage Near Minnehaha Creek.

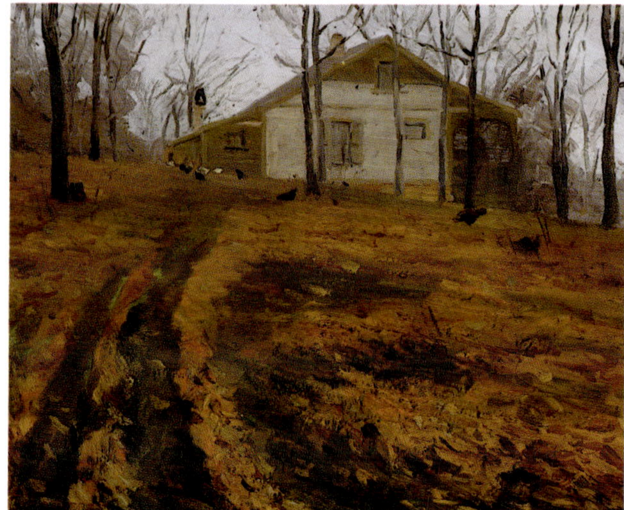

Fig. 13. Home of Alexis Jean Fournier.

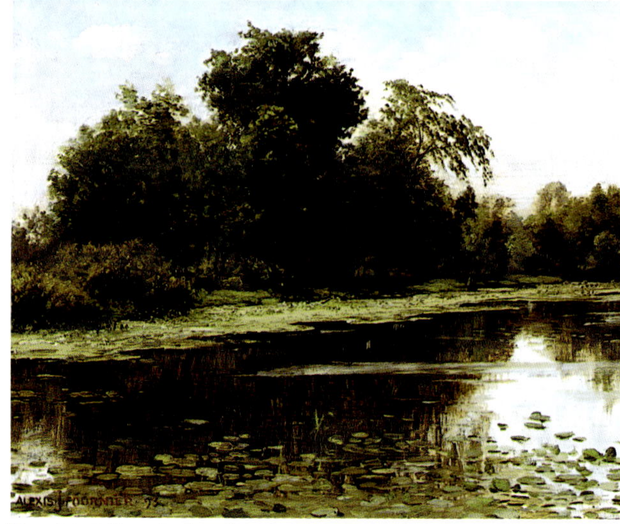

Fig. 14. Minnehaha Creek.

something of the state painter's craft, a number of tall pines rise above the horizon.

Though this water color of a twilight lake suggests a distance from civilization and the urban environment, Fournier did not need to go very far to find both inspiration and subject matter for his paintings. From his new house and studio on Columbus Avenue near Minnehaha Creek, a view of which was painted both by himself (Fig. 12) and by his friend and fellow artist, Emil Ahlberg (Fig. 13), Fournier could easily walk to Minnehaha Creek, the picturesque stream that winds through Minneapolis and its suburbs. In a painting of 1888 *Minnehaha Creek* (Fig. 14), the artist suggests a quiet Spring morning at this scenic landmark, a hushed and placid interlude in the middle of the city. Studies such as this were to lead to *Spring Morning Near Minnehaha Creek* painted later in Paris but based on sketches made near the artist's Minneapolis home. It won the much coveted honor of being hung in the Paris Salon of 1894.

Fournier's early urban scenes include several views of St. Anthony Falls, the earliest of which (Fig. 15), dating from 1886, was painted in honor of the bicentennial celebration of the discovery of the Falls of St. Anthony by Father Hennepin in 1686. This picture, executed in the harsh, linear style of Fournier's early period, is a copy of a painting by Alexander Loemans, a landscape painter who worked in Minneapolis in the 1870's before

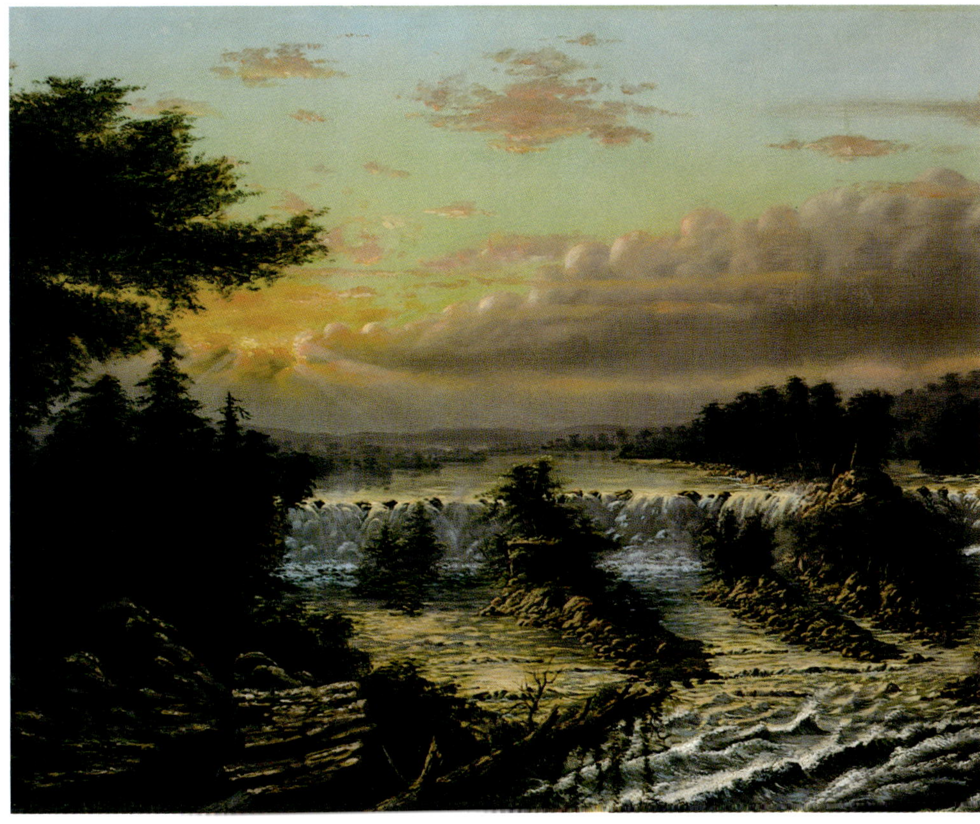

Fig. 15. St. Anthony Falls.

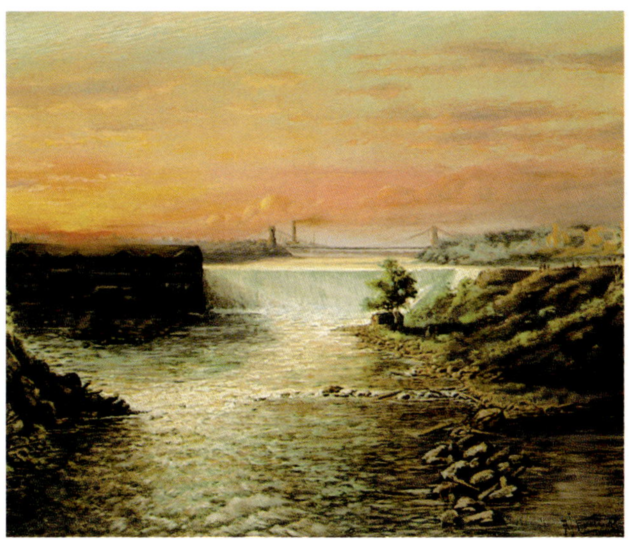

Fig. 16. St. Anthony Falls with Second Suspension Bridge.

moving further west to paint the Rocky Mountains and the Canadian Cascades.

This early view of St. Anthony Falls is similar to a view by Henry Lewis who, in 1855, had painted the Falls as they appeared in 1848. At that time the Falls existed in a remote and unspoiled wilderness when the population of the upper Mississippi still consisted of the native Ojibway and Sioux Indians painted by George Catlin in the 1830's and by Seth Eastman in the 1840's. Fournier, however, picked a later moment in the history of the area for two other versions of St. Anthony Falls. One of them, *St. Anthony Falls with Second Suspension Bridge* (Fig. 16) was not only exhibited at the Minneapolis Industrial Exposition of 1891 but was engraved, by J. Anderson, for the cover of its catalogue. Still another *View of St. Anthony Falls* (Fig. 17), painted in 1890, was purchased by James J. Hill.[19] It shows, above the Falls, and near the old Exposition Building, the church of St. Mary of Lourdes which still stands today. One of Fournier's most ambitious projects to date, its sheer size, over three feet by five feet, made it a fitting decoration for Hill's Summit Avenue mansion. The surging power of the Falls, cleverly depicted at an oblique angle from a vantage point below them, may have added to the appeal of the picture for the Northwest's energetic and forceful "Empire Builder." The painting retains some of the stiffness and linearity of the artist's earlier style, but it also reveals a new breadth of vision in its suggestion of the powerful force of the rushing waters.

By 1892 Fournier was sufficiently established to have a "Fournier Gallery" containing 193 of his paintings on display at the seventh annual Minneapolis Industrial Exposition, together with his drawings of the Indian Cliff Dwellers. As already noted, these drawings were worked into a panorama for the Chicago Exhibition of 1893 where his commentary on the scenes provided funds which helped to finance his first visit to France.

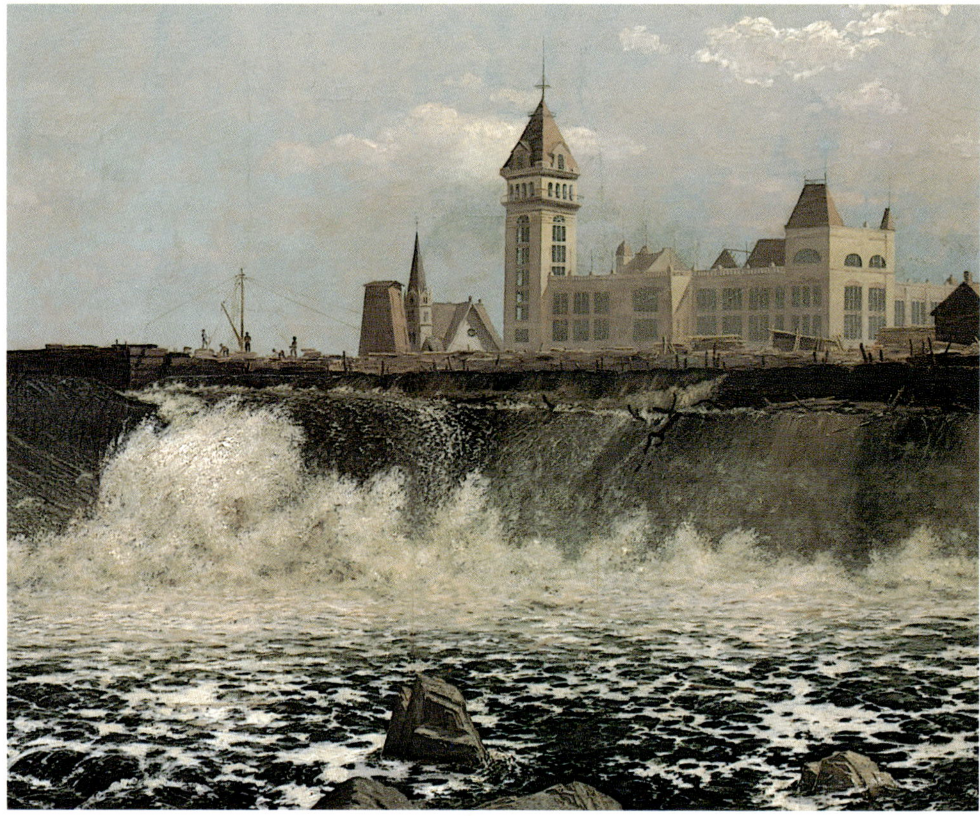

Fig. 17. View of St. Anthony Falls.

NOTES TO CHAPTER 2: Artistic Beginnings

1. "'Minneapolis is Home,' Said Alexis Jean Fournier." Unheaded, undated clipping in the artist's scrapbook, Minnesota Historical Society; and *Minneapolis Journal*, November 12, 1905, p. 18.
2. This was two years after the major outbreak of Indian hostilities in St. Cloud in 1863, but minor flare-ups continued throughout the decade. It may have been one of these later episodes that frightened the Fournier family.
3. *Minneapolis Journal*, November 12, 1905, p. 18. An address in Fournier's sketchbook mentions an "Alexis F (ournier?) Prefontaine, Lieut. de Police, Rue Chabourg, Montreal.
4. *Progressive Men of Minnesota*, St. Paul, 1915, pp. 445-6, and *Minneapolis Journal*, March 30, 1930, p. 2.
5. *Community News and East Aurora Chamber of Commerce News*, East Aurora, N.Y., July 10, 1946, p. 1.
6. *Progressive Men of Minnesota*, Op. Cit., pp. 445-6.
7. One wonders whether there was any relationship between this artist and Lawrence Mazzanovich (1871 or 1872-1959) who studied at the Chicago Art Institute and the Art Students' League in New York. He also studied in Paris but retained his connections with Chicago, exhibiting there fairly regularly from 1912 on. As Lawrence Mazzanovich was only seven or eight years old when Fournier was in Chicago in 1879, it is possible, given the Chicago connection and the unusual name, that Fournier worked under Lawrence Mazzanovich's father. It is interesting that much later Lawrence Mazzanovich was briefly associated with the Roycroft Community in East Aurora, N.Y. when Fournier was there also. For what little is known about Lawrence Mazzanovich see J. Gray Sweeney, *American Paintings at the Tweed Museum of Art*, University of Minnesota, Duluth, 1982, p. 182.
8. Research and inquiries to the Library of the Chicago Art Institute have failed to uncover any information about A. F. Jacassey.
9. *Progressive Men of Minnesota*, Op. Cit., p. 445.
10. *Brush and Pencil Magazine*, August, 1899, p. 243.
11. Ibid.
12. Laura Baldwin, "Minneapolis Artists at the World's Fair," *Literary Northwest*, Vol. 2, No. 4, Jan. 1893.
13. See Bertha L. Heilbron, "Making a Motion Picture in 1848," *Minnesota History*, June, September, December, 1936. Also, Bertha L. Heilbron, editor, *The Valley of the Mississippi Illustrated by Henry Lewis*, Minnesota Historical Society, 1967. Fournier may also have seen the studies for the panorama of *The Beach at Scheveningen* by the Dutch panoramist, Hendrick Mesdagh, which were exhibited at the Minneapolis Industrial Exposition in 1890.
14. The "Alumni Notes" of the *Sketch Pad* of the Minneapolis School of Art, 1922 do, however, list Alexis Fournier as an alumnus. The Notes say that "he began his studies under Volk in the old frame house next to the library."
15. This painting, now unavailable for photography, is clearly reproduced in *Iron Horse West*, The Minnesota Museum of Art, 1976, p. 50.
16. Quoted in Theodore C. Blegen, *Minneapolis, A History of the State*, University of Minnesota, Minneapolis, 1975, p. 156.
17. The quotations are from "Priceless Photographs of early Minnesota Saved by One Man's Foresight," *Minneapolis Journal*, April 30, 1922, Society Section, p. 1.
18. Reproduced in G. W. Sheldon, *American Painters, with Eighty-Three Examples of Their Work Engraved in Wood*, D. Appleton & Co., N.Y., 1879, opp. pg. 154, which Fournier may well have seen.
19. Laura Baldwin, Op. Cit. Also *Minneapolis Journal*, March 30, 1930, p. 2.

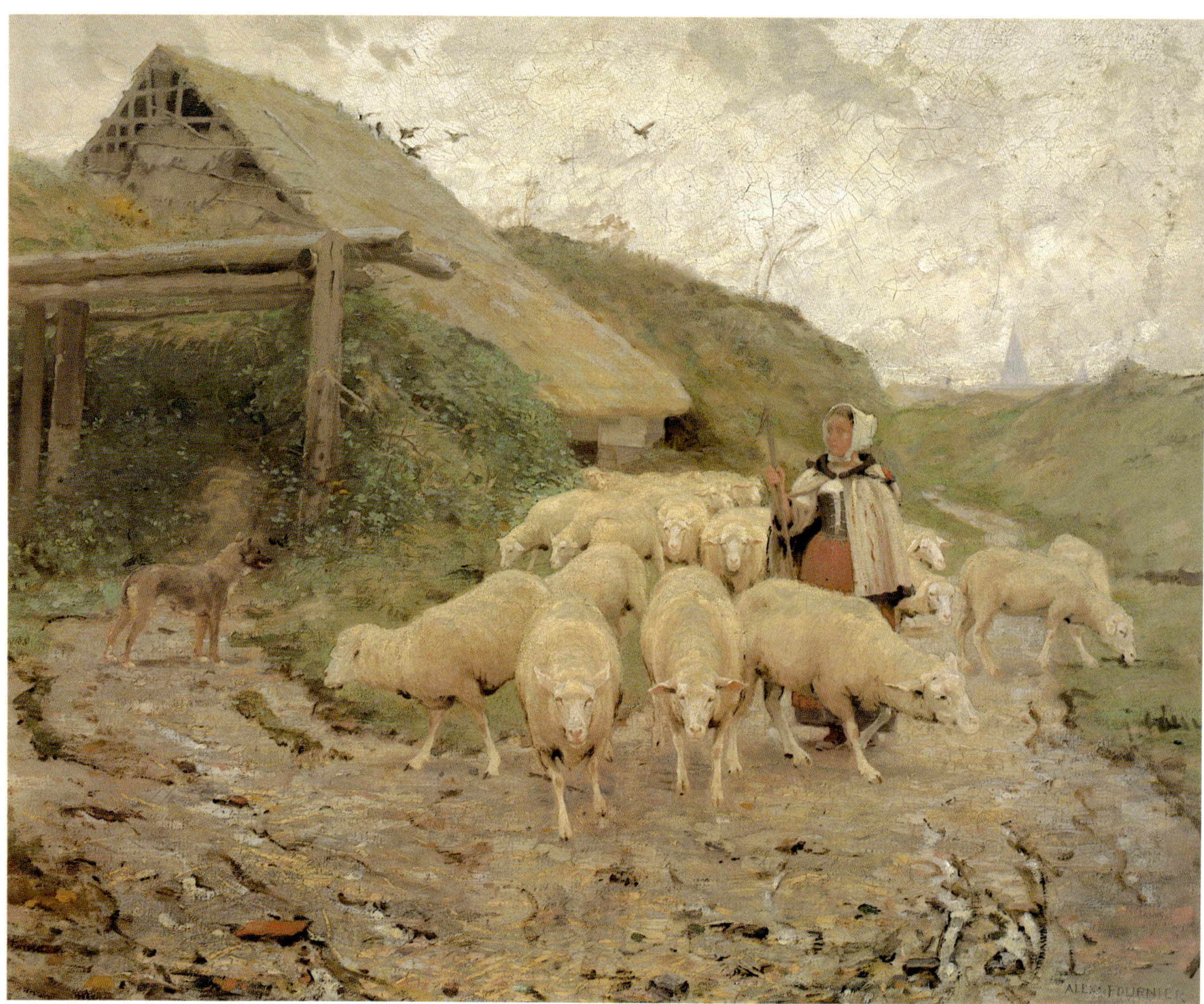

Fig. 1. Going to Pasture.

Chapter 3 France and America

With the money from the Cliff Dwellers' panorama, and with his travel purse augmented by Twin Cities patrons including James J. Hill, Ward Burton and Herschel V. Jones, Fournier set out on his first trip to France in late 1893. Emma and the two children stayed behind at 4811 Columbus Avenue for the generosity of Fournier's patrons did not extend so far as to permit the establishment of a second family residence in Paris.

Fournier's eagerness to go to France and study there was even greater for him than for most American artists in France. His genuine love of his native America had always been colored by his consciousness of his French ancestry and his fluency in the French language. For the rest of his life he cultivated a "French" appearance, occasionally even passing himself off as a French artist, for he felt himself

> "Sport of exiling winds of change and chance -
> Feet in America and heart in France."[1]

In Paris, Fournier enrolled at the Académie Julian, one of several studios operated by established artists. The method of instruction was fairly informal. Students would be assigned a particular subject, usually starting off with drawing from plaster casts of classical sculpture. When completed, the work would be criticized by the studio heads, and even from time to time by guest artists from the prestigious École des Beaux Arts. Fournier studied at the Académie Julian under Jean-Paul Laurens and Benjamin Constant, two nineteenth century French painters with a polished academic style.

Among the other students at the Académie Julian at this time were the Americans, Henry Ossawa Tanner, Joseph Pennell, Francis Hopkinson Smith, Fred McMonnies, and Lorado Taft. Fournier was living at the American Art Association Building at 131 Boulevard Montparnasse, in the heart of the colorful Latin Quarter. His roommate was the Canadian painter Ernest Thompson-Seton artist, naturalist, founder of the Boy Scouts of America and later a gifted writer and illustrator of children's books. His close friends included the etcher, George Plowman, a fellow Minnesotan born in Le Sueur, and the painters Sandor L. Landeau and Harry W. Sewell of San Francisco, whose portraits fill the pages of Fournier's notebook of 1894. In a pencilled autobiography written many years later, Fournier also listed other companions of the Latin Quarter days: the painters Charles Lazar, James McNeill Whistler, Frank Duveneck, John S. Sargent, George Elmer Brown, Edward Duffner and Herbert Waldron Faulkner, and the sculptors, Frederick McMonnies, Paul Bartlett, George Grey Barnard, Lorado Taft, Augustus St. Gaudens, John Flanagan and John Q. A. Ward.[2] His circle included writers, composers and musicians as well, for he also "saw much," he writes, "of friends, Israel Zangwill, Eugene Vail, Charles Sprague Pearce, Massenet, Grieg and Paderewski." He acknowledged, almost as an afterthought, the presence at one social gathering of "the master Impressionist, Claude Monet." But, as though to specifically deny Monet's influence on him, he says, "I was influenced in my work by J.M.W. Turner and Henri Harpigny (sic) whom I consider my master."[3] Indeed our artist never seems to have lacked for friends and companions, for he was possessed of a ready smile, an open and convivial personality and an irrepressible joie de vivre. His wit, his charm and his sense of humor are remembered still by those who knew him.

Husbanding his modest resources, Fournier wrote a careful account of his expenses in June, 1894. In the three week period from June 4th to June 30th he spent a total of $13.30 for artist's materials, meals, stamps, railway fare into the countryside, drinks, tobacco and even a straw hat.[4] He was obviously having a great time while, at the same time, devoting himself seriously to his studies at the Académie Julian.

Fournier's description of the Académie Julian is interesting both for his evaluation of his fellow students, especially the French ones, and for his perception of their attitude to the foreign students in their midst. "Julian's School," he reported, "is located in a big, barnlike structure and contains three studios all of them having painting classes and one also the sculpture department. In the middle of the winter season, when it is in full blast, there are about three hundred students there collected from every quarter of the world. Americans are well received by the French students, not so the German and English. The apparent carelessness and levity of the French students is a source of constant wonder to the Americans who see them accomplish so much with their air of never doing anything. They come to school in the morning laughing and singing and smoking cigarettes and then proceed to throw stools and paint brushes and raise the very devil. The point is that when they work, they do work. The average French student will do more in an hour than a foreigner will do in a day . . . The Frenchman is sui generis. He cannot be compared to other nations. This merry student who seems to have no time but for wine, women and song will astonish you by turning out a masterpiece just when you have begun to think that he is altogether worthless.

"In the atelier, clothes cut no figure whatever. Most of the French wear long hair and a peculiar sort of student costume while some of the Americans even wear cowboy costumes."

"Everybody is trying to get a picture into the Salon . . . The French call it 'arrived' . . . there are generally only about 700 pictures chosen out of 9,000 offered. Nationality has nothing whatever to do with the awards."[5]

Much to Fournier's delight, he himself "arrived" later the same year. His painting, *Spring Morning Near Minnehaha Creek*, unlocated today, was selected to be hung at the Paris Salon of 1894. Based on a number of earlier studies that had been done on location, it depicted Minneapolis' most picturesque landmark. Its lightness and clarity aroused the excited admiration of Fournier's fellow students and even the patriarchal Benjamin Constant, visiting the Salon exhibition on "varnishing day," insisted on being shown the painting by the artist himself. "Yes, it is a Spring morning and no mistake," he said. "You understand nature, I see that. Bon Courage."[6]

It was an understanding of nature that was uniquely Fournier's own. Curiously unmoved, at this time, by the dazzling, light filled canvases of the French Impressionists with their broad brush strokes and broken color technique, and even less attracted by the divisionist color method of their followers, Fournier developed his own ways of conveying air and light in nature. His was a gentle but nonetheless rigorous exposition of form and color in landscape painting that resisted the dissolution of objects in the haze of atmosphere. In this way he stood apart from true Impressionism, and also at this time from the "tonalist" landscapes of such fellow Americans as Robert Bruce Crane and Dwight William Tryon who concentrated on a single tone or color as a way of introducing a mood of revery or nostalgia in landscape art. Indeed, Fournier's manipulation of light and atmosphere retains something of the "luminist" tradition of earlier nineteenth century American landscapes, where light is used to define form and not to dissolve it. Fournier, at this time was still suspicious of the sensuous quality of the paint itself, though later he would come to understand and appreciate its uses.

Nor was he now concerned, as the Impressionists were, with the spontaneous recognition of a transient and fleeting moment. Fournier's vision was of a more permanent time and place, in the distilled image of an early Spring morning, for example, whenever and wherever it would occur. In this respect he was closer to the French Barbizon painters of a generation or so earlier than he was to the Impressionists who were his closer contemporaries. Like the so-called "men of 1830," those artists who, in the mid-nineteenth century congregated in the village of Barbizon near the picturesque forest of Fontainebleau, Fournier sought to escape from the increasing sordidness of nineteenth century industrialization into unspoiled nature and the rural past. His contact at the Académie Julian with Henri Harpignies, his chosen mentor there and the last of the great Barbizon painters, strengthened Fournier's conviction that their art was the model he would choose for his own. Indeed, it may have been during the summer of 1894, which he spent traveling through the French provinces (and in Italy), that Fournier first conceived the idea of what was to be his life's major project, a series of paintings depicting the homes and haunts of the French Barbizon masters.

Fournier's first sojourn in France ended in late 1895 when he returned to Minneapolis with some 60 oils and 20 watercolors painted in France and on trips he had taken to England and Italy. Two of these paintings had the honor of bearing Salon exhibition labels, for in 1895 Fournier repeated his success of the previous year by having *Le Repos* (now lost) accepted for the Paris Salon. This painting and *The Gathering Hour* (also lost), were sent by Fournier to New York where they were hung at the 1896 exhibition of the National Academy of Design. These exhibitions, and one the previous year at London's Crystal Palace where Fournier's *On the Road to Dieppe* was shown, gave the artist the sort of international reputation that made local galleries eager to display his work. Among them were Stevens and Robertson's Gallery on Sixth Street in Minneapolis, Clow's Gallery, and Harington Beard's Art House on Nicollet Avenue where his paintings drew lavish praise. A review of the paintings at Beard's in the *Minneapolis Journal* of January 14, 1896 commended his "native genius" and spoke admiringly of the artist's "energy born of the determination to succeed."[7]

Though no lists exist of the paintings that Fournier brought back from France, they may well have included *Going to Pasture*, painted in 1895, (Fig. 1) and *Evening in Normandy* (Fig. 2). Fournier had, by now, acquired something of a reputation as a painter of sheep grazing contentedly in a meadow or accompanied by their herders. Both paintings reveal a subtle luminosity and a subdued color palette in which soft tones of green, blue and grey predominate. Nature's humble creatures, both animal and human, aroused in the artist the same sentiments of reverence and quiet admiration as they did for such French Barbizon painters of the rural scene as Millet, or closer still, Charles Jacque.

But praise from the critics, though gratifying, was not enough to sustain a family and in the spring Fournier organized an outdoor sketching class where he introduced his students to the natural beauties of the local scenic spots. In his advertisement for the class Fournier begged leave "to mention that he (had recently) returned from abroad where he studied under the greatest men of today both in the academies and in the open air of France and Italy, and that he is fully capable of instructing all means of outdoor work. The location for class work," he goes on to say, "will be within a day's sojourn of Minneapolis such as Washburn Park, the Lakes, Minnehaha Falls, along the River and Minnehaha Creek . . . Although a pleasant time is assured," he cautioned potential dilettantes, "yet earnest work will be the motive of this class."[8]

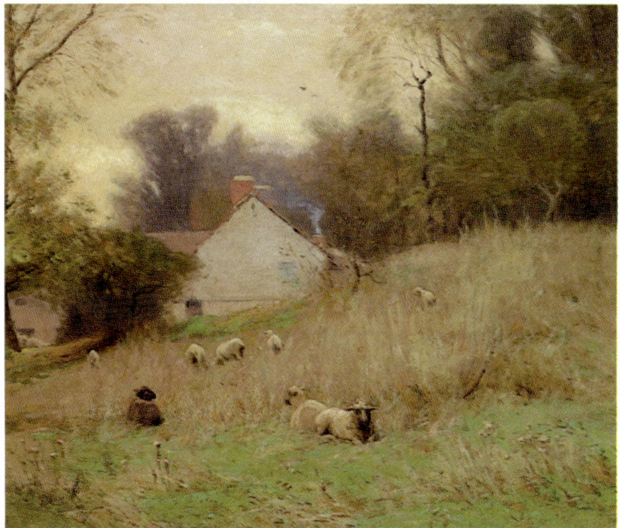

But Fournier was restless in Minneapolis. Scrapping together what money he could, he departed in the Fall of 1896 for his second trip to France, stopping on the way to visit the artists Max Weyl in Washington and William Merritt Chase in his New York studio. The introduction to the famous and successful Chase may have been furnished by Barton S. Hays, who had been Chase's first art teacher in Indianapolis many years before and who was living in Minneapolis and devoting himself to still-life painting in the 1880s and 90s. Fournier's second trip to France in which he briefly enrolled again in the Académie Julian, lasted only a few months, and by the spring of 1897 he was back in Minneapolis. Some months after his return, Fournier again painted the same Minneapolis landmark that had earned him so much praise at his first Paris Salon. *Indian Summer Morning Near Minnehaha Creek* (Fig. 3) pictures the small stream at a distance beyond a sunny field. Its clear, bright light and delicate harmony of color would no doubt have aroused the same kind of admiration as *Spring*

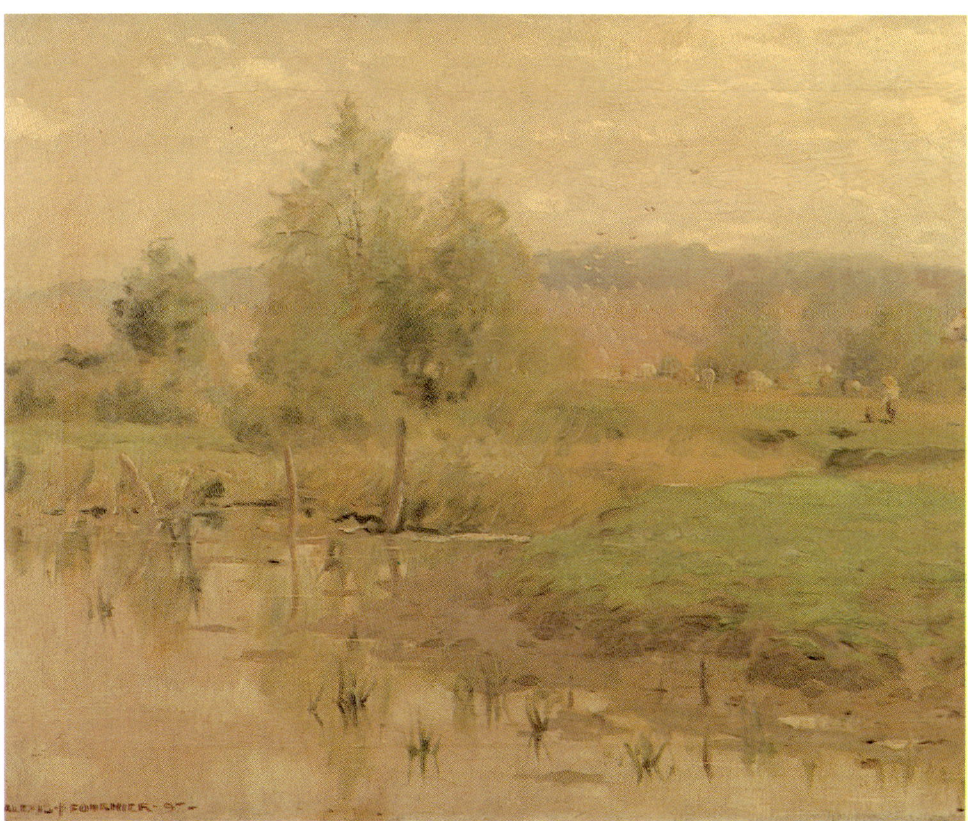

Fig. 2. Evening in Normandy

Fig. 3. Indian Summer Morning Near Minnehaha Creek.

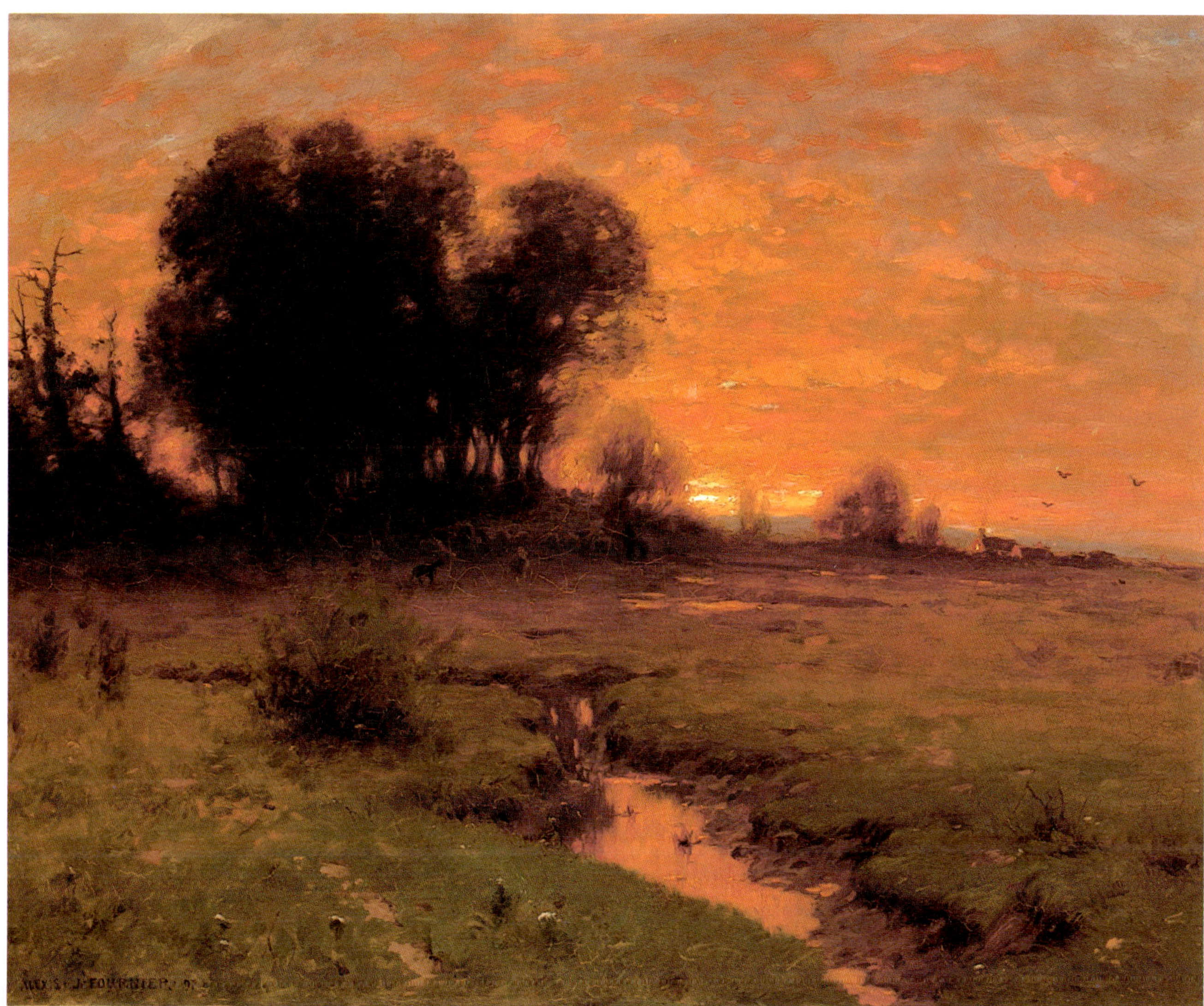

Fig. 4. When Golden Evening Fades.

Morning - Minnehaha Creek had three years earlier in France.

Fournier was exhibiting more widely and more frequently that year than ever before and his reputation as an extraordinarily able painter of the out-of-doors was spreading beyond the local community. The third annual exhibition of the Minneapolis Art League, which he had been instrumental in founding, exhibited seven of Fournier's canvases in 1897, while an exhibition at the Minneapolis Society of Fine Arts hung one. The 10th Annual Exhibition of the Art Institute of Chicago displayed three of his paintings and the National Academy of Design in New York showed two.

1897 was also the year that Fournier painted what is undoubtedly one of his masterpieces, *When Golden Evening Fades* (Fig. 4), also called, *Eventide: Normandie.*[9] The painting is typically Barbizon in its idyllic mood and poetic atmosphere as well as in the soft outlines of the objects fading in the evening gloom. A shepherd and his dog, barely visible in the darkening shadows, guides his flock up a slight rise to the farm whose roof appears just over the crest of the hill. Like the peasants of the Barbizon masters, especially Jean François Millet, the solitary shepherd is a part of the nourishing earth, sustained by the same spirit that gives life to the animals and vegetation around him. In the vast skies, the setting sun gleams between the lowering clouds in transient bursts of fiery glory, while the stream that winds through the meadow below, reflects in more subdued tones, the splendor of the evening sky. Though it is, of course, an intensely personal vision, its unity of the spiritual and material is held in common with such American followers of the Barbizon tradition as William Morris Hunt, Wyatt Eaton, and especially George Inness whom Fournier so much admired.[10] In its expression of the ideal of nature and of the artist's subjective appreciation of it, it signalled a change of course in Fournier's artistic direction.

"Feet in America and heart in France" was still an apt description of Fournier's restlessness and his longing to be in what he considered his second native land. On April 10, 1898 he again set out for the east, stopping to hold several exhibitions of his work, including one at the J. Eastman Chase Gallery in Boston. At the close of the Boston exhibit he sailed again for France on his third European trip, determined this time to strike out on his own and to travel and study independently of the Académie Julian. In 1898, and in the following three years, Fournier's paintings were again exhibited at the Paris Salon. Though he apparently had intended that his family should join him in France later in the year,[11] he changed his mind and returned to Minneapolis in the Fall of 1898 with twenty new canvases. He hoped to sell these pictures to his Minnesota friends and patrons in order to finance a more extended stay of several years in France. The money successfully raised, he again sailed for France in May, 1899 on his fourth trip in less than six years, this time taking his wife and children with him.

The family settled a few miles north of Paris at Auvers-sur-Oise in the former home of Charles François Daubigny, one of the French Barbizon masters, and near the home of Jules Dupré, another painter of the same school. The family had as a close neighbor, their friend, Charles Sprague Pearce, a Boston artist who lived in a remodelled chateau nearby. The Fourniers were "cosily situated, having a house and garden and some sheep and goats . . . models for his paintings," Fournier said.[12] Another friend and neighbor was the black Pittsburgh artist, Henry Ossawa Tanner, a former fellow student at the Académie Julian and Fournier's frequent companion on sketching trips into the surrounding countryside. He is portrayed in a drawing in Fournier's sketchbook of that year (Fig. 5).

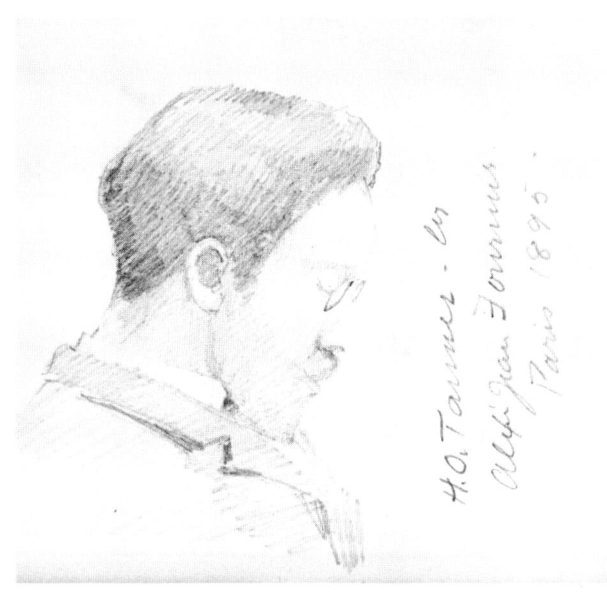

Fig. 5. Sketchbook Drawing of H. O. Tanner.

Another picture of this period is the much exhibited, *A Sylvan Melody* (Fig. 6). It was Fournier's Salon piece of 1901 and was purchased the following year by Mrs. Frank H. Peavey, widow of the Minneapolis grain merchant. The Peaveys had seen the painting on the artist's easel during a visit to France in 1899. They were old and loyal patrons of Fournier and were always welcome in his home. Frank H. Peavey died in 1901 and, in accordance with his wishes, Mrs. Peavey later donated the picture to the Minneapolis Public Library, which had not yet acquired any of Fournier's paintings.

The picture is more sentimentalized than Millet's subjects and accordingly, the shepherd boy is less heroic. As he sits on a grassy knoll piping dreamily on his flute, the boy, for whom Fournier's son, Paul, posed,[13] recalls instead the peasant figures of Constant Troyon, an older member than Millet of the Barbizon tradition. The atmospheric effects are also closer to Troyon, manipulating dark shadows for their pictorial effect. Each sheep in the flock is a study of passivity and contentment surrounding the shepherd boy as he plays on the flute. The late afternoon sun has begun its slow descent, illuminating the distant village in a bright shaft of light and bathing the tops of the foreground trees in its golden glow. The scene is one of tranquility and peace, of man and animal in harmony with nature. It is, perhaps, a more formal picture than many of Fournier's other paintings, lacking, to a certain degree, their spontaneity. Indeed, it has the aura of a studio piece, deliberately painted for an academic jury. But it captures, even celebrates, the nineteenth century ideal of the uncorrupted virtue of rural life, and this may have facilitated its acceptance by the Paris Salon.

At the same Salon Fournier also exhibited two drawings and a monotype. He had recently been experimenting with this graphic art form and had organized, with his friend, Herbert Waldron Faulkner, a monotype club in Paris. It was an informal organization, the members dropping in at Faulkner's studio, usually on a Saturday evening, to use his press. At the same time they enjoyed each other's companionship and comments. The club included Fournier's friend, the British novelist, Israel Zangwill, his artist brother, and also Louis Loeb, Francis Murphy, Albert Sterner and others. Fournier showed one of his monotypes to the aging Henri Harpignies who praised it so highly that he was encouraged to submit it to the Salon Jury. To his delight, it was accepted.

At about the same time, Fournier was also enjoying the honor of a one-man exhibition in the United States. From the 12th of April to May 13th, 1900, the Cincinnati Museum of Art showed twenty-five paintings by the artist, most of them scenes painted in Normandy. Later that year the prestigious annual exhibition of the Pennsylvania Academy of Art in Philadelphia showed an important Fournier painting, *The Crepuscle*, now lost. Some time in its history and for unknown reasons, this painting was erroneously identified as the Salon picture of 1901, but its subject is not at all like *A Sylvan Melody*. Instead of a shepherd boy piping to his flock on a late afternoon, it depicted a flock of sheep huddled on a cliff with the crepuscular moon rising in the distance.

Very different from his other pictures to date is a small painting entitled *Snow on the Village* (Fig. 7), done in Auvers in January or February, 1900. A low stone wall climbs into the picture creating an interesting curve in the composition of rectangles and inverted "V's," while a snow rimmed red roof provides a colorful note in the otherwise monochromatic description of winter in the village. Fournier exploits to the full here the pictorial possibilities of the huddled roofs of the village homes. It is a quiet, unforced landscape in which a certain calm restraint together with a cool delicacy in handling the architectural masses, mark it as one of Fournier's most interesting works. Resisting the painterly seduction of Impressionism to which Willard LeRoy Metcalf, John Twachtman and so

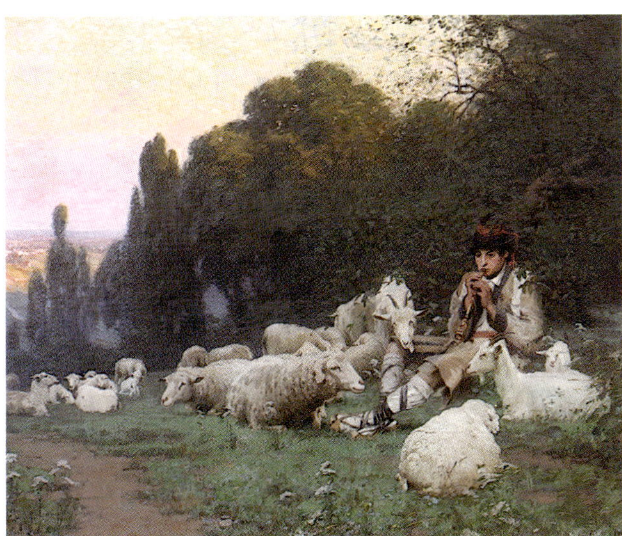

Fig. 6. A Sylvan Melody.

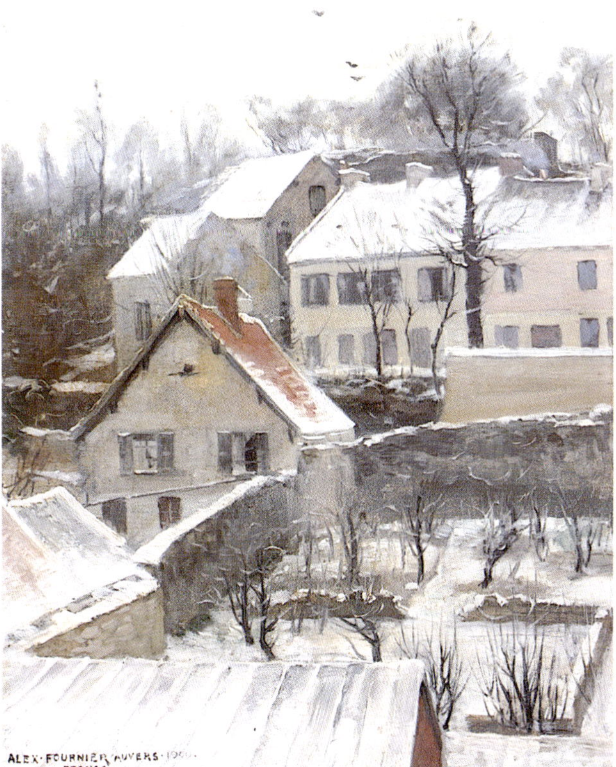

Fig. 7. Snow on the Village.

many of his American contemporaries succumbed, Fournier retains, in *Snow in the Village*, the linear precision and solid form of an older American tradition. The painting is signed Alex Fournier, instead of Alexis, a change which occurred around the year 1900.

Fournier at this time was, however, increasingly devoting himself to the same intense study of light and atmosphere in nature as the French Impressionists. Fournier's preference for an "American light" extended to a fondness for silhouetting form against a lighted sky, revealing a typical American concentration on the object itself, whether in the out-of-doors or, as in still life painting, on the table top. Thus, in a small landscape entitled *Twilight in Normandy* (Fig. 8) probably painted during this period, Fournier returns to the study of evening light evidenced in some of his early Minnesota pictures. We see a group of haystacks in the middle distance silhouetted against an evening sky. The setting sun is reflected against a low cloud in a sudden burst of gold and crimson while the muddy ruts of the country road in the foreground and a rough stone wall at the left have already begun to fade in the deepening evening shadows. One is reminded here not so much of the Barbizon masters whom Fournier so much admired as of the painters of the nineteenth century Hudson River School, and especially the landscapes of such artists as Martin Johnson Heade whose luminous views of haystacks on the Rhode Island marshes insist on

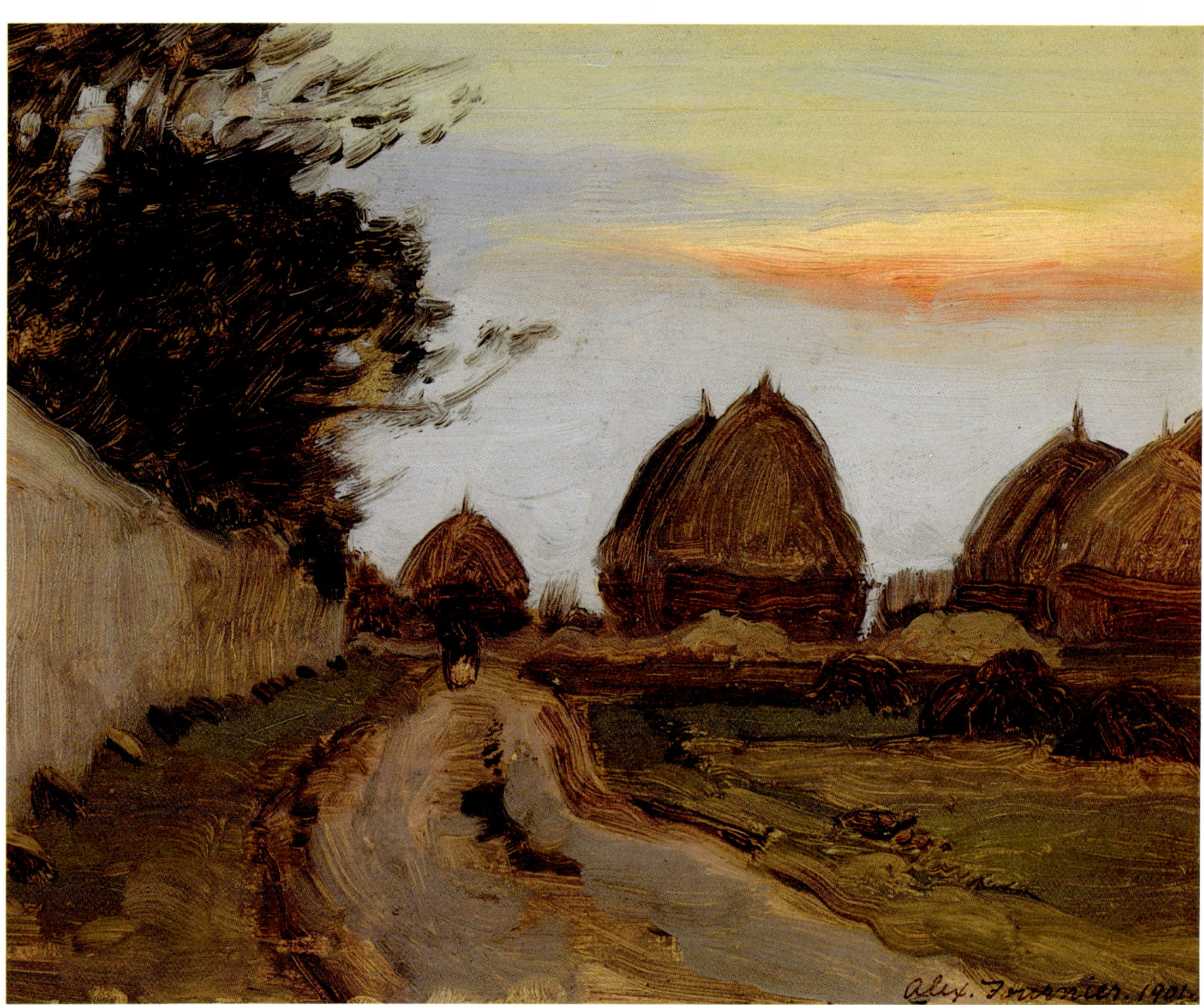

Fig. 8. Twilight in Normandy.

the primacy of tangible form as it is defined by a clear, revealing light. Monet's famous series of haystacks at Giverny that shimmer and dissolve in a haze of atmosphere as they seem to float on the picture's surface had not altered Fournier's perception of the out-of-doors, at least not yet.

In October, 1900, Fournier rented a temporary studio at 18 Impasse du Maine. He apparently divided his time for the next several months between Paris and Auvers-sur-Oise where the family continued to live for a few more months until Emma and the children returned to Minneapolis toward the end of 1900.[14]

In January, 1901, several of Fournier's canvases were hung at an exhibition of the American Art Association in Paris. A letter written by a Minnesota admirer who saw the exhibition and also visited Fournier at that time, gives us a glimpse of the esteem in which he was held by the Paris art community. "I must not forget to tell you about Mr. Fournier's pictures," the unnamed correspondent writes. "He invited us the other day to visit his studio . . . Never have I seen such rapid development. He had eight or ten perfectly exquisite pictures, so beautiful that I think his being an American, modest and not pushing, is all that stands in the way of a great reputation. Outside of the portraits shown by Whistler, Sargeant (sic), Cecilia Beaux and one or two others, there was nothing in the exhibit . . . that touched his landscapes . . . All artists seem to know him and think well of his work."[15] This report documents the fact that he was exhibiting with some of the best known artists at the turn of the century as well as being shown regularly at the Paris Salon.[16]

While Fournier was enjoying such success abroad, disaster struck at home. On Sunday afternoon, January 27, 1901, an overturned lamp caused a fire that destroyed his home in Minneapolis. The furniture and most of his paintings were saved, but a large portfolio which Emma had recently brought back with her from France and that contained most of the studies the artist had made the year before was lost. Fortunately, Emma and the children escaped unharmed and took up temporary residence with hospitable neighbors.

None of Fournier's letters to Emma (or hers to him) survive, but that he did not easily separate himself from his wife and children in order to study in France is attested by scattered notes in his sketchbooks. "Write to Emma," he reminds himself, or "Get gloves for me and Emma."[17] Tucked away in the artist's notebook on the homes of the Barbizon masters is a newspaper clipping reprinting James J. Metcalf's "Remember, Dear":

> "My darling when the morning comes
> And you begin your day,
> Remember that my loving heart
> Is yours in every way.
> Remember that I think of you
> Wherever you may be,
> And that you are the only one
> Who means so much to me."

NOTES TO CHAPTER 3: France and America

1. These lines appear on the bookplates which Richard Le Gallienne was affixing to his books in 1910. The sentiment, intended to define his own dilemma, applies as aptly to Fournier.
2. Undated, pencilled autobiographical sketch written in East Aurora, Collection of the Minnesota Historical Society.
3. Fournier Notebook, Paris, 1894, Collection of Willis Peterson.
4. Autobiographical sketch, Op. Cit.
5. Interview in *Minneapolis Journal*, November 18, 1895.
6. *Brush and Pencil Magazine*, 1899, p. 245.
7. *Minneapolis Journal*, January 14, 1896, p. 2.
8. Fournier Notebook, 1896, Collection of Willis Peterson.
9. Fournier had a disconcerting habit of giving the same painting different titles at different times in his life (as well as giving the same name to different paintings). *When Golden Evening Fades* may be the same picture that was called *End of the Day* when it was shown as No. 134 at the Art Institute of Chicago Exhibition of 1897, for the measurements and description match. *End of the Day* was also shown at the National Academy of Design in New York in 1897. However, in 1898 the Trans-Mississippi International Exhibition in Omaha, Nebraska, exhibited two Fournier canvases. One of them, No. 217, was entitled, *When Golden Evening Fades*. Again displayed under the same title, the painting was included among eight Fournier paintings exhibited in the art gallery and furniture shop of John Scott Bradstreet in Minneapolis the same year.
10. Fournier was a close friend in Paris of George Inness Jr. See *Minneapolis Journal*, May 17, 1899, p. 6.
11. *Minneapolis Journal*, March 29, 1898, p. 9.
12. *Minneapolis Journal*, November 21, 1899, p. 8.
13. *Minneapolis Society of Fine Arts Bulletin*, Vol. II, April, 1907, p. 6.
14. The length of Mrs. Fournier's stay in France with the children Grace and Paul, is unclear as newspaper accounts contradict one another on this subject. As closely as can be determined, Fournier's family was in France from the spring of 1899 to late in 1900.
15. *Minneapolis Journal*, January 31, 1901, p. 5.
16. The Paris Salon of 1901 exhibited Fournier's *Moonrise* as well as *A Sylvan Melody*. Fournier's friend, Burt Harwood, a fellow Minnesota artist then resident in Paris, also had two paintings hung there. The 300 pictures that passed the Salon Jury were picked from over 7,000 works that had been submitted.
17. Sketchbook 58B, Collection of Willis Peterson.

Chapter 4 Venetian Interlude

In the year 1867 William Dean Howells declared, in *Italian Journeys*, that "Venice is, and remains, the most beautiful city in the world."[1] His sentiments were echoed by at least three generations of American tourists, artists among them, who in the years following the Civil War flocked to Venice, the city on the lagoons, in ever increasing numbers. Lured by the city's Mediterrean light and color, as well as by its Byzantine and Gothic architectural splendor, Venice had by the last quarter of the nineteenth century supplanted Rome and Florence as a magnet for the American traveler. Indeed, in 1890 James Russell Lowell confided to a friend that "a longing has been growing in me for several years now, chiefly, I confess, for Venice, but with subsidiary hankerings after Rome and Florence."[2]

In truth, however, though the floodtide of American visitors began after the Civil War, the interest of American artists in Venice extended back as far as the early years of the nineteenth century to the painter Washington Allston. He was probably the first to acknowledge his indebtedness, if not to the city itself, at least to the Venetian colorists. "Titian, Tintoret and Paul Veronese absolutely enchanted me," he wrote, "for they took away all sense of subject . . . It was the poetry of color which I felt."[3] The color that Allston admired in the work of the Venetian Renaissance masters was a reflection of the city itself where the ancient stones of palaces, churches and plazas shone with the luminescence of the canals.

In any event, from Allston to Loren MacIver, whose *Venice* of 1949 is a semi-abstract reverberation of the shimmer and movement of the lagoons, the ancient city on the Adriatic attracted a host of American artists (as well, of course, as those of other nations). Some of them, like William Gedney Bunce established permanent residence there, and others, including Frank Duveneck, James McNeill Whistler, John S. Sargent, Theodore Robinson, John Twachtman, Maurice Prendergast and others, arrived for visits of varying lengths during the decades around the turn of the century.

In May, 1901 Alexis Fournier arrived in Venice in the company of his Paris friend and companion, Herbert Waldron Faulkner. He carried with him, on the front page of one of his sketchbooks, the admonition pencilled there by the French academician, Carolus Durand,

> "Aimez la Gloire plus que l'argent,
> L'art plus que la gloire,
> Le nature plus que l'art."

This was not Fournier's first visit to Venice—he had been there in the summer of 1894 and possibly again in 1895—but this time it was a more extended visit of two and a half months in which he attempted to master the peculiar light and atmosphere of the city.

The two friends, Fournier and Faulkner, rented a studio on one of the islands near San Giorgio. Every morning they packed their sketching materials and set out in the sandula, or flat bottomed boat, which they hired each day. As a later newspaper account describes it, the artists were often afloat at dawn, sketching or painting steadily until midnight on moonlit nights. "In the evening as the light faded, the boatman was dispatched to fetch the supper which had been ordered at noon and, taking this in the boat, the artists drifted out on the tide, to study the infinite changes of evening as it dropped over the city of the waters."[4]

Fournier was working hard but not neglecting his social life. At a restaurant in Venice called "Hole in the Wall," he and Faulkner met regularly with a group of writers and artists that included Israel Zangwill, Eugene Vail, Burt W. Johnson, Fritz Thaulow, Joseph Pennell, the resident expatriot American William Gedney Bunce, and "many well known Englishmen."[5] Fournier was particularly close to Israel Zangwill whom he had met on one of his previous visits to Venice. At that time the novelist was just completing his best known work, *Children of the Ghetto*, and Fournier had accompanied him on some of his tours through Venice's ancient Jewish quarter. During this visit of 1901, the painter and the novelist again toured the ghetto and other historic sites together, Fournier much enjoying the writer's profound knowledge of the history of the ancient city.

Like other artists to whom landscape was the quintessence of the painter's craft, Fournier saw in Venice the opportunity to flavor his views of nature with the picturesque. Indeed, his pictures of the Adriatic city are rare exceptions to his commitment to rural subjects since his early paintings of Minneapolis and St. Paul. Venice's elaborate palaces shining golden in the sun, the deep blue of the Mediterranean sea and sky, the graceful churches and ancient stone walls, even the colorful boats tied up at the quays, all appealed to his sense of the piquant while still affording him the opportunity to study nature in an unusual and exotic environment.

Yet Fournier's view of Venice was different from that of his American compatriots. Unlike Sargent or Duveneck, he never allowed the brush stroke itself to dominate the picture nor did he fall into the kind of semi-abstract revery for which Whistler is justly famous. Twachtman and Robinson succumbed to the bright colors of the Impressionists and allowed light itself to master their compositions, while Prendergast, emerging from the Impressionist aesthetic of broken color and light-filled landscapes, developed his own highly individual style of tapestry like forms that weave across the picture plane in a flat pattern of shape and color. But Fournier was too much of a traditionalist to venture out stylistically so far on his own. His views of the city, such as *Evening in Venice* (Fig. 1), exploit the poetic light and gentle lyricism of Barbizon rather than the bold patterns of Prendergast or the simplification and pictorial innuendo of Whistler. Indeed, Fournier never relinquished his fidelity to the visual experience or his conviction that it should serve as the primary foundation for art. In this he clung to the conservative aesthetic conventions of his native land, resisting the new tendencies manifesting themselves in Europe. What he did add to the American tradition was a unique sense of color and a feeling for its dramatic possibilities.

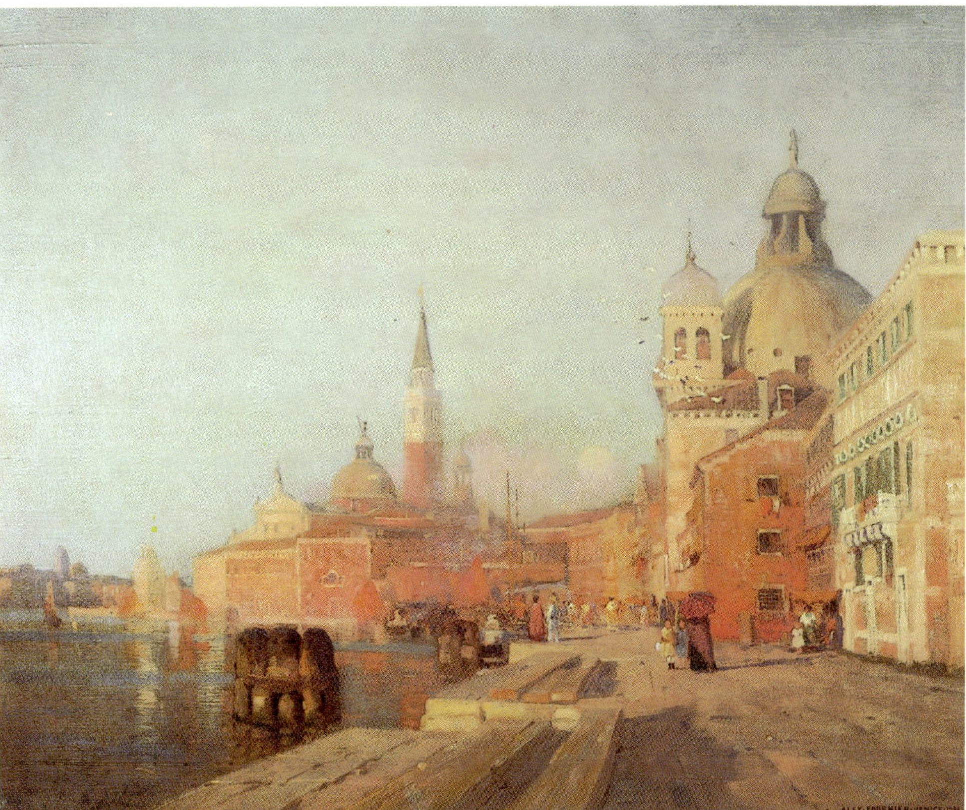
Fig. 1. Evening in Venice.

A group of Venetian paintings based on this summer trip to Venice was exhibited at Beard's Art Gallery in Minneapolis at the end of December, 1901, and later shown in St. Paul. These pictures mark a significant departure from Fournier's landscapes because the trees and foliage which play such an important compositional and coloristic role in his French and American subjects are almost entirely absent here. The light defines form here not in terms of nature's own organic structure but in buildings, stone quays and boats tied to their moorings. The shimmering, ever present water reflects shifting patterns of light and shadow. A few of the Venetian pictures are almost entirely sea and sky coming close to marine painting, a subject rare in Fournier's oeuvre.

A large painting of 1901, *Venetian Sunset*, depicted a twilight scene on the Guidecca canal. This painting was bought by Dr. Soren Rees, a prominent Minneapolis physician who may have seen it when it was exhibited at Beard's. It was so admired by Rees' close friend, Dr. Frederick Wulling, first dean of the School of Pharmacy at the University of Minnesota, that Fournier painted a smaller copy for him in 1903 (Fig. 2). The tighter composition and even more spectacular color palette of the smaller version place it among Fournier's most accomplished works.

The picture shows the Church of the Gesuati appearing at a short distance beyond a stone wall

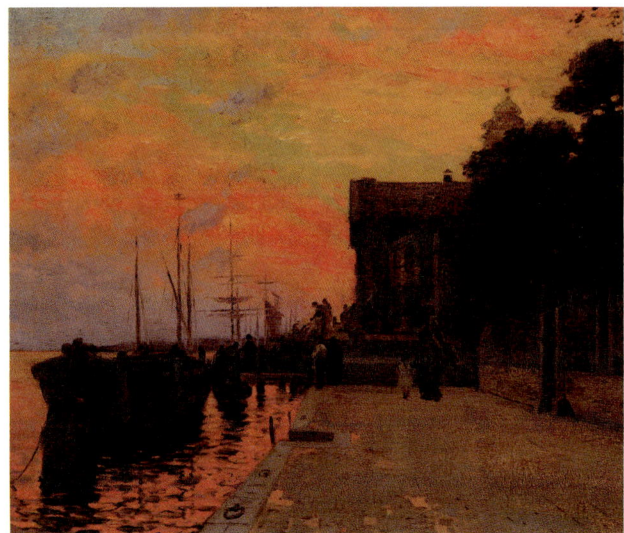
Fig. 2. Venetian Sunset.

and some intervening buildings. The wall is softened by the darkening foliage of a few trees that hide the main dome of the church and reveal only one of its two turrets. Some boats are tied up at a jetty close by and pedestrians climb the steps of a bridge spanning the entrance to the Rio di San Vio, one of the very small canals feeding into the much broader Guidecca. A pencil sketch in Fournier's Venice notebook shows the same scene from the opposite direction (Fig. 3). In the painting, a recent rain shower has drenched the foreground pavement and little puddles of water, caught in the rough stones, still reflect the colors of the evening sky. Those colors, the crimson, saffron and violet hues of the setting sun are also reflected in the water of the canal as, far in the distance, the purple hush of night settles over the horizon. For sheer coloristic bravura Fournier occasionally equalled, but never surpassed, this picture.

Fournier's delight in color is an element that

Fig. 3. The Gesuati.

sets him somewhat apart from the mainstream of American art as it had developed in the eighteenth and most of the nineteenth century, though Frederick Edwin Church had earlier painted some glorious sunset scenes. But Church and Fournier too are typically American in their preservation of fact and the palpable presence of the object. The dissolution of form practiced by the Impressionists reached the United States relatively late in its art history and American artists only rarely succumbed to the disintegration of form practiced by their French colleagues and even earlier by the English painter, Joseph Mallord William Turner. Sunsets are, almost by definition, a vehicle for the study of color and light effects and had been painted in America frequently enough. But even the well known *Twilight in the Wilderness* by Frederic Church scarcely achieved the coloristic splendor of Fournier's sunsets. Fournier's roots, of course, were not in the United States but in French Canada, and therefore, his identification with France and French culture was more intense and personal than for his American compatriots at the turn of the century. Perhaps this explains, to some degree, his sensitivity to color, his awareness of its dramatic possibilities, and his growing appreciation of the esthetic and sensuous quality of the texture of paint itself.

Perhaps the most important of Fournier's Venetian paintings is *The Entrance to the Grand Canal* (Fig. 4), which, like many of his major works, exists in several versions. The largest and most impressive is a four by six foot canvas which was the chief ornament of the dining room of the Roycroft Inn in East Aurora, N.Y. It is the most classical of Fournier's Venetian pictures in its clear, unambiguous form and its sure line. It shows a staircase near St. Mark's Square leading down to the blue waters of the canal. A photograph of that summer shows Fournier on the very same steps, knapsack on his back and portfolio in hand (Fig. 5). In the painting the white stone balustrade flanking the stairs is drawn crisply and precisely though it is

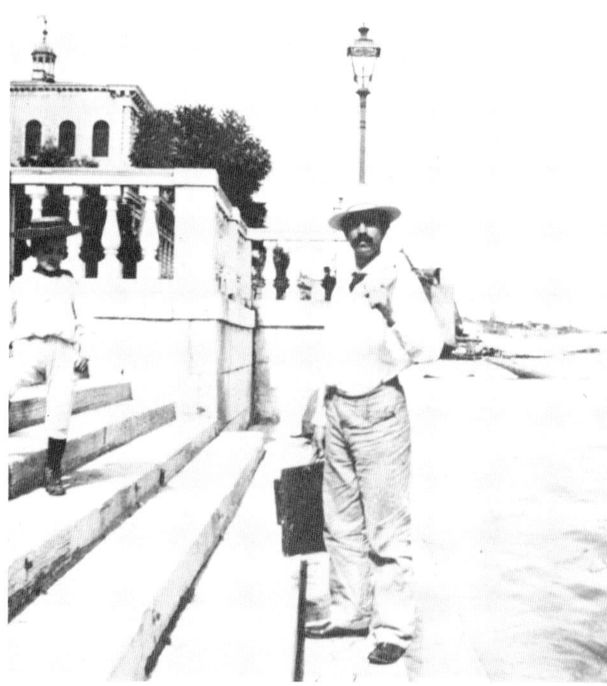

Fig. 5. Photograph. Alexis Fournier in Venice, 1901.

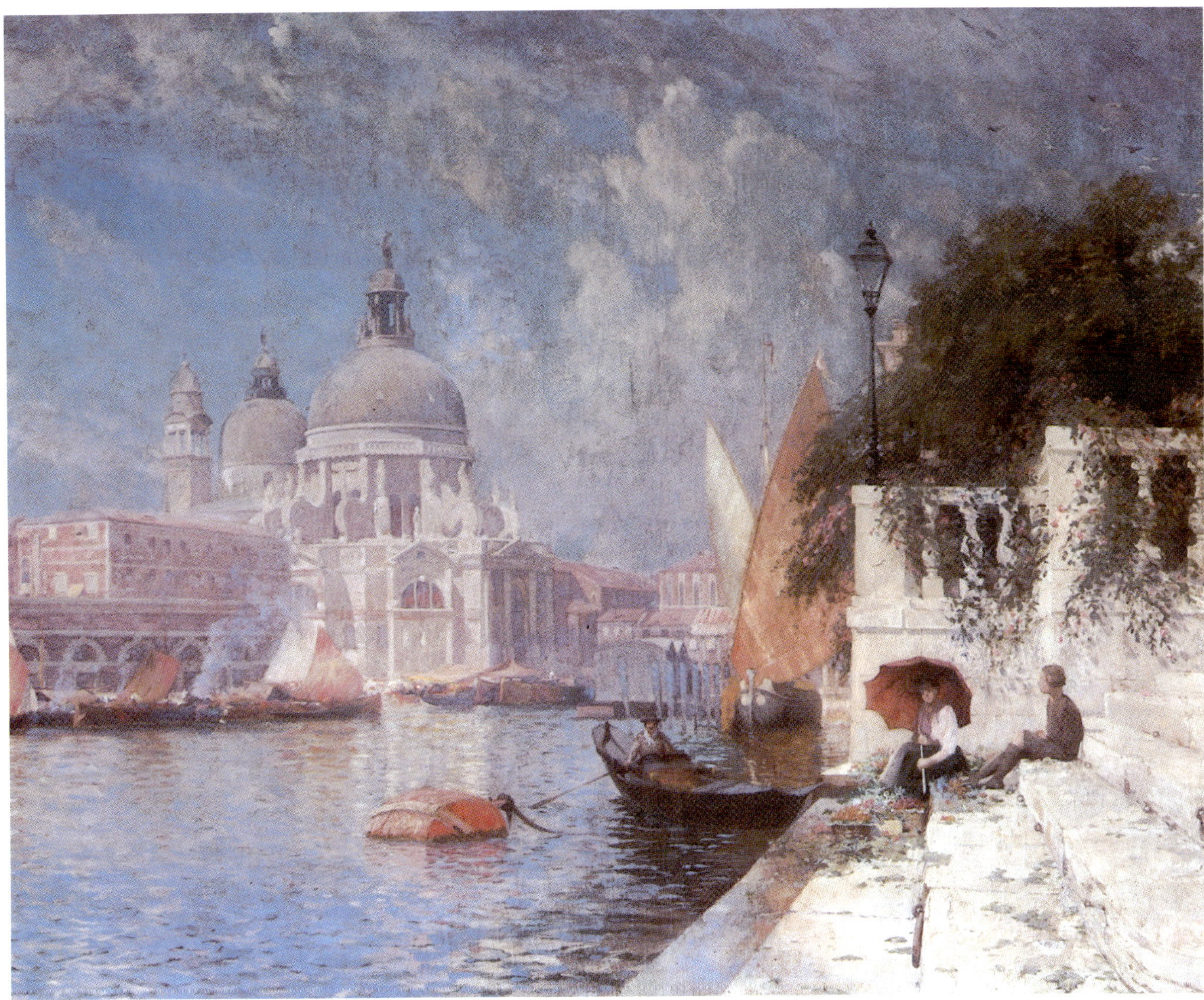

Fig. 4. Entrance to the Grand Canal.

somewhat softened by the foliage spilling over from an adjacent garden. A couple, sitting on the steps, look across the canal to one of Venice's proudest monuments, the church of Santa Maria della Salute, with dome upon dome rising above its picturesque base. With the morning sun glinting on its volutes and ornamental stonework, the building almost seems to float on the water like Kubla Khan's "stately pleasure dome" in the Xanadu of Samuel Taylor Coleridge's imagination. This image of a fairy tale world is reinforced by the opalescent blues of sea and sky and by the violets, pinks and oranges that carry out the artist's symphony of color. The picture clearly reveals the artist's enchantment with Venice, with its shimmering canals, its colorful boats, its open plazas and ancient stone monuments, all shining in the brilliant light of a Mediterranean sky.

Of the large number of oils, watercolors and drawings of Venice done by Fournier some are preserved today only in old photographs in the artist's album and some just mentioned in old exhibition catalogues or newspaper reviews. One that does survive, again in several versions and different sizes, is *On the Zattera* (Fig. 6), a view of one of Venice's main landing places near its Custom's House. Here Fournier exploited the pictorial possibilities of the forest of masts and colorful sails on the boats tied up at the quay. The cool shadows cast on the stone pavements seem to reflect the quiet waters of the canals and enhance the peculiar luminous sheen that distinguishes Venice. But even when water is not shown, as it is not, for example, in *The Campo Mauritzio* (Fig. 7), that luminous quality still persists. Here Fournier used a very impressionistic brush to depict both the pedestrians and the flock of pigeons alighting on the street, but he combines it with the flat, reflective surfaces of buildings, pavement and sky. The picture exhibits what has been called the "glare aesthetic," practiced by many American artists in Venice, in which intense daylight, portrayed in strong tonal contrasts, achieves the effect of glare from reflecting surfaces. Flat, or nearly flat, planes of buildings and pavement offer background "support" to the figures in the foreground. These planes function as mirrors reflecting the bright sunlight against which the shadows of clearly defined objects are cast, intensifying color and light without dissolving form.[6]

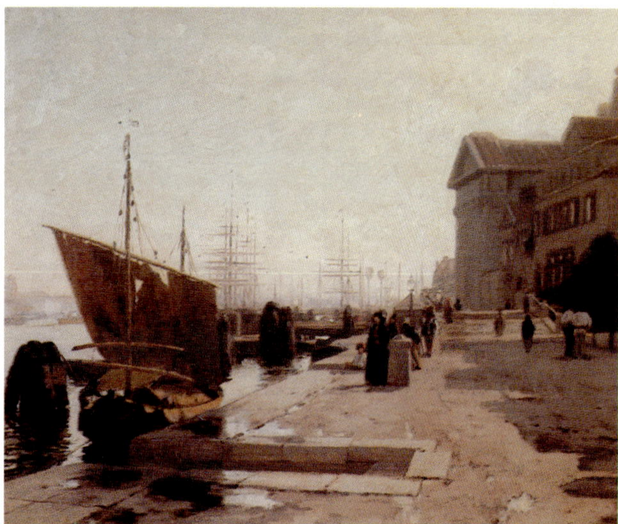

Fig. 6. On the Zattera.

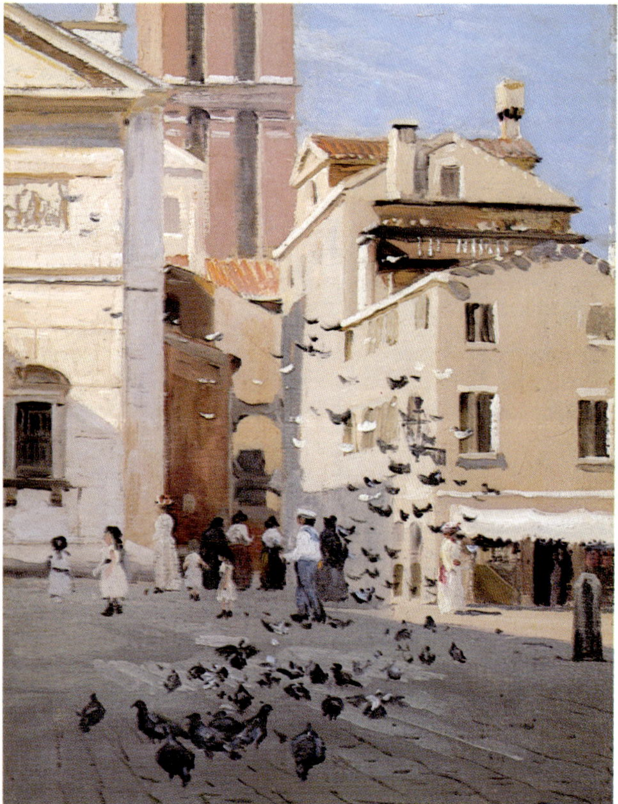

Fig. 7. The Campo Mauritzio.

It was Fournier's special skill in depicting color and light that was singled out for special praise in a picture entitled *Fiesta Scene* (now lost), when it was exhibited with the artist's other Venetian paintings in Minneapolis at the end of the year. A critic noted: "An odd and interesting bit of Venice that is full of cheerful suggestion is a fiesta scene. The arches and white electric lights and myriad red lanterns cast broken reflections in the softly lapping waters . . . (above which rise) towers and roofs faintly illuminated from the lights of the canals . . ."[7]

Apparently Fournier never tired of observing the city, its buildings, plazas, boats, quays, water and sky. The spontaneity and apparent effortlessness of his finished work belie the many hours spent in the studies and preparatory sketches which fill his notebooks (Fig. 8). "Paint some studies," he admonishes himself, "of gondolas, sandulas, sailboats in the sun, red buoys, doors, cupolas, grills, etc., San Marco and palaces from Lagoon, San Giorgio, Salute from the Zacharia."[8]

Some time during the summer Fournier travelled to Rome and a number of delightful paintings are the result of what was probably a rather brief stay. *Vatican Gardens* (Fig. 9) is a small painting that again reveals the "glare aesthetic" of tonal contrasts evident in many of the Venetian paintings. The strong Italian sunlight defines the surfaces of buildings and garden walls with a crispness and vitality that creates a significant spatial division in the painting. The clearly defined planes reflect the bright light back toward the spectator, and contrast with the cool green shadow of the foreground space.

Toward the middle of July, 1901, Fournier packed his gear and set out on a leisurely trip back to France, stopping en route in Switzerland where he entered a few more sketches into his notebook. In August he was in Paris where he retrieved the studio easel, bicycle, writing desk and lamp that he had left at Faulkner's place before his trip to Venice. He devoted the late summer and early fall to forays into the French countryside where he continued to sketch and paint, but he was beginning to think of home. By the end of November he was ready to return, especially as a number of exhibitions were being planned after his arrival in the United States. The Paris edition of the New York Herald took note of his departure in an account of a farewell party held in Paris in his honor. "The poetic quality of his work," wrote the Herald correspondent, "which is, after all, but his gift of portraying nature, . . his sincerity, and his tremendous capacity for hard work, were a source of constant inspiration to everyone who knew him."[9]

Fournier arrived back in Minneapolis on November 17, 1901 after an absence of two and a half years. On some occasion during that period he

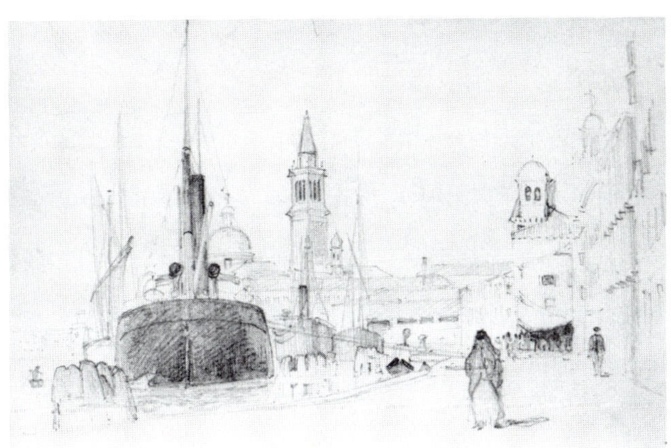

Fig. 8. Scene in Venice.

may have visited Minneapolis briefly, perhaps to accompany his family when they returned at the end of 1900. He brought back with him thick rolls of studies and a wealth of drawings and sketches which served as the basis for much of his later work. Though he apparently did not set foot again in Venice, he returned to it in memory and imagination throughout the rest of his life.

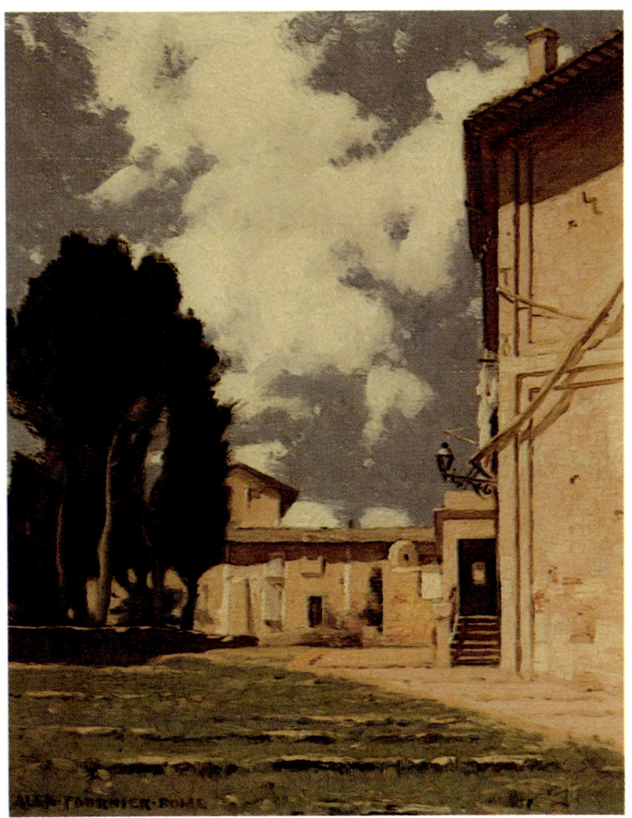

Fig. 9. Vatican Gardens.

NOTES TO CHAPTER 4: Venetian Interlude

1. William Dean Howells, *Italian Journeys*, Boston and New York, 1867, pp. 157-8.
2. Quoted in Charles C. Eldredge, Introduction, *The Arcadian Landscape: Nineteenth Century American Painters in Italy*, University of Kansas, 1972, p. viii.
3. Quoted in Barbara Novak, *American Painting of the Nineteenth Century*, New York, 1969, p. 57.
4. *Minneapolis Journal*, November 23, 1901, p. 24.
5. Ibid., p. 24.
6. William H. Gerdts describes this phenomenon in *American Impressionism*, Henry Art Gallery, University of Washington, Seattle, 1980, pp. 17-18.
7. *Minneapolis Journal*, December 21, 1901, p. 14.
8. Fournier Sketchbook, Collection of Willis Peterson.
9. *Minneapolis Journal*, December 2, 1901, p. 4.

Chapter 5 Bradstreet - The Arts and Crafts Movement

The emotional and professional dilemma of the foreign-trained American artist returning to his native land was a common enough experience in Fournier's time to have become the subject of a novel published in 1893 by William Dean Howells. In *The Coast of Bohemia*, Ludlow, the artist-hero, articulates the predicament of those nineteenth century American artists who returned from abroad determined to adapt the art of one culture to the reality of another. If Ludlow had the courage of his convictions, Howells remarks, a "purely American event could be reported on his canvas with all its native character, and yet it could be made to appeal to the enlightened eye with the charm of a French subject . . . he owed a duty to France no less than to America and wished to fulfill it in a picture which should at once testify to the excellence of the French method and American material."[1]

A further problem for the returning artist, as Fournier himself said, was the absence of a conducive environment in America for the artist to work in. That he missed the professional and personal support which he had felt in France is revealed in a talk he gave to the Women's Civic League of St. Paul on February 21, 1902. The Latin Quarter in Paris, he said, was the mecca of ambitious, young American artists for precisely the reason that there "he is surrounded by ambitious workers like himself, all anxious to accomplish something, all eager to succeed." As drawing and painting are purely mechanical attainments, true artistry depends on the painter's "ability to see and feel," an ability that flourishes only when supported by a conducive atmosphere. "Even in the East," the artist said, "there is growing up a little coterie of earnest believers in and workers for art whose influence is felt, but there is no art atmosphere here in the northwest, for there are no workers."[2]

Nevertheless, Fournier was not one to mope and mourn for what was unavailable. In spite of his longing for France, once back home, he plunged eagerly into a flurry of activity. He rented the studio at 719 Hennepin Avenue that had just been given up by Robert Koehler, the second director of the Minneapolis School of Art after Douglas Volk's departure in 1893. The studio was in the little building set back from Hennepin Avenue that T. B. Walker, Minneapolis art patron, had built in the early 1880's to house the newly formed Minneapolis School of Art, before it moved to other quarters at the Minneapolis Public Library. To save money Fournier sublet the big back room of the studio with its wide, comfortable fireplace to the Art League, a rather cosmopolitan art club formed largely through Koehler's efforts. The studio had also been previously occupied by Douglas Volk (when Fournier briefly shared some of its space with him) and John Scott Bradstreet, a Minneapolis furniture dealer, furniture designer, collector, gallery director and arbiter of Twin Cities taste. The Skylighters' Club, an arts and culture club which Bradstreet founded together with Edwin H. Hewitt, a Minneapolis architect, also had at one time occupied space in the Hennepin Avenue studio. The Skylighters later became the Minneapolis Arts and Crafts Society which, under Bradstreet's guidance, established an important niche for itself in the American Arts and Crafts movement.

There were a number of exhibitions for the artist to attend to, either just closing or planned for the near future. One was at Harington Beard's Gallery in Minneapolis in January, 1902, an exhibition that was moved to St. Paul in the following month. The newly founded Art Workers' Guild bought *Moonlight* from that show, a painting that later passed into the possession of the St. Paul Institute when it was founded, in 1905, through the merger of the Guild with the Art Museum Association of St. Paul. This may have been the same picture that the Carnegie Institute in Pittsburgh had recently exhibited.

More important was a letter Fournier received in August, 1902 from William French, director of the Chicago Art Institute, informing him that the Art Committee had acted favorably upon his application for a special individual exhibition, and that one of the Institute's galleries would be at his command from October 3rd to October 19th. It directed him to send to Chicago twenty to thirty paintings. The exhibition was to prove a resounding success. It was much praised in the Chicago press and the artist was hailed as one of the greatest of America's landscape painters. Several Fourniers were bought from that show for Chicago collections and, in fact, Director French later wrote Fournier that the exhibition had attracted more visitors and more purchasers than had ever been known at any one man show at the Chicago Art Institute. "It has been decidedly the most interesting (such show) that the Institute has arranged," wrote French, and, he added, "The variety of your works is remarkable."[3]

One of the many visitors who purchased from that exhibition was Elbert Hubbard. He bought *Silvery Moonlight* (also called, *The Shepherd's Return*) painted in 1898 (Fig. 1), for the art gallery of the Roycroft community at East Aurora, N.Y. It is particularly noteworthy as an early painting by Fournier in a tonalist mood, a style to which he occasionally turned in his later life. In it the artist has relied on the silvery tones of blues and greens to suggest a mood of stillness and revery in the quiet of a moonlight scene as a shepherd guides his flock through the evening streets of a Normandy

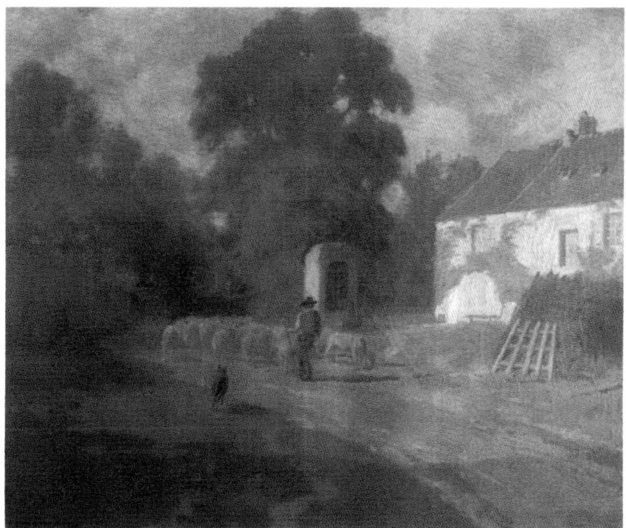

Fig. 1. Silvery Moonlight.

village. It is far from the pragmatism of earlier works such as *Millpond at Minneapolis* or even the nocturnal *Moonlight on Lake Harriet.*

At the same time as the Art Institute exhibition, Fournier was invited to exhibit with Adam Emory Albright, a painter of America's country children, at the Tenth Annual Exhibition of the Chicago Ceramics Association. In September Fournier also exhibited at the Third Annual Exhibition of the Minneapolis Society of Fine Arts, where he showed a recently completed painting entitled *Great Oaks from Little Acorns Grow* (Fig. 2). The title is more allegorical than is usual for Fournier but appropriate in this case because the painting shows a corner of the still young University of Minnesota campus. Both of the buildings in the background reveal the strong influence of the Romanesque

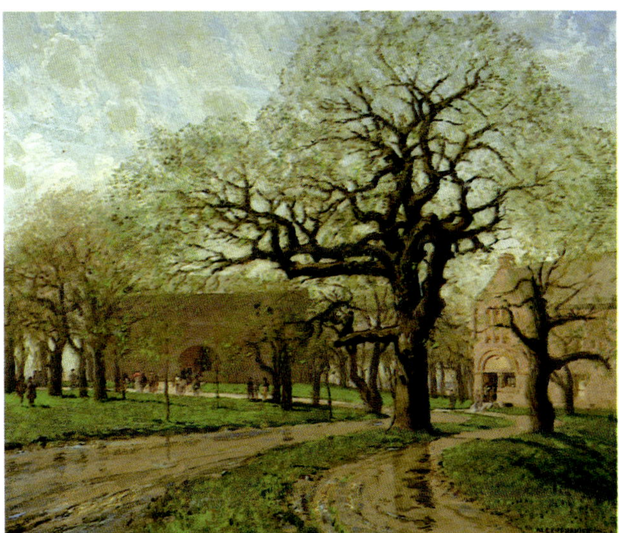

Fig. 2. Great Oaks from Little Acorns Grow.

style of Henry Hobson Richardson's architecture as it was interpreted by his local followers. This style, emphasizing wide, low-springing arches, rough stone or brickwork and solid impressive façades, was especially fashionable during the early 1890's when the University, and the Twin Cities, experienced a period of expansion and great building activity. There is a rawness in the painting, a sense of new beginnings that contrasts sharply with the mellowness of the artist's French landscapes. Instead of Daubigny and Harpignies, or even Corot, whom Fournier later claimed as his models, this painting recalls the direct, uncompromising style of the foremost French advocate of realism, Gustave Courbet.

But the influence of the French Barbizon masters is still evident in the idyllic, pastoral landscapes of France that Fournier painted during the early years after his return to America. Contradicting his own stated ambition to "become not a European artist but an American painter of American landscapes . . . proud to be described as 'that fellow from Minnesota'"[4] (meant, perhaps, to ingratiate himself with the local market), Fournier devoted considerable time during this period to translating sketches and notes made during his travels in France into finished canvases.

Afterglow: Normandie (1901) (Fig. 3) is typical of Fournier's French landscapes in its rich color, its effective contrast of bright light and strong shadow, its ability to make the spectator feel the immediate presence of the scene, and its creation of drama out of a simple and familiar country scene.[5] Three small canvases entitled *A Silvery Day, France* (Fig. 4), *Normandie* (Fig. 5) dated 1900 and *In Normandie* (Fig. 6) capture in vivid detail the atmospheric conditions of the moment. In the first, a hilltop tree bends to a sudden gust of wind beneath the cool colors of a windswept sky. In the other two, the first of which, *Normandie*, may be a study for the more finished *In Normandie*, the day is an intermittently overcast one in which the clouds cast a transient light on a French country scene showing the cone topped round haystacks of rural Normandy. These landscapes are infused with life—vibrant scenes of nature breathing in time to the shifting patterns of light and shadow. In the painting, *Normandie*, particularly, the artist has lowered the horizon line enough to make the landscape essentially a cloud study, with the earth reflecting the ephemeral patterns determined by the changing architecture of the cloud masses above. In its suggestion of nature's evanescent moods this picture is reminiscent of Dutch landscapes of the 17th century and John Constable's early 19th century studies of the English countryside in its constantly shifting light.

The persistence with which Fournier clung to the inspiration of France, however, was entirely typical of the American expatriots' dual allegiance in matters both artistic and personal after he returned home. Indeed, during the same period, especially during the years 1902-03, Fournier, frequently posing as a Frenchman, dress, accent and all, was engaged in painting the local scene in Minnesota. He was commissioned to do a number

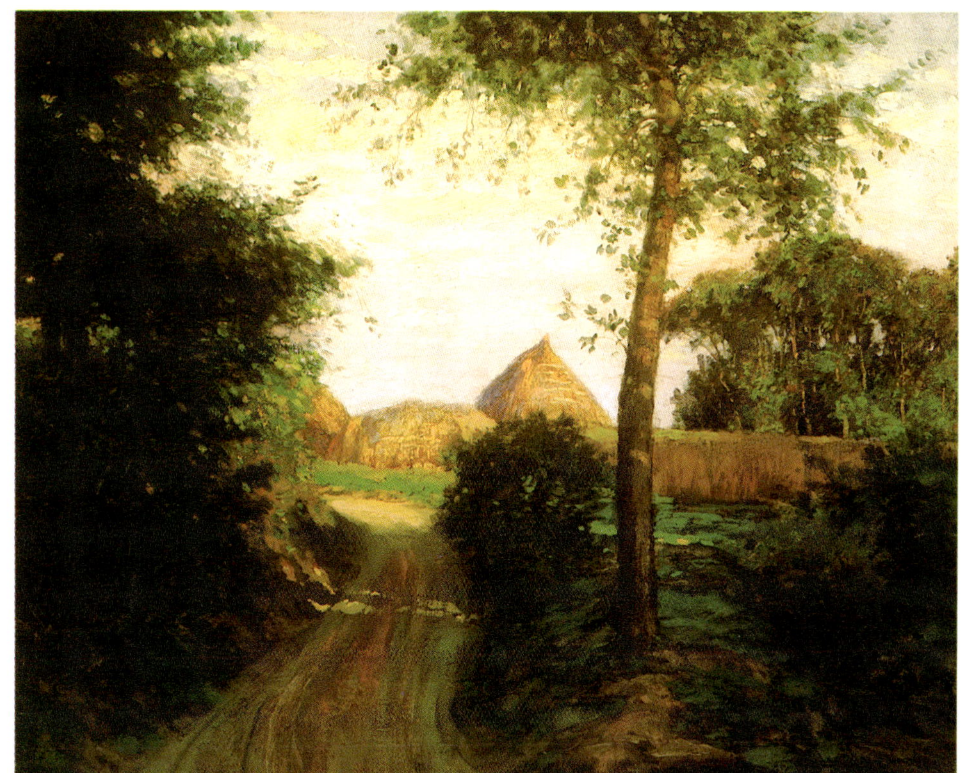

Fig. 3. Afterglow: Normandie.

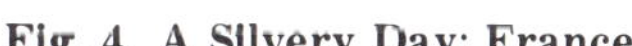

Fig. 4. A Silvery Day; France

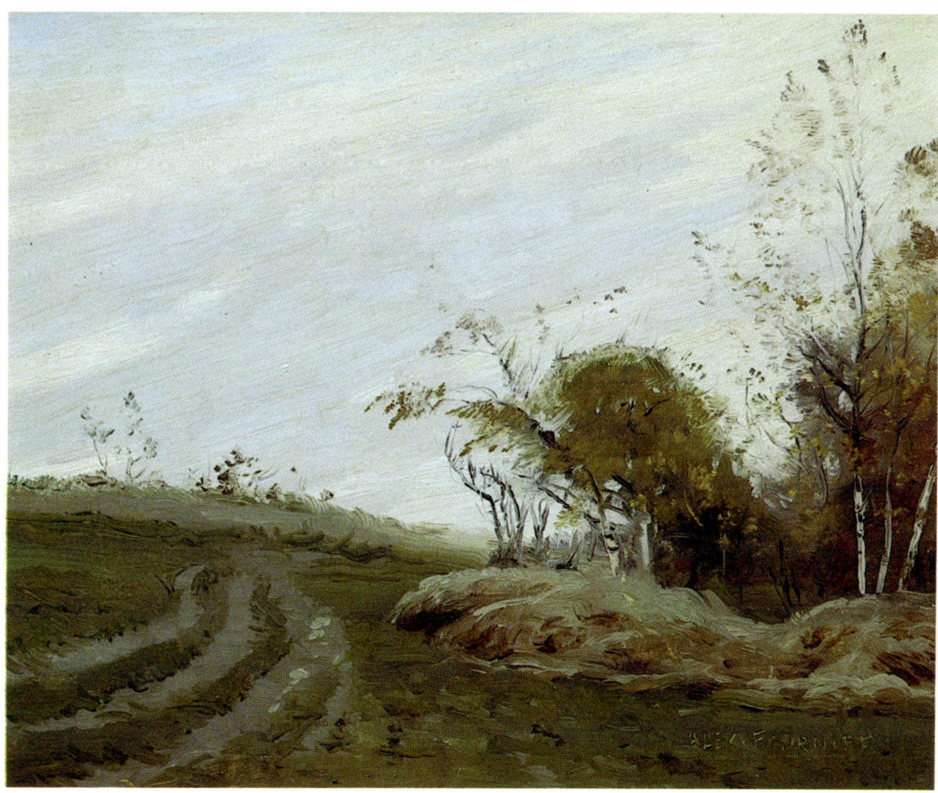

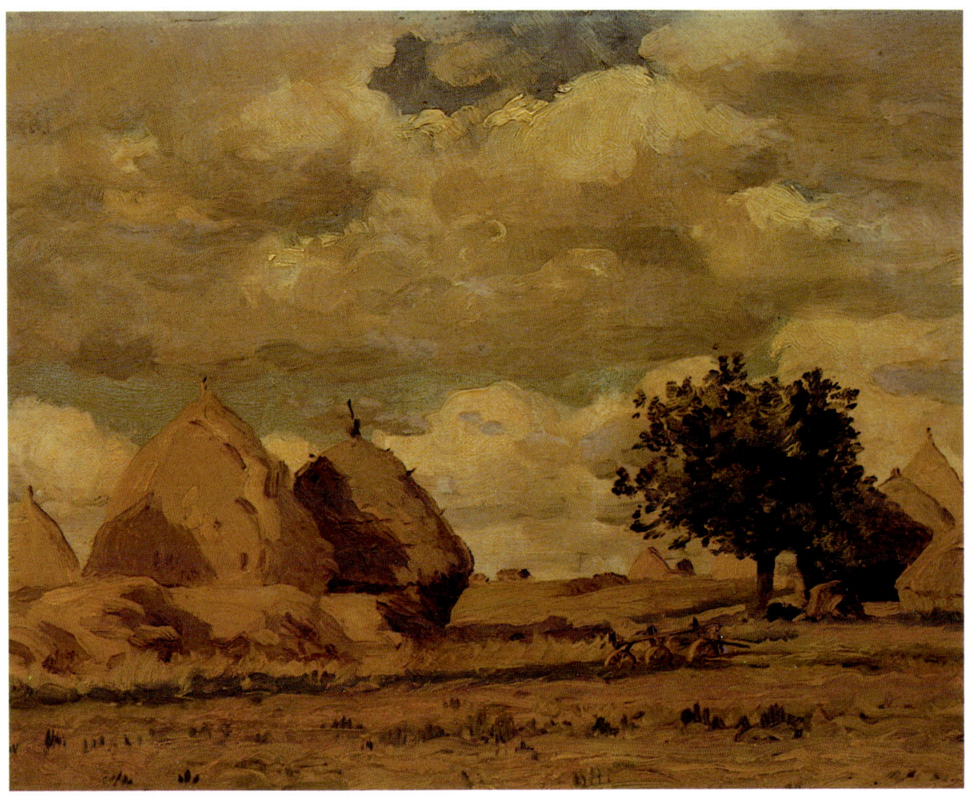

Fig. 5. Normandie.

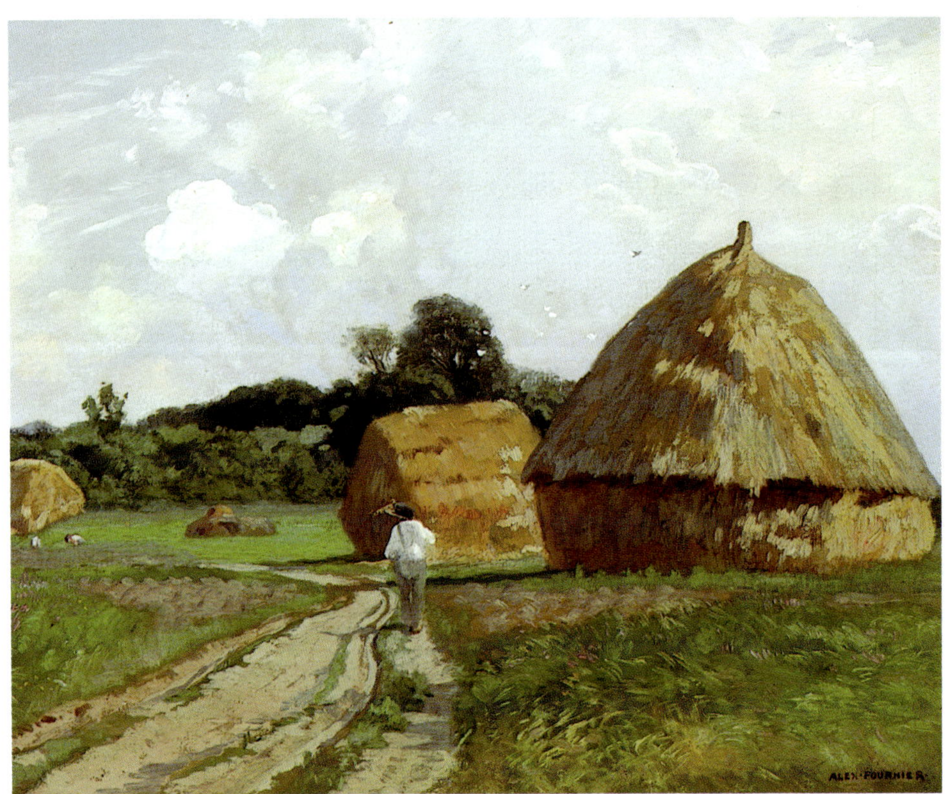

Fig. 6. In Normandie.

of "portraits" of the homes of Minneapolis businessmen. Among them was *Old Orchard*, the Excelsior, Minnesota estate of John F. Wilcox, a wealthy Minneapolis contractor and builder. Wilcox asked Fournier to paint five separate views of Old Orchard for each of his five daughters. One of them (Fig. 7) shows the house screened by the blossoms of the orchard's apple trees in the full bloom of a Minnesota spring. There were also several views of *Highcroft* (Fig. 8), the Wayzata, Minnesota home of grain entrepreneur Frank H. Peavey. Fournier even painted a portrait of Peavey himself, assuming a rather debonair pose as country squire with Highcroft in the background (Fig. 9). This picture represents a rare foray by the artist into the field of portraiture for Fournier did not enjoy painting portraits and few from his hand exist. But the artist was willing to overcome his reluctance in this case, for Mr. and Mrs. Peavey were old friends and loyal patrons and deserved special favors. They had encouraged Fournier through his early career and had made a point of visiting him both in Auvers and Paris where Fournier had introduced them to his circle of friends in the art community.

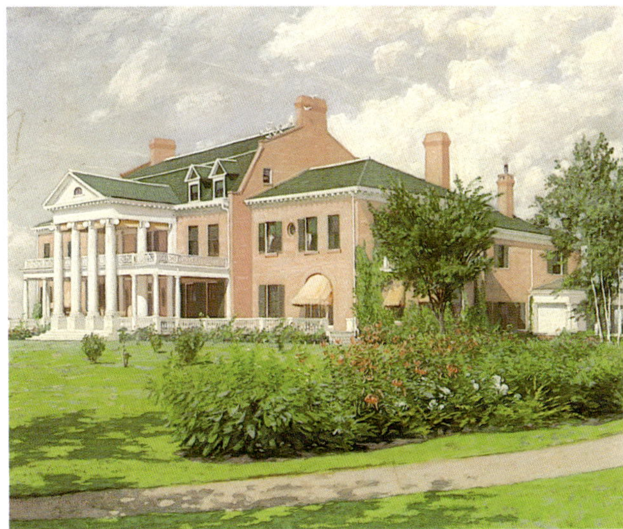

Fig. 8. Highcroft.

To return to the picture of Highcroft, however, it is literally a portrait of a house, illustrating Peavey's colonial revival style home. It was situated on a scenic rise amidst the woods and meadows surrounding Lake Minnetonka in Minneapolis' western suburbs. While H. H. Richardson's Romanesque revival style dominated public architecture, the colonial revival style, featuring red brick trimmed in white and an evenly spaced and harmonious facade, was favored for domestic architecture at the turn of the century. Peavey's house, which the artist has shown in its flowery summer setting, was built in this lighter, more elegant colonial style.

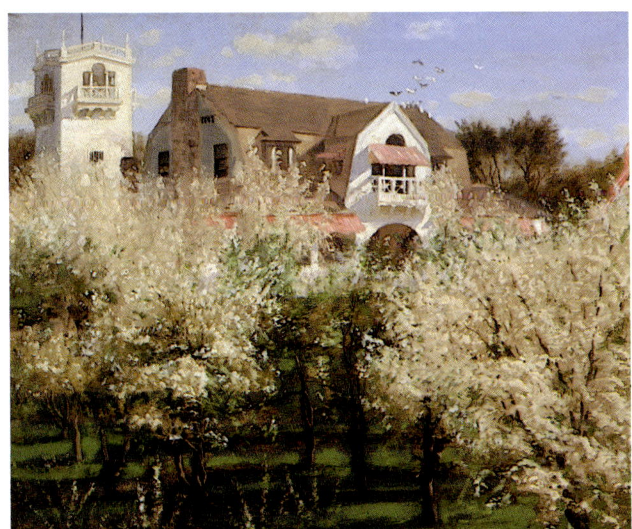

Fig. 7. Old Orchard.

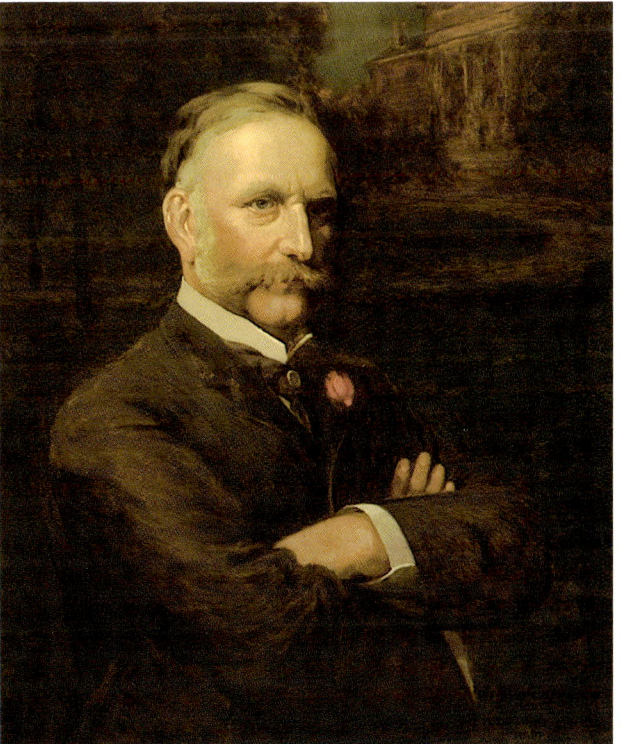

Fig. 9. Frank H. Peavey.

During the period immediately following his return from France, Fournier renewed his contact with two important local organizations involved in the arts. One was the Art League, still revolving around its founder Robert Koehler, and the other was the arts, crafts and furniture firm of John Scott Bradstreet. The Art League was an informal association of artists, musicians, architects, craftsmen and even engineers that held weekly discussions ranging over a wide variety of topics, at the "round table" of the Hennepin Avenue studio. Besides Koehler, its artist members included Burt Harwood (who eventually made Paris his permanent home), Herbjørn Gausta, a Norwegian born artist of Viking proportions, Fournier himself, Gustav Goetsch, an instructor in the Art School, Allen Smith and Mr. Lloyd, workers in stained glass. There were also a number of art patrons, including some from the academic community of the University of Minnesota, such as Dean Frederick J. Wulling of the School of Pharmacy, Professor McClumpha of the Department of English, S. C. Burton, the Gale brothers, Harlow and Robert, and many others. Distinguished out-of-town guests were also welcome around the cozy fireplace of the Hennepin Avenue studio, and Francis Hopkinson Smith, Ernest Thompson-Seton (Fournier's Paris roommate), Richard Le Gallienne and "Fra Elbertus" Hubbard participated in the round table discussions on their occasional visits to Minneapolis.

Of great immediate value to Fournier was his association with John Scott Bradstreet, art dealer, furniture designer, and leader of the growing Arts and Crafts movement in Minneapolis. Indeed, Bradstreet's reputation was more than merely local. An article in the *Pittsburgh Dispatch* of October 10, 1904 took admiring note of the Crafthouse that Bradstreet had established at 327 South Seventh Street in Minneapolis "for the express purpose of housing workmanship executed there as well as artifacts of beauty collected from all over the world. It is a manifestation of the revolt against the cheap, the tawdry and the commonplace." The article then went on to describe its leading spirit as "a man cultured not alone as regards his sense of artistic development but from many and long sojourns in the orient, and this unique building is the outgrowth of years of study of eastern art and its . . . bearings on the development of the art sense wherever found. As a result, Minneapolis can boast of a Crafthouse as distinctive . . . as the renowned Kelmscott Manor beloved of Morris and his associates."

The reference to Morris and Kelmscott Manor is particularly interesting for it links Bradstreet directly to William Morris and the Arts and Crafts movement in England. Indeed, in the decade following the establishment of the influential Arts and Crafts Exhibition Society in London in 1888 there was a rapid proliferation of arts and crafts organizations in the United States as well.[6] This growth was particularly strong in the Boston and Providence, Rhode Island area, and later in western New York state, though the movement was never limited to those two regions alone. Both in England and America the Arts and Crafts movement was born of a desire to return to the careful craftsmanship and pride of work of the pre-industrial era as an antidote to the shoddy products of the industrial revolution. Through John Scott Bradstreet and the Crafthouse in Minneapolis and Elbert Hubbard and the Roycrofters in East Aurora, N.Y., Fournier was intimately associated with the movement, though it is doubtful that he ever saw himself (or that others saw him) as a "craftsman" rather than as an "artist." Bradstreet, however, would undoubtedly have countered that the two terms are synonymous and that he, for one, was both craftsman and artist.

Bradstreet sprang from an old New England family, a direct descendant of William Bradford, governor of the Plymouth Colony in the seventeenth century. He was born at Towley, Old Ipswich, Massachusetts on December 14, 1845 and was educated at the Putnam Academy at Newburyport. He started his business career as an employee of the Gorham Manufacturing Company in Providence, Rhode Island. But in 1873, seeking relief from the chronic respiratory illnesses from which he suffered, he came to Minneapolis which was believed to have a salubrious climate for such conditions.

The move to the raw frontier town of scarcely 50,000 souls must have been a jolt for Bradstreet, a man of cosmopolitan interests and a refined aesthetic sensibility. On the other hand, the level of local taste was a challenge to which Bradstreet felt he could, and would address himself. After two years as a salesman for a local furniture manufacturer, Bradstreet opened his own furniture business at the first of several locations on Nicollet

Avenue. The quality of the furniture he offered moved one visitor to note that "the place was so obviously in advance of its surroundings, it . . . evidently did not belong to the town."[7] In 1885 Bradstreet formed a new business partnership, Bradstreet, Thurber and Company, which allowed him the financial freedom to pursue his interest in interior design.

The following year he made the first of his biennial buying trips to Japan. His lifelong fascination with *Japonisme* may have started during his employment by the Gorham Manufacturing Company in Providence which, in the post Civil War period, produced silverware incorporating oriental, particularly Japanese design. In the same year as his new business partnership, Bradstreet also moved into the "Judd House," a boarding house catering to a well-to-do clientele, where, as a long term resident, he was permitted to decorate his rooms according to his taste with a melange of oriental furniture and objets d'art.

In 1888, or perhaps early in 1889, he acquired an old Victorian house on a large lot at 327 South Seventh Street, and he spent the next four years transforming it into what came to be known as the Crafthouse, "an unusual structure, having more the appearance of an art institute than a place of business."[8]

The Crafthouse was a combination of furniture factory, showrooms and cultural center. Concerts were held there and so were special exhibitions of arts and crafts. The Crafthouse also boasted a Japanese style garden, designed by Bradstreet himself and displaying indigenous Minnesota plants as well as a Japanese bronze fountain, miniature pines and a plank bridge acquired from the Japanese Pavilion at the St. Louis World's Fair of 1904.

The Crafthouse was an Arts and Crafts establishment in that it encouraged the appreciation of beauty and pride of craftsmanship which was the basis of the American Arts and Crafts movement. Behind the public reception rooms of the Crafthouse, which Bradstreet constantly compared to William Morris' Kelmscott Manor, his workshops produced many contemporary crafts including carving, gilding, furniture making, and stained glass. He also undertook commissions for murals which he invited Fournier to execute.

Bradstreet's true love, perhaps, was designing furniture. The day after his death on August 10, 1914, the lead editorial in the *Minneapolis Journal* had this to say: "Bradstreet was a man who did his work for the love of it and for the love of the beautiful . . . His work showed a . . . delicacy and strength and had a lacework beauty about it that was characteristic."[9]

As a corollary of his attempts to promote good taste and appreciation for art, Bradstreet was active in many civic enterprises as well. He was one of the founders of the Minneapolis Society of Fine Arts in 1883 and helped organize its first loan exhibition. He was also a member of the Park Board, president of the Municipal Art Commission and a founding member of the Skylighters Club, devoted to the appreciation of art and fine craftsmanship.

These clubs existed side by side with other art organizations that were beginning to appear on the scene. One of them was the Chalk and Chisel Club which was formed in 1895 and later changed its name to the Arts and Crafts Society. Its purpose was to develop all types of art work and to hold biannual exhibitions. There was also the Handicraft Guild, established in 1904. It maintained a school of design in which there was instruction in pottery, metal and leather work, book binding, wood carving and other arts. These organizations were formed by and for women, though they acknowledged the influence of John Scott Bradstreet and regarded him as something of their mentor.

The portrait of John Scott Bradstreet by Douglas Volk (Fig. 10), probably dating in the early 1890's, is a presentation that stresses his patronage of the arts and his discriminating taste. Indeed, he is as much displayed in the picture as are the rich carpets, the fine furniture and the exotic bric-a-brac surrounding him. It is just the sort of elegant portrait that was much in demand by the wealthy middle class of that time and that was produced so successfully by such "society" painters as John Singer Sargent and William Merritt Chase.

In addition to undertaking mural commissions that Bradstreet put in his way, Fournier also exhibited his paintings at the Crafthouse on various occasions. The first such exhibition, from March 21st to March 31st, 1899, displayed some of the

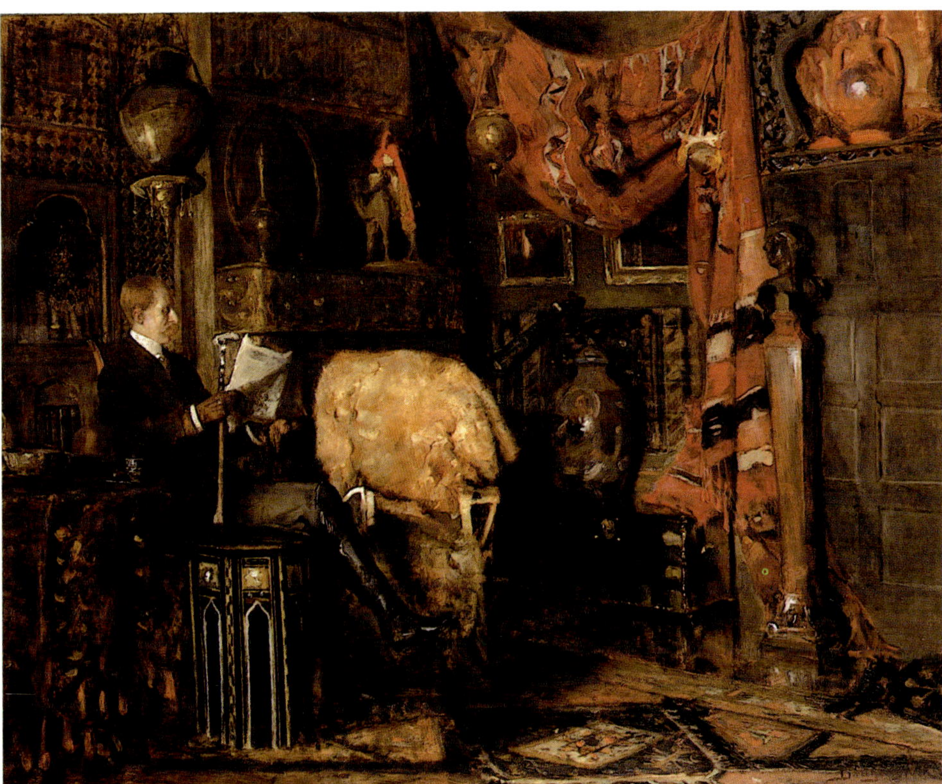

Fig. 10. John Scott Bradstreet.

paintings he had completed the previous summer in France, though it also included *When Golden Evening Fades* and another much exhibited work, *Peace and Plenty,* now lost. *Silvery Moonlight,* later exhibited at the Chicago Art Institute where it was bought by Elbert Hubbard, was also shown. A local critic, while praising Fournier's pictures in the Bradstreet show, lauded the setting almost as much as the paintings themselves. "Minneapolis has never had a more interesting or delightful exhibition," he wrote, "than the one . . . of Alexis Joseph (sic) Fournier's recent paintings which are shown in the harmonious and splendidly effective setting afforded by the exquisitely decorated and furnished rooms of John S. Bradstreet's new establishment on Seventh Street."[10]

Fournier exhibited at Bradstreet's again from January 14th to January 28th, 1902, including in the show a number of his Venetian pictures. It was from this exhibit that Mrs. Peavey bought *A Sylvan Melody* to donate to the Public Library in her husband's memory. She also bought two other important Fourniers, both now lost but one preserved in an old photograph in the artist's album. It is *Moonlight on the Lagoon,* which was praised at the time as a painting of "great power, fidelity and delicacy . . . (in which) the silver track of the moon leads one's vision out into the immensity of the open sea. A group of moored boats are seen dimly, with their signal lanterns . . . The sky is filled with that curious but beautiful effect of fleecy clouds just breaking up into a wavelike appearance, and the moon is dimmed by one of these wavecaps."[11] The other painting bought by Mrs. Peavey and later extensively exhibited was *Peace and Plenty,* which was admired for the "brilliancy and hot stillness of the afternoon (which) is represented in glowing colors (while) sheep stray between broad fields of grain toward an invitingly cool grove."[12]

Nearly all of the paintings shown at Bradstreet's gallery in January were moved the following month to an exhibition of the Minneapolis Society of Fine Arts at the Public Library. Here again Fournier's versatility, glowing colors and deep and sympathetic observation of nature drew admiring comment.[13]

The mural commissions that Fournier received through Bradstreet resulted in the decoration of a number of Twin Cities dining rooms. Many of them have disappeared behind subsequent layers of paint or wallpaper, so that it is difficult to know just how many were done. The few that do survive show that these were not really murals in the strict sense of the word, but rather, in the not uncommon practice of the time, pictures that were painted on canvas that had been cut to fit above the wainscoting and then attached to the wall. The murals in the home of Dr. Arthur Strachauer were typical (Figs. 11-14). They represent the four seasons—the subject usually chosen by Fournier for this type of work, and are executed with the broad compositional masses that recall something of the scene painter's technique. There is more subtlety here, however, than in a stage backdrop and also a closer and more sensitive observation of nature, in spite of the great breadth and freedom with which the artist has handled the subject. On one wall the sun delicately feels its way through the foliage of a forest grove, fitfully illuminating the tree trunks and the ground, while another wall depicts an expansive meadow whose shadows seem to move as the wind sends great volumes of high-piled clouds sailing across the sky. Similar murals of the four seasons were painted to decorate other Twin Cities homes, the Roycroft Inn at East Aurora, New York, and even Fournier's own house at East Aurora to which he eventually moved at the invitation of Elbert Hubbard, the eccentric founder and guiding light of the Roycroft Community.

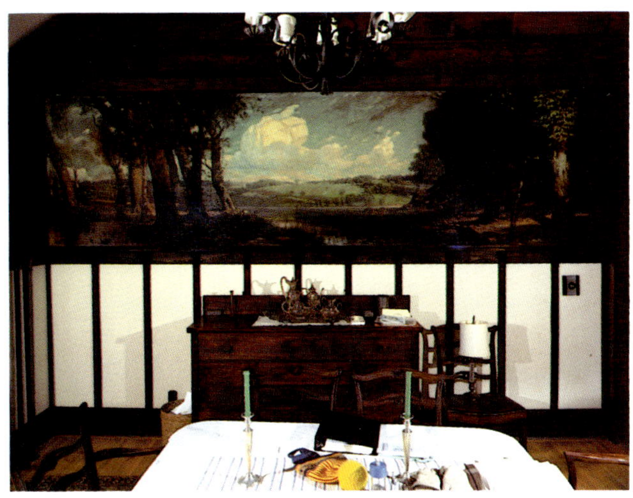

Fig. 12. The Seasons.

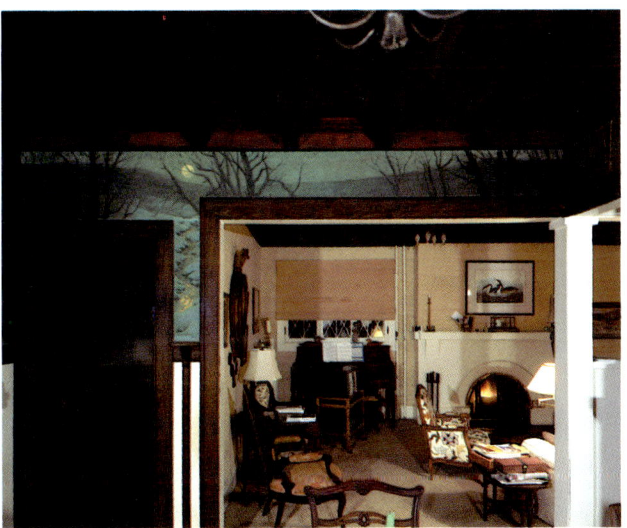

Fig. 13. The Seasons.

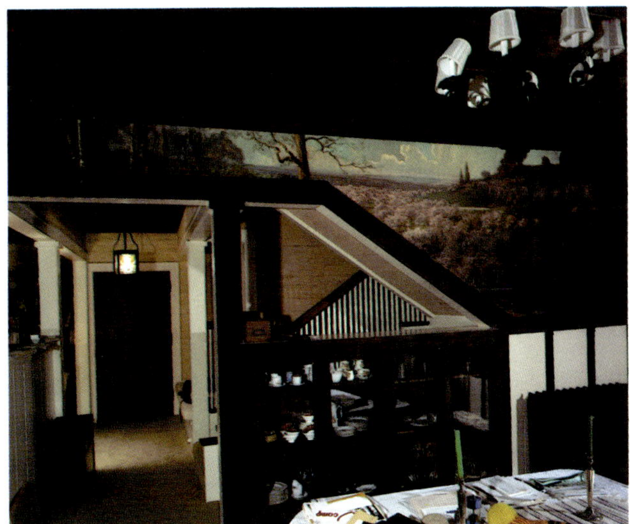

Fig. 11. The Seasons.

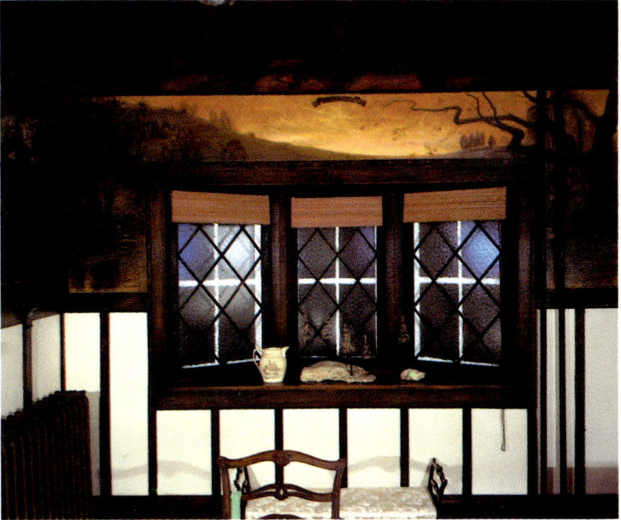

Fig. 14. The Seasons.

Meanwhile, however, oil paintings continued to emerge from his Hennepin Avenue studio. In a rare attempt at illustrating contemporary poetry, Fournier painted two versions of *The Old Swimming Hole* in 1903, one in bright sunlight, now lost, and the other, a version in the early evening (Fig. 15). The latter was copyrighted in 1905, and in 1906 appeared together with James Whitcomb Riley's poem and his portrait on an art calendar published by Edward Osborne & Company of New York City. Fournier sent the poet a copy of the published picture and in return received a beautifully bound copy of Riley's poetry with the autographed inscription, "To my friend, A. J. Fournier whose picture far surpasses the poem."

One can readily understand Riley's admiration for the painting because it captures the same spirit of childhood innocence and nostalgia inherent in the poem itself. Painted with a looser, broader brush than the artist normally used at this time, the painting represents two boys enjoying the cool waters of the swimming hole on a summer evening. One of them scrambles up the mossy bank after his swim, while the other sits by a campfire they have built against the chill of the evening air. The nude body of the boy in the foreground shines translucently, as though absorbing the glow from the flames that warm him and light up the darkening shadows. A wisp of blue smoke curls up from the campfire in the still evening air and beyond it the quiet waters reflect the shore and distant woods. A rough plank diving board and primitive dugout canoe by which the boys have reached this quiet spot complete the composition.

It is instructive to compare this painting with a more famous one of the same subject painted in 1883 by the Philadelphia artist, Thomas Eakins. Eakins' painting, *The Swimming Hole* (Fig. 16), is an intellectual exercise, a rigorous exposition of balanced composition and unified design, completely lacking the nostalgia of Fournier's picture. The figures in Eakins' representation form a pyramid whose base is the rocky ledge that rises from the stream. The emphasis here is not only on classical structure but on visual objectivity in describing the human body in motion—an objectivity

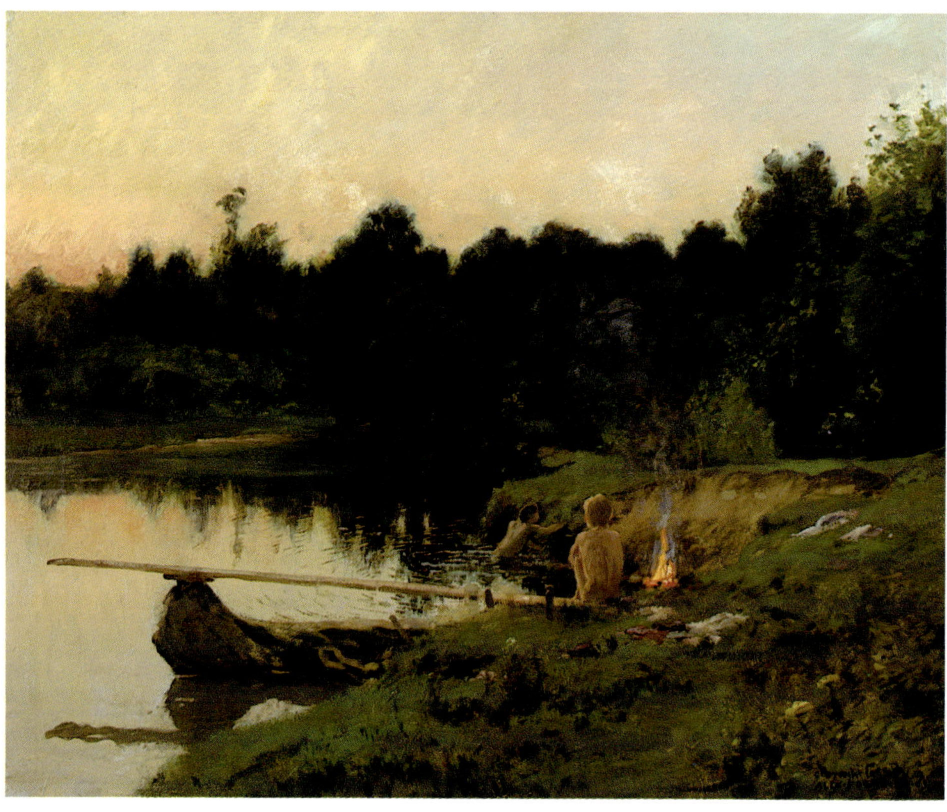

Fig. 15. The Old Swimming Hole.

facilitated in this case by the use of a camera. Fournier's painting, on the other hand, exploits the expressive quality of color and emphasizes the sense of man in harmony with, indeed as part of, nature. The soft tones, the evening light, the shadowy depths and even the nude figures absorbing the glowing light of the campfire underscore the artist's passion for a poetic mood and for ephemeral atmospheric effects. It is a lyrical style based on firm execution but inspired more by the music of nature than by its organization.

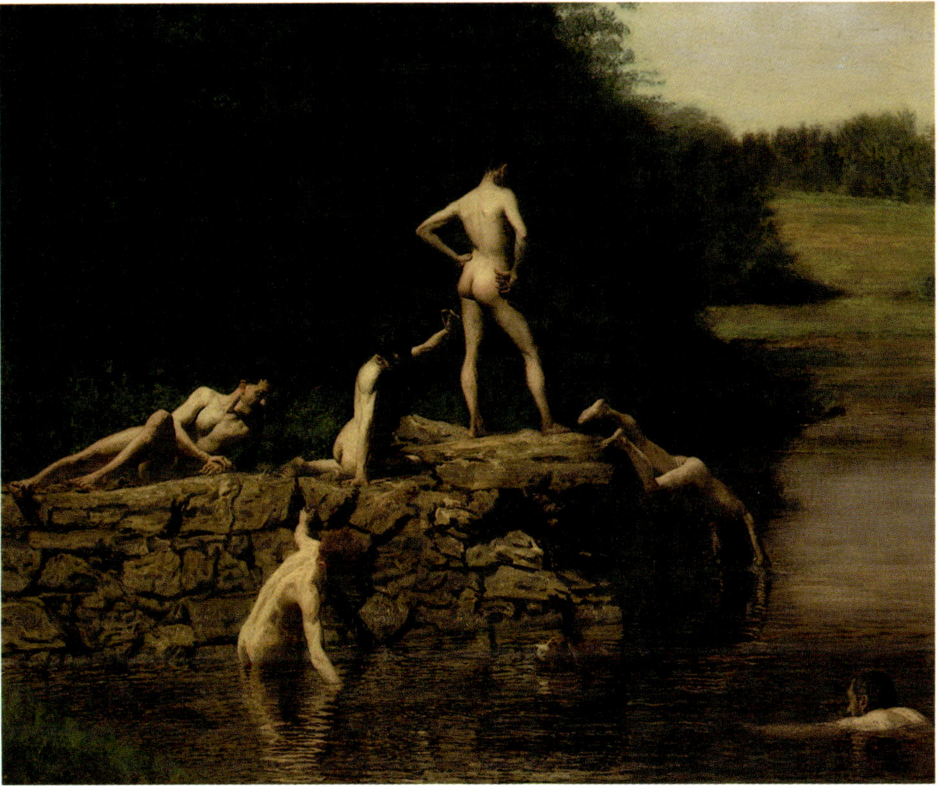

Fig. 16. The Swimming Hole.

NOTES TO CHAPTER 5 - Bradstreet - The Arts and Crafts Movement

1. For a good discussion of the problem of the expatriot American artist returning home, see Laura R. Meixner, *An International Episode: Millet, Monet and Their North American Counterparts*, Memphis, Tenn., 1983, from which the quotation is taken.
2. *Minneapolis Journal*, February 22, 1902, p. 5.
3. *Minneapolis Journal*, October 27, 1903, p. 7.
4. *Minneapolis Journal*, May 4, 1901, Part II, p. 1.
5. For an excellent discussion of French-influenced American landscapes at this time, see William H. Gerdts, "Post-Impressionist Landscape Painting in America," *Art and Antiques*, July-August, 1983.
6. See Robert Judson Clark and others, *The Arts and Crafts Movement in America*, Princeton University Press, 1972.
7. Quoted in Ronald L. M. Ramsey, "John Scott Bradstreet and the Minneapolis Crafthouse," *The Tiller*, Vol. 1, No. 4, March-April 1983, p. 39.
8. *Minneapolis Journal*, August 10, 1914, p. 1.
9. *Minneapolis Journal*, August 11, 1914, p. 6.
10. *Minneapolis Journal*, March 22, 1899, p. 6.
11. *Minneapolis Journal*, January 16, 1902, p. 7.
12. *Minneapolis Journal*, January 25, 1902, p. 5.
13. *Minneapolis Journal*, February 26, 1902, p. 7.

Chapter 6

With the Roycroft Community

On June 1, 1903, Alexis Fournier moved to the village of East Aurora, N.Y. at the invitation of Elbert G. Hubbard, businessman, writer, utopianist and eccentric. Fournier had met Hubbard at least as early as 1896 when Hubbard was on a lecture tour that included the city of Minneapolis.[1] The writer came to Minneapolis again in November, 1900 to give another lecture at the Lyceum theatre on the Roycroft Arts and Crafts Community that he had established in East Aurora. Afterwards he was entertained by the Minneapolis Arts and Crafts Society at a party at which, interestingly, Richard Le Gallienne was also a guest of honor. As the correspondent of the *Minneapolis Journal* remarked the following day, "the presence of these two . . . distinguished literary men made the occasion one of unusual interest."[2] Fournier was in France in 1900 and missed the opportunity to renew his acquaintance with Hubbard and to meet Le Gallienne at this time.[3]

Nevertheless, Fournier and Hubbard apparently maintained some contact in the coming years for the week after Christmas, 1902, Fournier was in East Aurora at Hubbard's invitation to supervise the rearrangement and installation of the art gallery there. The current art director of the Roycrofters, Jules Maurice Gaspard who was primarily a portraitist, was about to leave and it may be that the idea of moving permanently to East Aurora was first suggested to Fournier at this time. The artist wanted time to think it over. His hesitation was not, it seems, because of reservations regarding Hubbard, "Fra Elbertus" as he was affectionately called in his community. "A man of marked peculiarities he (Hubbard) undoubtedly is," remarked Fournier to a newspaper interviewer when he returned to Minneapolis in early January. "One who has undertaken the great work which he now has so well in hand, must necessarily be of such a type." In spite of those "marked peculiarities" Fournier maintained that Hubbard was "utterly unselfish, and that his sole aim is to advance the interests of those working under him. Out of a generous gift of perseverance, a strong physique and personality . . . this man of ideas has built up an institution which is at once the wonder and admiration of the civilized world. Europe and the very cradles of art," he continued, "take off their hat to this man who, in the face of ordinarily crushing obstacles of modern commercialism, . . . has reincarnated such a distinctively old school in modern garb, as is embodied in his Roycrofter's shop."[4] Nevertheless, Fournier was reluctant to give up his residence in Minneapolis with all its personal associations and its growing circle of rich and admiring patrons.

After further correspondence Hubbard and Fournier met again in April, 1903 at the Chicago Art Institute where the "Fra" had been invited to lecture about his beloved Roycrofters. This time Fournier succumbed to Hubbard's blandishments and to his dream of an integrated, self-supporting artistic fellowship. Less than two months later, on June 1, he moved, though tentatively at first, to the village of East Aurora, New York.

Who then was this Elbert Hubbard who was to become a cultural messiah to thousands of Americans and under whose skillful managerial hand the Roycroft community became both an artistic and commercial success?

He was born in Bloomington, Illinois on June 19, 1856, the son of Dr. Silas Hubbard, a country doctor, and his wife, Juliana Frances Read Hubbard. At the age of fifteen Elbert left home, heading for Chicago where he worked for several years for a number of Chicago papers. Fiercely independent, even at this early age, he apparently sold his services on a free lance basis in whatever capacity the newspapers would accept. It was here that he laid the groundwork for his future as publisher, editor and writer. In 1875 Hubbard took a position with his brother-in-law's soap manufacturing company, the Larkin Soap Company of Buffalo, N.Y., and for the next seventeen years he was engaged in sales and promotion for the firm. He introduced such innovative (for that time) techniques as extensions of credit and sales premiums, devices which he later employed just as successfully to promote the circulation of his own magazine. It was in Buffalo too that, on June 30, 1881, he married Bertha C. Crawford of Hudson, Illinois with whom, shortly afterward, he moved to the picturesque village of East Aurora, about 20 miles from Buffalo. By 1892, when he was thirty six years old, Hubbard had become successful enough to be assured of a modest but secure income and, with larger ambitions than selling soap for the rest of his life, he retired from business.

Ever a man to flout convention and follow his own path in life, he decided at the age of thirty nine to enroll in Harvard University as an undergraduate. He was, however, too mature for the narrow and rigidly defined curriculum in effect at Harvard at that time, and after spending a year there, he withdrew from the University. Of far more value to him as an educational experience and of much greater significance for his future, was a trip to Europe that he took with his twelve year old son, Bert, in 1894 when he visited the Kelmscott Press and its community of workers in Hammersmith, England. There he fell under the spell of its charismatic leader, William Morris, as unconventional and visionary a leader as Hubbard himself was later to become. Hubbard was enchanted not only by Morris as a person but by his philosophy of work. He described Morris as "a man of marvellous power . . . frank, bold, gruff, tousled and dressed in overalls and blouse like a workingman . . . He gloried in doing things with his hands . . . and the only thing that gave William Morris more joy than to do things with his hands . . . was to show others how to do things with their hands. He always made things as well as he could. His motto was not how cheap but how good."[5]

The Kelmscott Press itself and the way it was run also struck a responsive chord in Hubbard, for he saw it as a practical model for community life and not merely as a romantic's empty yearning for the past. Hubbard was just as suspicious of the forces of industrialization and urbanization as Morris and as hostile to the kind of materialistic society which he felt it fostered. And like Morris too, Hubbard felt that the material objects of the industrial society were common and shoddy, lacking style and pride of craftsmanship. "Work is for the worker" he later wrote. "It doesn't matter what happens to your product . . . what matters is how you do it." "We are what we are on account of the things we have thought and the things we have done."[6] It was this integrative view of individual personality and achievement that formed the basis of the Roycroft community of workers.

Upon his return from England, Hubbard entered the employ of the Arena Publishing Company in Boston. It was there that he published his first two novels, *One Day: A Tale of the Prairies* (1893) and *Forbes of Harvard* (1894), as well as two essays. In 1894 he also published in New York his third and last novel, *No Enemy (But Himself)*, and in January, 1895 the first volume of his *Little Journeys* appeared. This was a collection, which eventually reached 170 volumes, of breezy, informal accounts of Hubbard's "visits" to the homes of the famous writers, artists and philosophers of the past, from Socrates to Thorwaldsen.

In 1895, carrying the example of William Morris' Kelmscott Press to America, Hubbard founded the Roycroft Printing Shop in East Aurora. Among its first undertakings was the publication of *The Philistine*, the first issue of which appeared in June. Conceived in a spirit of intellectual challenge and mutual exchange with its readers, Hubbard worked on the early issues of the magazine with the assistance of a number of contributors. However, with the appearance of the forty-fifth issue in January, 1899, Hubbard announced that thereafter he himself would write everything including the journal's essays, the aphorisms that he constantly pronounced, and even the advertisements and testimonials for the books that were being published in ever increasing numbers by the Roycroft Press. By the time of Hubbard's death in 1915, *The Philistine* had achieved a circulation of 225,000 and was so completely Hubbard's own mouthpiece that it was discontinued when he died. In 1908 Hubbard also started the publication of *The Fra*, a more formal periodical than *The Philistine* and less Hubbard's personal instrument. That journal ceased publication in 1917.

In January, 1904, following his divorce from Bertha under circumstances considered highly scandalous at the time, Hubbard married Alice Moore, a writer and former schoolteacher.[7] She became Hubbard's surrogate as director of the Roycrofters during his frequent absences from East Aurora on lecture tours. On at least one such trip he even ventured onto the vaudeville stage, more, however, for his own amusement than for any aspirations toward show business. Indeed, Hubbard's flamboyant style and dress were drama enough in themselves. From his many lectures his audiences absorbed more of a sense of contact with a vibrant and unique personality than with the content of the lecture itself. In the same way readers of *The Philistine* and *The Fra* gathered from these journals not so much the substance of what Hubbard wrote as his breezy and informal style and the sense of having been personally addressed in a continuing correspondence. For Hubbard was a pioneer in popularizing an informal, personal style in literature as a revolt against the stiffer conventions of polite and formal writing. Indeed, *The Philistine* was the longest lived and most substantial of a large number of small, informal periodicals which were born during the 1890's and the first years of the twentieth century.

Hubbard's unconventional style in dress, writing, and even in his personal life led to his being regarded in some circles as a radical. This suspicion was reinforced by the cooperative nature of his Roycroft community. But though Hubbard flaunted his unconventionality at least in outward appearance, he was distinctly conservative in his economic views. Like many self-made men he loved to pontificate about the virtues of hard work and frugality. The tone of his well known *Message to Garcia* published in 1899 was one of impatience with the inefficiency of employees and the justifiable frustration of their employers. It was very popular with the industrial magnates of the time, was translated into many languages, and was distributed successfully in Europe as well as America. A collection of his *bon mots* on efficiency in business and in life was issued posthumously as *Efficiency in Business* in 1921 and again was popular with America's "bosses."

Elbert Hubbard and his wife, Alice, died on May 7, 1915 when, on a trip to Europe, they went down with the torpedoed liner, *Lusitania*. For a number of years the Roycroft community survived without them under the direction of Bert Hubbard, Elbert's son, but the spark that had kindled its creative energies was no longer there. In 1938 the Roycroft shops fell victim to the depression and were sold at auction to a religious organization.

The Roycrofters were revived, however, on the 120th anniversary of Elbert Hubbard's birth, June 19, 1976 and reestablished on a more modest scale as a modern Arts and Crafts community, still located in the village of East Aurora.

It is hardly surprising that Fournier should have admired, and to a certain informal extent, even joined the Roycroft community. He undoubtedly hoped to find in East Aurora that "coterie of earnest believers in and workers for art" whose absence in the midwest he had deplored when speaking to the Women's Civic League of St. Paul in February, 1902.[8] Moreover, the Roycrofters were a major component in the American Arts and Crafts movement, a movement with which Fournier had already been at least partially identified through his association with John Scott Bradstreet and the Crafthouse in Minneapolis. Like the Crafthouse, the Roycrofters were very much the personal creation of one man. But Hubbard went further than Bradstreet in his vision of what an Arts and Crafts community could, and should, achieve. He saw the Roycrofters and their work as an answer to the problems spawned by the industrial revolution and an increasingly urbanized society. Basically the community was designed to further spiritual growth and at the same time to make money, "a place where men and women can work up to their highest and best—a place where they can get an education and a living at the same time."[9] Through such workers Hubbard hoped not only to improve the quality of machine made manufactures but, even more importantly, to alleviate the increasingly impersonal character of the American artist's life.

The Roycrofters, who began as a printing shop devoted mainly to Hubbard's publications, evolved into a society of bookbinders and designers, and, later into a full fledged artistic community engaged in the production of books, pottery, copper and other metal work, jewelry and even a distinctive style of furniture. Eventually, the Roycroft enterprises even included an inn, that opened for guests in 1903 and for which Fournier painted a number of murals.

It is difficult to clearly define the scope and membership of the Roycrofters as an organization. They developed a core of about five hundred workers who were engaged in the various crafts and enterprises of the Roycroft community. The workers followed an apprenticeship system in which they learned the various crafts while moving from shop to shop. There was also, however, a much larger group of sympathizers and interested participants who took classes, attended the lectures offered by the community, or who simply admired Elbert Hubbard and his philosophy of life. They called themselves Roycrofters-at-large and, together with the actual workers, made up the community.

When Hubbard established his press in East Aurora in 1895 he took the name Roycroft from a pair of seventeenth century English bookbinders and, in fact, a bindery was soon added to the press. Though it was mainly devoted to the publication of *The Philistine*, the press also issued a number of books. These were produced on a hand press modeled after that used by Benjamin Franklin and often took four or five months to complete. The first book to bear the Roycroft colophon was *The Song of Songs* published in 1895-96. The books were bound at first in a soft chamois, but later the Roycrofters also made a more unique binding with elaborate high relief designs in molded leather. A leather shop that made table mats, boxes and other small items was added to the Roycroft enterprises, and in 1901 the Roycroft book catalogue first mentioned a line of furniture including a Morris chair.

Roycroft furniture has recently been enjoying a revival of interest as an important part of the American Arts and Crafts movement. It was beautifully made in the plain "mission" style (supposedly based on that of the old mission monks), popularized by Gustav Stickley and his brothers, Leopold and J. George Stickley of nearby Fayetteville, N.Y.[10] One of Gustav Stickley's chief furniture designers, interestingly, was Harvey Ellis, a Rochester, N.Y. artist and architect. Ellis, who began working for Stickley in 1903, probably forms another link in Fournier's involvement with the Arts and Crafts movement. During the 1880's and 1890's Ellis was in Minneapolis working for Leroy Buffington and other midwestern architects. Undoubtedly, Ellis, with his interest in contemporary arts and crafts, would have known John Scott Bradstreet, founder of Minneapolis' Crafthouse, with whom Fournier had also established both a personal and professional relationship. In any event, Ellis produced for Buffington a number of beautiful drawings of architectural elevations and furniture designs. Many of them appeared in *The Craftsman*, a journal established by Gustav Stickley as an organ for his workshops. These were organized on the lines of a medieval guild and were called "United Crafts." The first issue of *The Craftsman* was devoted solely to Stickley's (and Hubbard's) English mentor, William Morris and was, as the introduction noted, "intended to mark the beginnings of a new and unique labor association, a guild of cabinet makers, metal and leather workers, formed for the production of household furnishings."[11]

Both Stickley's furniture and that made in the Roycroft shops was characterized by simplicity of design and a truly functional style. Its satisfying proportions and straightforward rectilinear lines were devoid of the elaboration of Victorian furniture. It was much influenced by the cabinet work of such British furniture designers as Arthur Mackmurdo, C.F.A. Voysey, Scott Baillie, John Ruskin and William Morris. As the first Roycroft furniture was made in 1896, two years before Gustav Stickley's first experimental efforts, the Roycrofters were, in fact, among the first to make Arts and Crafts furniture in America and therefore they were a strong influence on its subsequent design. By 1899 Hubbard was successfully promoting and selling Roycroft furniture through advertisements in *The Philistine.*

The variety of designs in Roycroft furniture indicates that there was probably no single major designer working for the Roycroft shops, though Victor Toothaker was undoubtedly its most important contributor.[12] Santiago Cadzow was the first of the Roycroft designers and cabinet makers, and a German artisan named Albert Danner joined him in the early 1900's. Herbert Buffum also came about the same time as Danner and he eventually became the superintendent of the Roycroft furniture shops.

Of all the useful objects made by the community, book manufacture and design probably ranked first from the beginning of the Roycroft enterprises. Hubbard, who was always "discovering" artists to bring to East Aurora, brought, as his first "find," the English graphic artist, Samuel Warner, Fellow of the Royal Society of Artists. He joined the Roycrofters as a book designer in 1895. Another early "discovery" was William Wallace Denslow of Chicago who began his association with the community in East Aurora in 1896, designing book illustrations, title pages and cover designs for the Roycroft books. He even had a share, with Hubbard himself, in designing some of the Roycroft buildings, notably the Chapel-Library. Where Warner's style was a simple one, more traditionally in the Arts and Crafts mode, Denslow introduced the free flowing, graceful Art Nouveau style in his book illustrations. A small but elegant seahorse was his signature in the Roycroft books, as it is also of his pencilled portrait of Fournier dated Sept. 1, 1906 (Fig. 1). Denslow later achieved national fame as the illustrator of L. Frank Baum's *The Wonderful Wizard of Oz.*

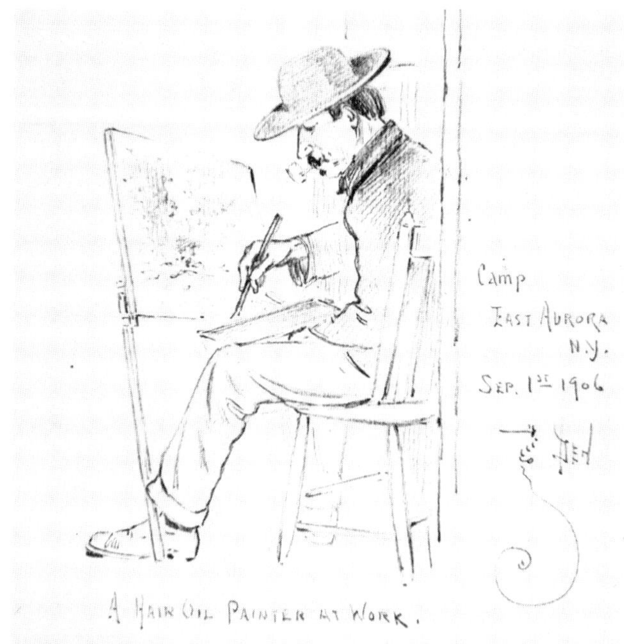

Fig. 1. Portrait of A. J. Fournier.

1903, the year that saw Fournier's arrival in East Aurora, was also Dard Hunter's first year there. He was a nineteen year old student at Ohio State University when Hubbard hired him and sent him to travel extensively in Europe in order to learn a variety of skills that he thought would be useful to the Roycroft community. Eventually Hunter became the epitome of the all-round Roycroft artist who was a master of many media. He was skillful as an architect, book designer and pen and ink artist, as well as being an expert craftsman in designing jewelry, lamps and stained glass windows.

The "fine arts" of sculpture and painting also interested Hubbard and he pursued their practitioners with an almost equal zeal. Jerome Conner, for example, was a young sculptor working in Salem, Massachusetts when Hubbard "discovered" him in 1898 and persuaded him to join the Roycrofters in East Aurora. There he developed not only a sculpture department but also one devoted to ironwork, stonecutting, and ceramics. His three-quarter life size statue of Elbert Hubbard stands today in front of a school facing the Roycroft campus.

Besides Fournier, there were also a number of painters who joined the Roycroft community. Sandor Landeau was a Hungarian born painter of landscape and genre subjects whom Fournier had known in his student days in Paris and who was a particularly close friend. Like Fournier, Landeau had studied in both the United States and Paris and, in fact, had lived in the French capital for twenty-five years before returning to America. He joined the Roycroft community in 1915 and lived there until his death in 1924. Other Roycroft artists included Lawrence Mazzanovitch, Carl Ahrens, Raymond Nott, Albert Miller, Otto Schneider and Lillian Bonham. They remained at East Aurora for periods varying from a few months to a few decades. Alexander Levy, art director of the Larkin Soap Co. of Buffalo with which Hubbard had been associated, was also a frequent visitor to East Aurora and another of Fournier's good friends. Herbjørn Gausta and Nicholas R. Brewer, Minnesota artists and longtime friends of Fournier, were also occasional visitors, Brewer frequently accompanying Fournier on sketching and painting expeditions in the countryside nearby.

Both of these Minnesota friends left portraits of Fournier, probably painted around the time of his move to East Aurora. Gausta's portrait (Fig. 2) shows Fournier in his artist's smock and cap, holding his palette and brushes, and painting a landscape already framed. In Brewer's portrait (Fig. 3) Fournier is shown in three-quarter length, holding a walking stick and wearing a hat and coat as though he had just dropped in for a chat. Brewer has captured something of Fournier's nervous energy, his intensity and the seriousness of his purpose despite the fact that underneath his sober demeanor there lurked a fun loving imp with a sense of humor that was as ready to laugh at himself as at

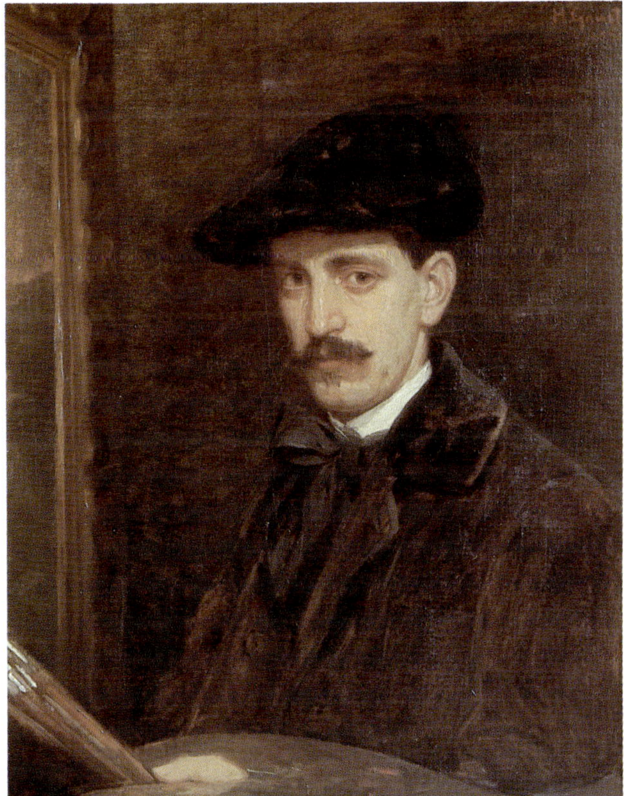

Fig. 2. Portrait of A. J. Fournier.

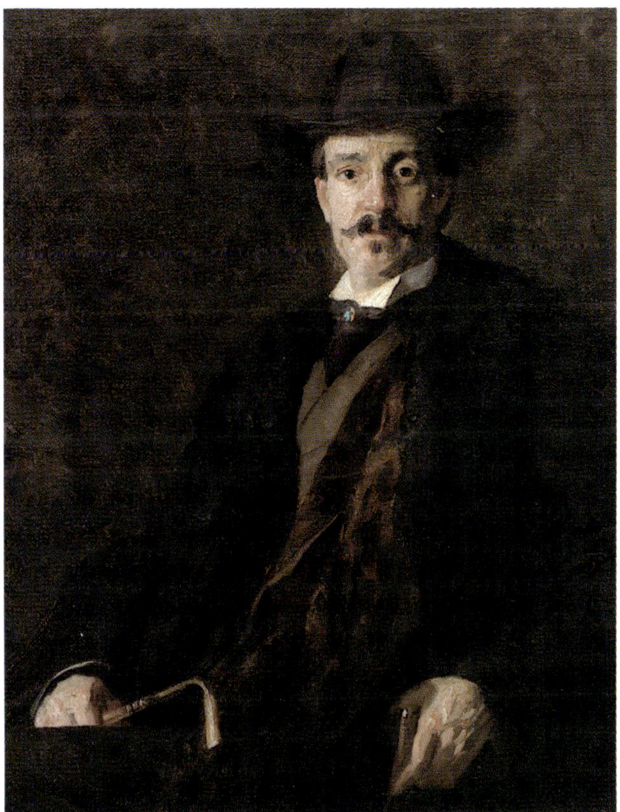

Fig. 3. Portrait of A. J. Fournier.

the foibles of the rest of the world. Both portraits depict a man in his late thirties or early forties which would coincide with Fournier's early years at East Aurora. A slightly later portrait by Margaret Evans Price of East Aurora is a pen and sanguine drawing depicting an older, seated Fournier, shown in profile (Fig. 4). The subject seems more relaxed here, as though reflecting on half a lifetime of good times and good work.

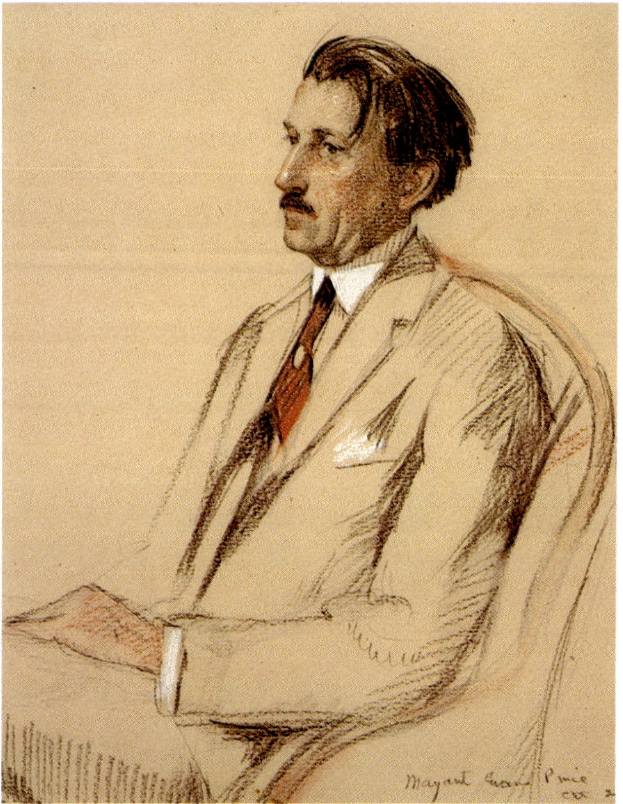

Fig. 4. Portrait of A. J. Fournier.

Though Fournier remained with the Roycrofters longer than any other artist, indeed outliving the end of the enterprise in the late 1930's, his move to East Aurora was not to be complete for many years. Fournier kept his studio and home in Minneapolis, returning there periodically. Later he also maintained a residence in South Bend, Indiana. East Aurora, however, became, after 1903, his permanent summer home, and from 1938 until his death, it was his year round residence.

When Fournier first joined the Roycroft community, his duties as its "art director" were more in the nature of lecturer and "artist-in-residence" than as an administrator. Twice a month he lectured on art at the Roycroft chapel and, according to his Minneapolis admirers, these lectures attracted "not only the two hundred members of the Roycroft community but visitors from the surrounding villages."[13]

He was also invited to accompany the "Fra" on his lecture tours to Boston, New York and other cities in order to tell the audiences who came to hear Hubbard about the art opportunities offered by the Roycroft community. Best of all he could exhibit his own paintings at these gatherings and thus acquire a larger reputation for himself. As for Hubbard, he not only admired Fournier's paintings, but enjoyed his cheerful company, his fund of entertaining stories, his dark good looks and his slightly unconventional dress. "You *ought* to be able to paint," he told his friend, "you look the part."[14]

Their relationship, however, was not all sweetness and light. There was more than a little mischief in Fournier's make-up, and enough of a sense of humor to prevent him from taking the Fra's pontificating too seriously. The messianic streak in Hubbard and the self-conscious earnestness of the Roycroft community led him to maintain some emotional distance. With the writer, Richard Le Gallienne and his old friend from Minnesota, the artist Nicholas Brewer who frequently visited East Aurora, he formed what the three friends called the "Tommyrotters' Club," an irreverent group of free spirits in the Hubbard camp. Dedicated to pure fun and high jinks, their antics were enough to earn a shake of Hubbard's finger and, on at least one occasion, "a severe reprimand from His Majesty, Fra Elbertus," as Nicholas Brewer put it.[15]

The *Minneapolis Journal*'s art correspondent, as late as 1909, noticed Fournier's reluctance to be formally identified with the Roycroft community. After mentioning that "Alexis Fournier . . . is spending some weeks in his old home," the writer went on to say that the artist lives in East Aurora and although he steadfastly denies that he is a Roycrofter, he admits to an admiring fondness for Elbert Hubbard . . . What principally holds Mr. Fournier in East Aurora, however, is the lovely country in the vicinity which in summer offers so many attractive subjects for his brush."[16]

It is probable that Fournier's move to East Aurora was motivated by more than the local scenery and his personal admiration for Hubbard. In order to support himself and his family primarily from the sale of his paintings, it was desirable, perhaps even essential, that he seek out potential customers and patrons wherever they could be found. It is unlikely that he could have maintained an adequate income if he had been dependent exclusively on his reputation in and around Minneapolis and St. Paul, even though Fournier appears to have been unusually adept and persistent in cultivating profitable contacts. In this light, the following comment in the *Minneapolis Journal* of August 29, 1903, is particularly significant. Fournier "has decided to make his temporary stay in East Aurora, N.Y., a permanent one . . . because the Philistine man is making him known to his patrons and has offered him tempting inducements to remain."[17]

In East Aurora in 1904 Fournier built a comfortable house for himself and his family near the Roycroft buildings on a plot of land that Hubbard had given him. He decorated the interior—the hall, living room and dining room—with the same kind of scenic murals he had previously painted in Minneapolis and St. Paul dining rooms. His studio was a large and comfortable room on the third floor extending over the entire length of the house (Fig. 5). Displayed in it were a number of the artist's own paintings, pictures by fellow artists with whom he had exchanged paintings, and a large collection of curios and mementos. From the rafters hung an old fish net acquired from a fishing colony on the coast of Massachusetts. On one side was a large organ operated by rolls similar to those in player pianos, on which Fournier loved to entertain himself and his guests. There was an old desk of illustrious pedigree (it had belonged to the French Barbizon painter, Daubigny) and a large carved antique chest from the Black Forest of Germany. It was a room for both relaxation and work, for Fournier was as industrious and prolific as he had always been and paintings continued to be produced on his easel from sketches made on his frequent rambles into the countryside. The studio even boasted its own separate outside door and staircase upon which the neighborhood boys would clamber to peer through the glass window at the artist at work. They must have known that he was aware of their presence and that he accepted their homage with a twinkle in his eye for he had a genuine affection for children and felt that they, as much as adults, could be taught to appreciate and practice art.

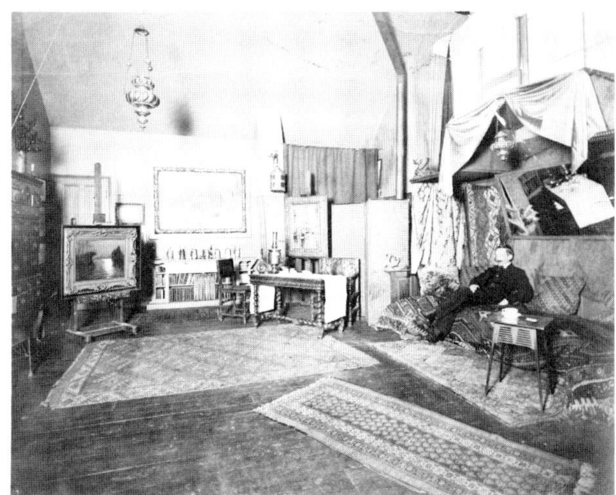

Fig. 5. Fournier's Studio in East Aurora.

The artist was by no means severing his ties to Minneapolis. In fact, as early as November, 1903, he was back at work in his studio on Hennepin Avenue with his family again installed at the Columbus Avenue address. In the same month he also had an exhibit of his work on display at the Detroit Museum of Fine Arts and had just recently returned from Boston where his paintings had been shown at the "Fine Arts Building" there. He was also acquiring some important patrons in addition to Elbert Hubbard. They included Mrs. Charles Schwab, wife of the United States Steel magnate, who had acquired *Daubigny's Neighbors*, and George Wharton Jones, a then well known authority on the American Indians who bought *Springtime*, a French scene with a flock of sheep ambling along the road. Vanderbilt University at about this time, acquired two canvases, *Boulanger's Hamlet* and a twilight scene, *On the River Oise*.

That Fournier was being increasingly appreciated is also evident from the fact that in the month of January, 1904, his works were on display in Nashville, Tennessee, St. Louis, Missouri, Columbus, Cincinnati and Cleveland, Ohio, Detroit, Chicago, Boston, New York and Pittsburgh.[18] From April 30th to December 1st, 1904, Fournier was represented at the St. Louis World's Fair Exposition commemorating the centennial of the Lousiana Purchase, and in the fall of 1905 he was back in Minneapolis preparing for an exhibition that was held from November 15th to December 15th at J. A. Clow and Co., which was, like Bradstreet's, an art and furniture establishment. His pictures there included a number of Venetian scenes, a few French views and some new landscapes from East Aurora.[19] One of the paintings, *In Corot's Home*, presents a new theme entirely and one that presaged his major achievement a few years later, a series of paintings called *The Homes and Haunts of the Barbizon Masters*. At the same time as the Clow exhibition, he was also showing, with Douglas Volk, a number of canvases at the Minneapolis Society of Fine Arts Exhibition at the Minneapolis Public Library.[20]

In December, 1905, the Art Museum Association exhibited paintings by Fournier at the State Capitol in Albany, N.Y. The cover for the exhibition catalogue, which was used again eleven years later for an exhibition at Broderick Galleries, Buffalo (Fig. 6), was designed by Fournier's friend and fellow Minnesotan, Paul Manship, better known in later years as a sculptor than as a graphic artist. In January, 1906, there were forty-nine Fournier paintings exhibited at Louis Sweet's Photographic Studio on Hennepin Avenue. These canvases were later shown at Anderson's Galleries in Chicago. It may have been in connection with this last exhibition that Fournier, together with Herbert Waldron Faulkner, lectured to the Palette and Chisel Club in Chicago.

It seems also at about this time that Fournier rented a small studio near Lee, Massachusetts. A large number of his canvases have recently come to light there and several of his paintings of this period are landscapes of western Massachusetts and northern Connecticut. In fact, at the exhibition at J. A. Clow's in November, 1905, many of the pictures were of New England scenes though others, also in the exhibition, were views begun in France and Venice a few years previously. *The Gleaners*, discussed in the next chapter, was one of the paintings found in the Lee studio.

Two pictures painted during Fournier's early East Aurora years and that reflect his new surroundings, are *The Roycroft Chapel* (Fig. 7) and *The Roycroft Inn* (Fig. 8), both of which were painted for Elbert Hubbard in 1903. Though they are rather intimate and unpretentious pictures, like *Corot's Home*, they both also herald the series,

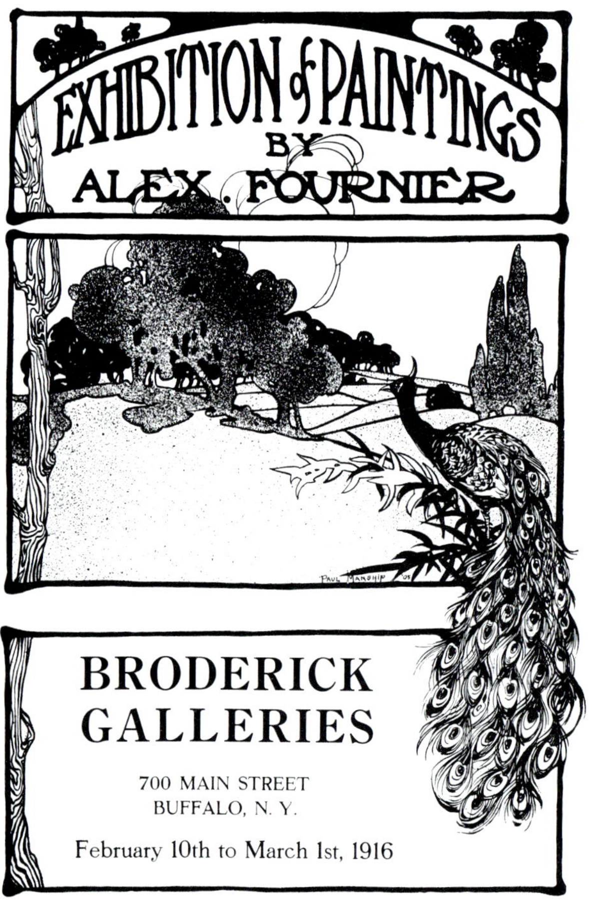

Fig. 6. Cover for A. J. Fournier Exhibition Catalogue.

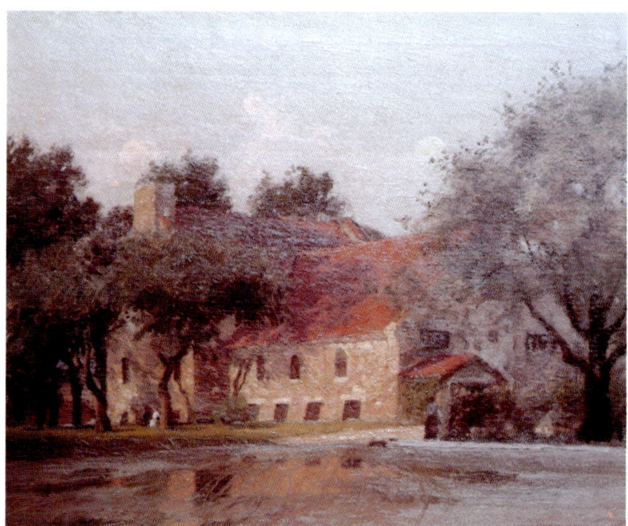

Fig. 7. Roycroft Chapel.

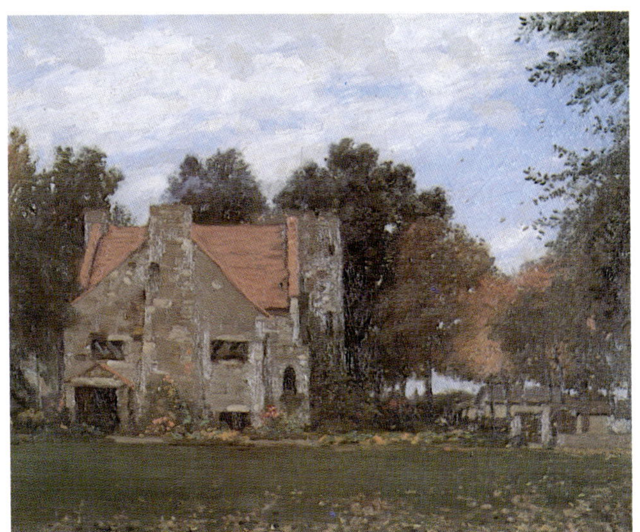

Fig. 8. Roycroft Inn.

the *Homes and Haunts of the Barbizon Masters* to which they bear more than a passing resemblance.

There are also a number of paintings of Cazenovia Creek and Valley, some of them dating around 1903 and most of them painted in the spring and autumn. Autumn was Fournier's favorite season for its colorful foliage seen through an Indian summer haze, provided just the light and color he most admired. He compared the Cazenovia Valley to Normandy, commenting many years later that "I love that valley as much, if not more, than I did Normandy. It possesses all of the brightness of Normandy and it is so near home."[21]

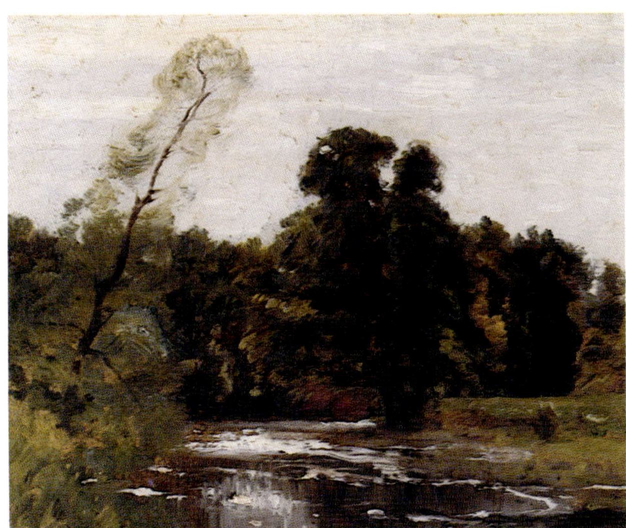

Fig. 9. Cazenovia Creek.

The sociable Fournier was always an organizer and joiner. Soon after his arrival in East Aurora he formed a Paint and Varnish Club. With his students and friends he would rent a boat and float down Cazenovia Creek, looking for especially scenic spots to sketch and paint. Some of Fournier's pictures of Cazenovia Creek reveal a looser, more impressionistic technique than was his usual style at the time. One of them (Fig. 9) is perhaps a study or sketch for a more ambitious picture of the creek. With just a few deft strokes, applied broadly and loosely to the canvas, the artist has managed to suggest the swift waters of the stream breaking above the boulders in their shallow path. On the banks of the creek the trees are beginning to show, amidst the many shades of green, the colors of approaching autumn.

Fournier was, however, increasingly using the Impressionist *plein air* mode of painting, for large pieces as well, abandoning the refinements of the studio for a direct confrontation with nature. In 1909 the art critic for the *Minneapolis Journal* would write, on the occasion of one of Fournier's periodic visits: "Of late Mr. Fournier has been making his paintings direct from nature . . . He has brought with him a large number of new canvases which have been made with the quick, direct broad style that the new practice begets."[22]

Fournier was also busy with a series of "murals" (as in the Minneapolis examples, these were really canvases that were cut and fitted to the walls above the wainscoting) which were taking shape under his hand at the Roycroft Inn. The ceiling was painted in a soft sky effect, and on the four walls were pictures of well known European sights. One was a picture of Venice, one a glimpse of the ruins of an ancient Greek temple, another a misty view of London, and still another a typical street scene in Paris. The original quality of these murals is hard to judge today because they are now in very bad condition and, though still in situ, have deteriorated quite beyond repair.

Other, more intimate pictures continued to be painted as well, Elbert Hubbard still serving as Fournier's most important patron. *The Pumpkin Patch* (Fig. 10), painted in 1906 for Hubbard, is the quintessence of October in the country. The globes of orange, distributed throughout the canvas with a deceptive casualness, are actually carefully arranged to create a balanced and coherent composition. Their bright color provides a lively note against the duller hues of the background, and suggest the final gleams of a sun preparing to abandon, for the time being, the warmth and vitality of the summer season.

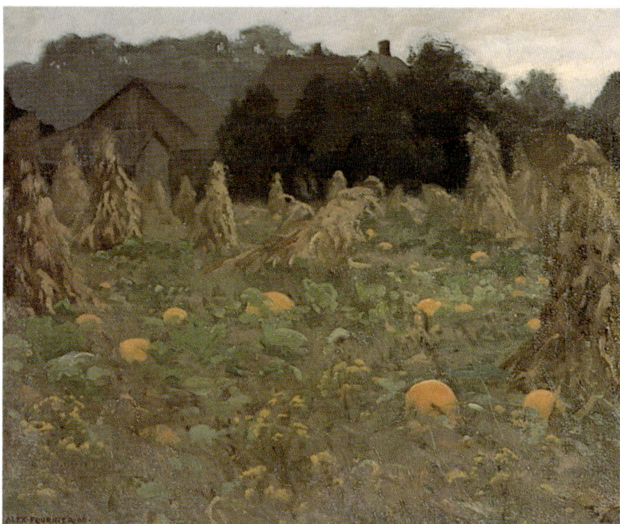

Fig. 10. The Pumpkin Patch.

Though periodic visits to Minnesota continued, and though he was still traveling widely, Fournier was becoming more and more identified with East Aurora and the Roycrofters as the decade wore on. An undated photograph taken probably around 1907 or 1908 (Fig. 11) shows Fournier with a group gathered around Elbert Hubbard at whose right sits Richard Le Gallienne who had become a frequent guest at East Aurora. Fournier and Le Gallienne maintained close ties through the years, and in the summer of 1923 Fournier visited Le Gallienne at the writer's cottage in Woodstock, New York, where another artists' colony existed. It was from the porch of Le Gallienne's cottage that Fournier painted a number of Catskill Mountain views, including *Clearing in the Catskills* and *Clouds and Shadows*, both much admired by contemporaries and both now lost. The latter was painted in Fournier's typical style revealing a wide sweep of valley with mountains in the distance and a stately cloud shadow floating over the foreground. The picture was later exhibited, together with twenty-one other Fournier canvases at Mohr's Art Gallery in Toledo, Ohio, where it was singled out for special praise.[23]

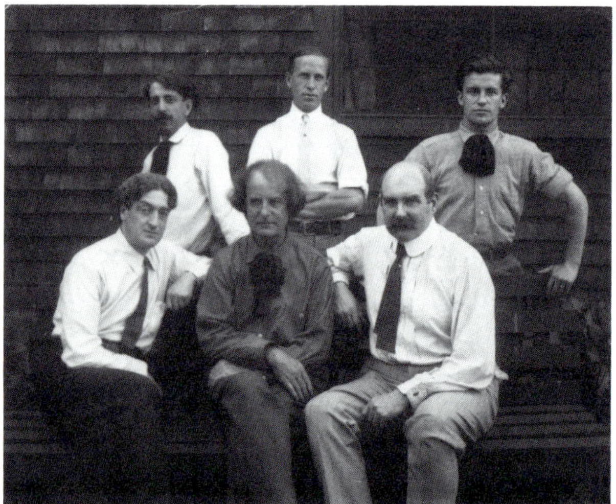

Fig. 11. A. J. Fournier, Elbert Hubbard and Richard LeGallienne with Burr McIntosh, Ed Shay and McDougall.

Some time toward the end of the decade, Fournier moved from his large house in East Aurora to a smaller bungalow next door, retaining, however, the use of the third floor studio in the larger house. The bungalow had previously seen duty as a collection of small buildings, including a chicken coop and a blacksmith's shop, set in the midst of an apple orchard. When these structures were consolidated and adapted to human needs, some of the apple trees were incorporated into the new dwelling and allowed to continue growing through its roof. The artist relished the unusual and piquant note this detail added to his "bungle house" as he liked to call it and which he photographed in its spring glory (Fig. 12). The inside was equally picturesque. It was decorated with paintings, brightly

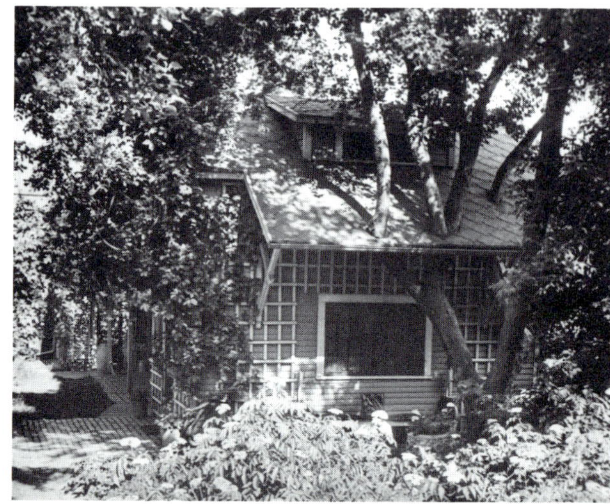

Fig. 12. A. J. Fournier's "Bungle House."

patterned dishes and shawls collected from far and near. There was also a blue room, painted to match a large, blue vase of which Fournier was particularly fond.

Fournier painted pictures of this "bungle house," his own home and haunt, several times. One of them, *My Bungalow: Blossom Time* (Fig. 13) of

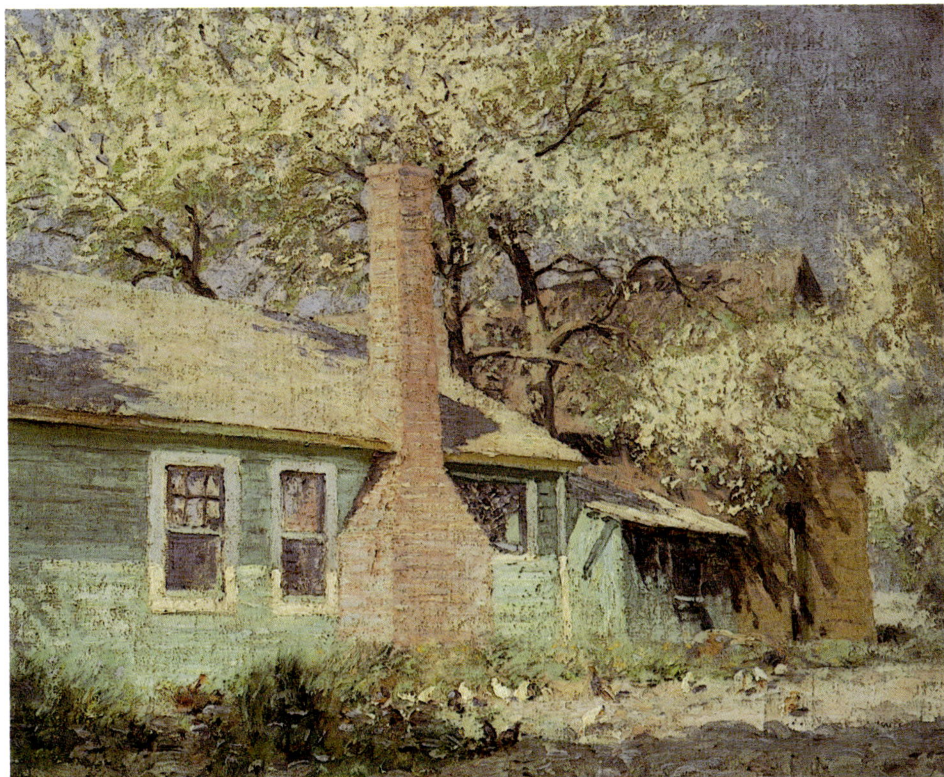

Fig. 13. My Bungalow: Blossom Time.

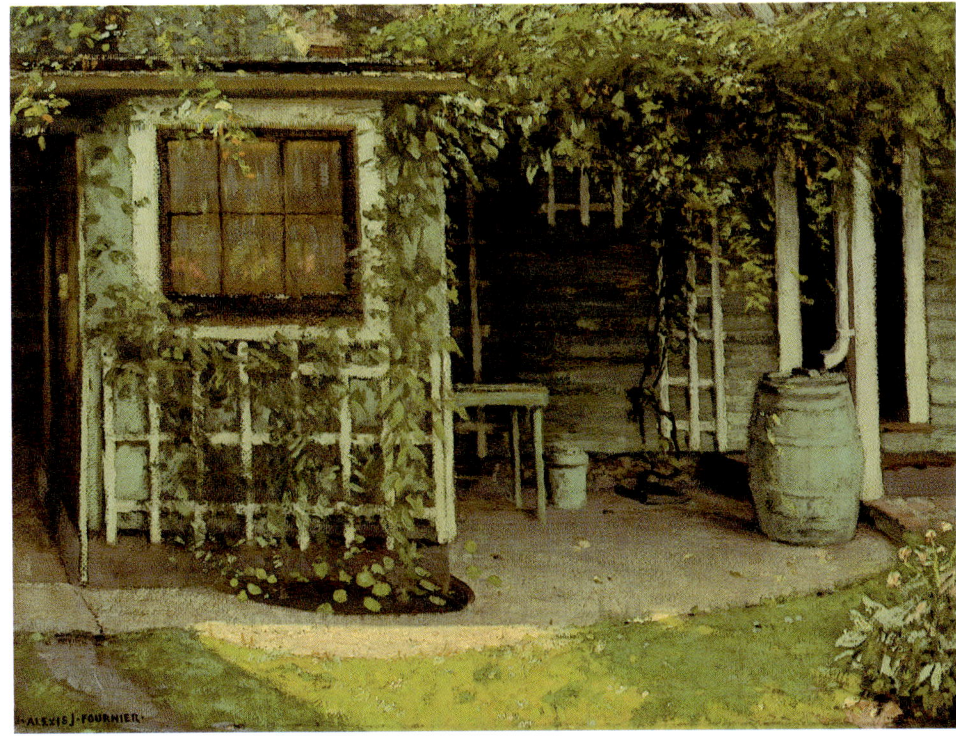

Fig. 14. Our Rain Barrel.

around 1920, is executed in the impressionistic, loose brush technique that Fournier developed in the late teens and early twenties. The apple trees are in full bloom and their profusion of blossoms seems to shelter the modest wooden dwelling. The soft tints of blues and greens, the white cloud of blossoms, the bright and sunny day, and even the chickens pecking in the yard, all create a feeling of joy and optimism in keeping with the promise of the new season. *Our Rain Barrel* (Fig. 14), painted at about the same time, describes something of the artist's modest living arrangements and interjects a genre note not usually present in his paintings of this period. Both pictures are springtime views for Fournier did not like to paint during July and August. The late summer light was too hard to reveal the various nuances of greens that he loved,—"everything on just one note," he said. "Tiresome."[24]

Fournier liked better the gentler colors of spring as is evident in *The Awakening* (Fig. 15), a study of the pastel cadences of early May. In a scene veiled by the gentle mists of spring, a flock of sheep is depicted on an upland meadow overlooking the village of Holland, N.Y. nestled in the valley below. It is a sweeping panorama of the countryside near East Aurora and of the rolling hills that eventually rise into the rugged peaks of the Allegheny Mountain range. Through the mists are revealed the soft harmonies of greens, violets and pinks that announce the arrival of the new season. The picture was painted originally for Elbert Hubbard and, as one of his favorite Fourniers, it occupied a prominent place in his home in East Aurora.

But the autumnal scene was still first in the artist's order of preference, as is evidenced by a number of canvases in which the more dramatic colors of that season are exploited. *October Afternoon* (Fig. 16), probably painted near East Aurora, is typical of these. In a glowing image of a harvest field, the sunlight outlines the corn shocks in the meadow and defines, with a transparent clarity the little stones in the foreground. The vivid scarlets, golds and greens of the trees in the middle distance, as they contrast with the cooler blues and greens of the more distant fields, reveal the artist's

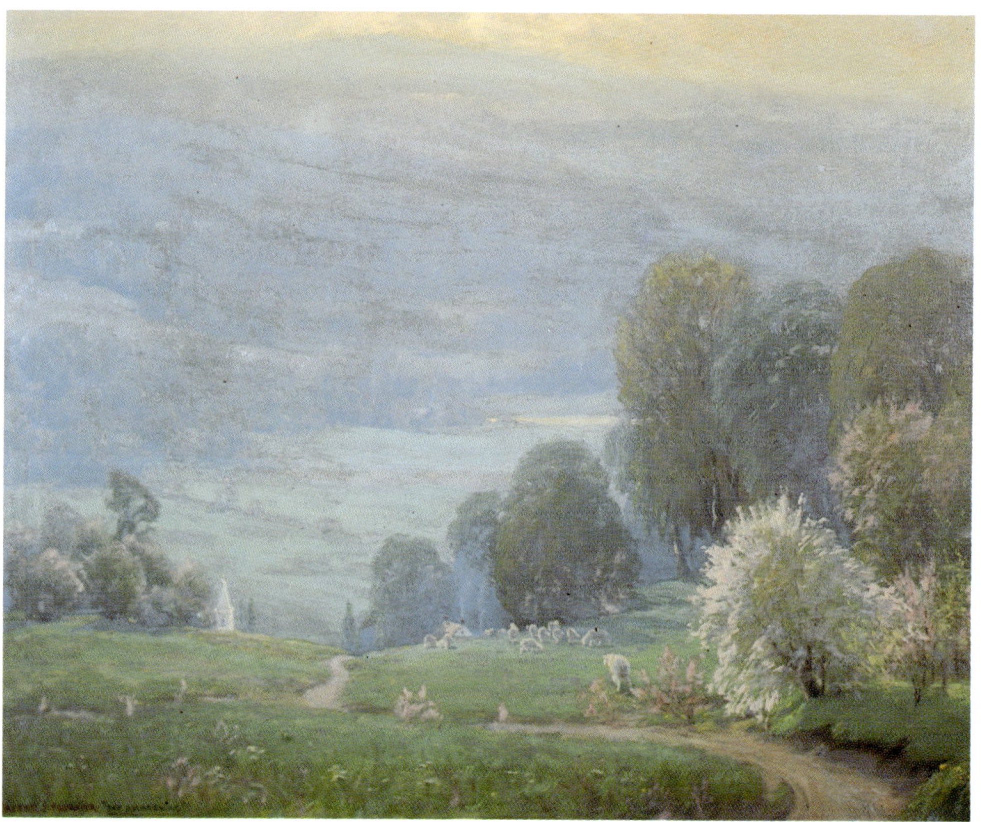

Fig. 15. The Awakening.

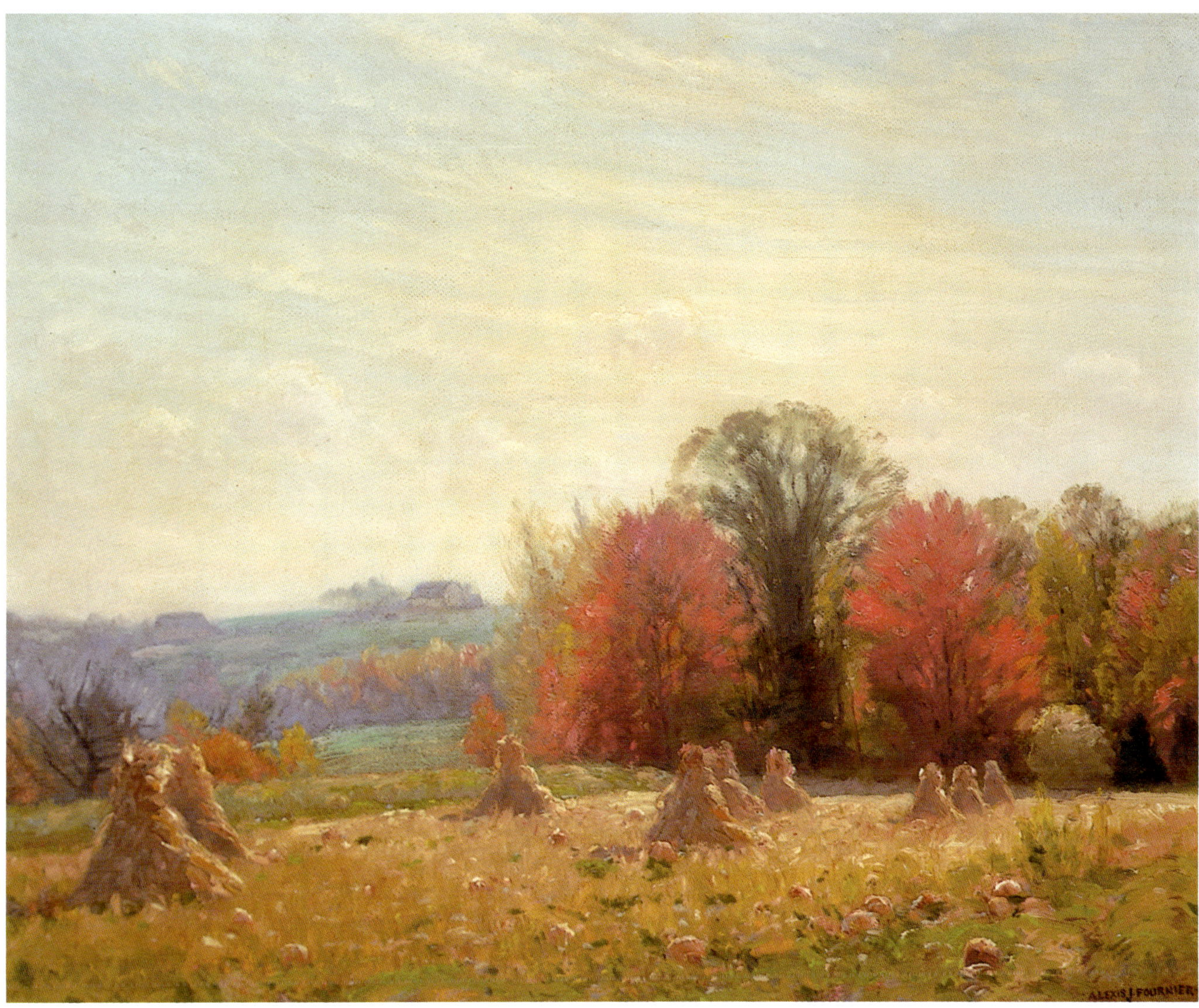

Fig. 16. October Afternoon.

delight in the radiant colors of nature and his complete mastery at depicting the out of doors with a sparkling freshness and vitality.

Late in the winter of 1907, Fournier was back in Minneapolis, exhibiting for the second time at J. A. Clow's art and furniture gallery. Included in this exhibition were *The Old Swimming Hole* (whether the daylight or evening version is unknown), *Summer Skies* (Fig. 17), a cheerful picture of rolling meadow land under the high banked clouds of a summer sky, and other paintings with such typical Fournier titles as *Twilight After the Storm*, *The Sylvan Pool*, *A Golden Sunset*, *The Valley*, *Early Spring in Normandy*, and *Autumn Morning*. The artist was producing about forty major paintings a year at this time and apparently finding a ready market for his work. His touch was ever a gentle one and, as a reviewer described the second Clow exhibition, "to look at Alex Fournier's pictures is like greeting charming acquaintances with the pleasant feeling that they will become good friends."[25] Eleanor Jewett, a Chicago critic, was later to add, "One can live with these pictures. One can keep rational with them, they belong to the circle of Emerson's essays and Thoreau's rambles. They are confident and secure in their perfect relationship to nature."[26]

For some time Fournier had had in mind the idea of starting a painter's colony in East Aurora, a Roycroft school of landscape painting that would, he hoped, become as famous as the Barbizon school had been in France.[27] This hope would never be fulfilled. But a kindred aspiration was to have more success. As early as 1904 he had begun to plan for and work on what would become his major project for the decade, a series of paintings of the homes and haunts of the Barbizon painters in France. Corot, Diaz, Daubigny, Millet and Dupré had not only inspired Fournier's brush but had guided his spirit in its love of nature and in celebrating that love on canvas. He wished to leave a lasting tribute to their memory, one that they would have understood and appreciated. To this end he would return once more to France. In the late spring of 1907, with "The Fra's" blessing, and probably financial backing as well, the artist left on his sixth trip to Europe.

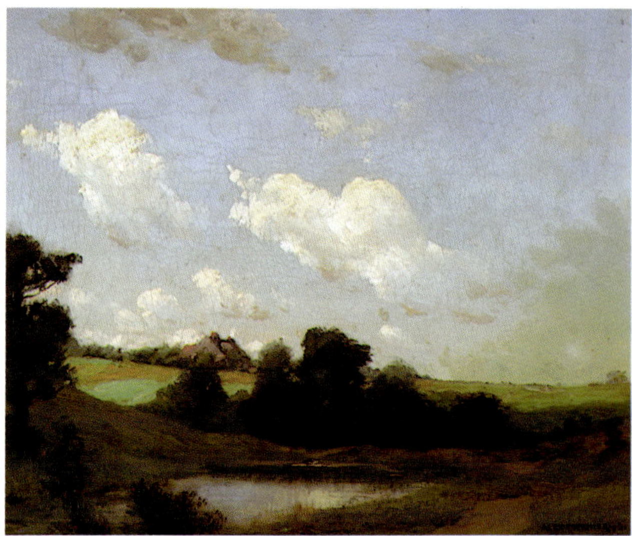

Fig. 17. Summer Skies.

NOTES TO CHAPTER 6: With the Roycroft Community

1. This early connection with Hubbard is mentioned in *The Minnesotan*, Vol. 1, No. 6, January, 1916, p. 15 and *Buffalo Evening News*, January 20, 1948.
2. *Minneapolis Journal*, November 15, 1900, p. 6.
3. Le Gallienne was the house guest of the James Carlton Youngs from the fall of 1900 to February, 1901. During that period the young Winston Churchill, on his own lecture tour in the United States, was also a guest in the Young's house in Minneapolis. Le Gallienne had an unflattering opinion of the future statesman. See Richard Whittington-Eagan, *In Quest of the Golden Boy, A Life of Richard Le Gallienne*, London, Unicorn Press, 1960, p. 382.
4. *Minneapolis Journal*, January 2, 1903, p. 11.
5. Albert Lane, *Elbert Hubbard and His Work*, Worcester, Mass., 1901, pp. 12, 13, 62.
6. Janice C. Crumrine, "Elbert Hubbard: Pragmatic Romanticist," *The Roycroft Movement: A Spirit for Today*, Burchfield Center, State University of New York at Buffalo, 1979, p. 3.
7. Charles F. Hamilton, *As Bees in Honey Drown: Elbert Hubbard and the Roycrofters*, A. S. Barnes, Cranbury, N.J. 1973, contains a sensitive description of Elbert Hubbard's long affair with Alice Moore.
8. *Minneapolis Journal*, February 22, 1902, p. 5.
9. Crumrine, Op. Cit., p. 5.
10. For an excellent discussion of Roycroft furniture see David M. Cather, *Furniture of the American Arts and Crafts Movement: Stickley and Roycroft Mission Oak*, N.Y., 1981, Ch. V., "The Roycroft Shops." Robert Judson Clark, *The Arts and Crafts Movement in America*, 1876-1916, Princeton University Press, 1972, also contains a brief discussion of Roycroft furniture, as does Charles F. Hamilton, *Roycroft Collectibles*, A. S. Barnes, New York, 1980.
11. Cather, Op. Cit., p. 23.
12. Ibid., p. 87.
13. *Minneapolis Journal*, October 27, 1903, p. 7.
14. *East Aurora Advertiser*, August 8, 1938.
15. Nicholas R. Brewer, *Trails of a Paintbrush*, Boston, Christopher Publishing House, 1938, pp. 168-9.
16. *Minneapolis Journal*, January 31, 1909, Second News Section, p. 2.
17. *Minneapolis Journal*, August 29, 1903, p. 16.
18. *Minneapolis Journal*, January 23, 1904, p. 6.
19. *Minneapolis Journal*, November 12, 1905, Second News Section, p. 18.
20. Ibid., p. 13.
21. *East Aurora Advertiser*, January 22, 1948.
22. *Minneapolis Journal*, January 31, 1909, Second News Section, p. 2.
23. Undated, unheaded clipping, Fournier's Scrapbook, Collection of Allan Bartlett.
24. *Buffalo Evening News*, January 24, 1909.
25. *Minneapolis Journal*, March 20, 1907, p. 4.
26. Undated, unheaded clipping in Fournier's Scrapbook, Collection of Allan Bartlett.
27. *Minneapolis Journal*, November 12, 1905, Second News Section, p. 18.

Chapter 7

The Homes and Haunts of the Barbizon Masters

Fournier arrived in France in the late spring or early summer of 1907. Though he settled in Auvers, he made frequent trips to Barbizon to study the environs of the village made famous by the so-called "Men of 1830."

The village of Barbizon was a cluster of about two hundred cottages on the edge of the forest of Fontainebleau, situated on the west bank of the Seine about thirty five miles south of Paris. This was the place where, about the middle of the nineteenth century, a group of French artists went to seek a new freedom from the restraints of academic convention in a direct communion with the changing rhythms of nature. But their direct translation of nature, observed and recorded *en plein air*, was not the only thing that set them apart from their contemporaries. These artists sought in nature a new way of life, a daily source of inspiration as both men and artists, much as the peasant who tilled the fields identified himself with the land that sustained him. Closeness to nature, these artists felt, expressed through a simple rural life, was the true measure of an artist's success, rather than academic prizes or artistic renown.

The Forest of Fontainebleau, which these artists chose as the center of their artistic life, was a rather tame wilderness of shallow pools, narrow streams, and clusters of oak, birch and elm. The "sublime" wilderness of dark, mysterious forests, craggy mountains, deep chasms and remoteness from civilization was not to be found at Fontainebleau. Here the woods were rarely so dense that sunlight could not easily penetrated to the forest floor and the forest itself was traversed by many well trodden paths.[2] Nevertheless, suitable subjects for the painter abounded, not only in the forest itself but in the carefully tended fields that surrounded it. Nature here offered not "sublimity" but domesticity, peace and tranquility.

Because the Barbizon landscapes stressed a "natural" environment rather than the classical compositions of the accepted academic tradition based on Claude Lorraine and Nicolas Poussin, they had a significant impact on a whole generation of American artists and collectors. Barbizon seemed to represent for the American audience an idyllic environment similar to the natural utopia that had once existed in the new world but now was being threatened by the spread of industry and urbanization. Still, Barbizon was different from the depiction of nature as a national and religious symbol that had characterized the landscapes of Thomas Cole and his followers in the tradition of the Hudson River School. It was more gently didactic and its pervasive sentiment was not drama but nostalgia. Its appeal was more to the imagination than to any patriotic impulse and indeed, Barbizon implied a faint decadence born of the centuries old continuity of peasant life. Indeed, that very decadence of old world peasantry provoked the same delicate melancholy that accompanied the portrayal of the new world Indians, those "noble savages," whose fate was doomed by the westward expansion of white civilization. Both groups, American Indians and French peasants, satisfied a romantic yearning for the primitivism associated with Rousseauian innocence and virtue, and for the "natural man" as opposed to the "civilized man" who was necessarily corrupted by centuries of false values, political and social intrigue and, more recently, industrialization.

Jean Baptiste Camille Corot was among the earliest visitors to Barbizon around 1825. He was followed by Theodore Rousseau who was to make it his permanent home in 1848. In the following year Jean-François Millet moved into a three room cottage in Barbizon where he would live until his death in 1875. Others who became well known and influential members of the group were Charles François Daubigny, Virgile Narcisse Diaz de la Pena, Jules Dupré, Charles Emile Jacque and Constant Troyon, though not all of them actually resided in Barbizon. After 1860, for example, Daubigny lived at Auvers-sur-Oise, a short distance north of Paris, while Dupré's home was at L'Isle Adam, also on the River Oise and just a few miles east of Auvers.

Among the first American artists to come under the spell of the Barbizon masters was a Bostonian by the name of William Perkins Babcock. He was a painter whose assimilation of the Barbizon aesthetic was a highly idiosyncratic one, for it was combined with a bent toward the classicism of the nineteenth century academic tradition. Nevertheless, he became an admirer and life-long friend of Millet and, even more importantly, served as an intermediary through whom a number of his American compatriots were introduced to the French artist and became disciples of the Barbizon tradition.

Probably the most important of these American artists was another Bostonian, William Morris Hunt, who, while a student at the Paris atelier of Thomas Couture, first encountered Millet's work at the Paris Salon of 1850.[3] The following year, through the good offices of Babcock, he met Millet himself and early in 1853 he gave up his lodgings in Paris and settled in Barbizon where he remained until his return to the United States in 1855. Millet's influence was apparent in the increased monumentality of Hunt's style, a new economy of means, and an incorporation in his own work of Millet's "solid painting, simple, full and round."[4] Later, when Hunt became Boston's most influential artist and teacher he advised his students to learn not from his own example, but from that of the Barbizon masters. "The artist is an interpreter of nature," he wrote. "When I look at nature I think of Millet, Corot, Delacroix and sometimes of Daubigny."[5]

Hunt was not only a friend and admirer of Millet, he was his patron as well. He bought as many of Millet's paintings as he could afford, including *The Sower* now in the Boston Museum of Fine Arts, and then introduced him to buyers among his well-to-do American friends who were making the grand tour of Europe. Through the efforts of Hunt, and others like him, the pictures of the Barbizon master quickly found their way into the collections of America's industrial tycoons, James J. Hill of St. Paul among them. Indeed, it could have been in Hill's Summit Avenue mansion that the young

Fournier was first introduced to, and fell under the spell of, the masters of the Barbizon school.

At about the same time that Hunt was becoming Millet's friend, patron and disciple, George Inness, a painter from New York state, was making his own discovery of the Barbizon artists, particularly Theodore Rousseau. Though his initial reaction to the Barbizon landscapes was guarded, they nevertheless profoundly influenced his later style. Forsaking the inherent optimism of most American landscapes of the nineteenth century, and even of his own earlier work, Inness' later pictures take on something of Barbizon's "dreamy obscurity" and the "sad and heavy tone" that contemporary American critics disliked in his work.[6] It has been pointed out, however, that many of the Barbizon elements in Inness' paintings were not so much additions to his art as modifications of qualities that had previously existed in it.[7]

Inness' subjective view of nature and his conviction that the presence of the divine Creator was manifest more in nature's moods than in the infinite variety and detail of the landscapes of the Hudson River School, marks him as a close spiritual counterpart of Alexis Fournier. Both artists sought to express their emotional response to nature's ephemeral and mysterious moods, through the sparkle of raindrops on a grassy field after a summer shower, or the golden light of a setting sun still illuminating the highest branches of a darkening grove of trees. Both relied on the memory of a scene as much as, if not more than, the sketches they had made *en plein air*, and for both artists it was the intrinsic poetry of the natural world that provided the essential ingredients for their translation of the visual experience.

There were, of course, many other Americans who were influenced, to a large or small extent, by the French painters of the Barbizon school and who became their admiring devotees. They included Winkworth Allan Gay, Wyatt Eaton, Will H. Low, J. Foxcroft Cole, John LaFarge, Mark Fischer, and Homer Dodge Martin. None of them, however, went so far as to devote themselves to the kind of artistic tribute that Fournier was determined to pay them in his projected series of paintings of their homes and haunts.

The idea of painting a group of pictures devoted to the homes of the Barbizon masters, was an idea that had been in Fournier's mind for a number of years. It may have occurred to him as early as 1894 when he first roamed the French countryside, and been further focused in 1902 when Charles Sprague Smith published a small volume reminiscing about a summer he had spent a decade earlier at the village of Bourron, just a few miles from Barbizon. The book, entitled *Barbizon Days: Millet-Corot-Rousseau-Barye*,[8] was a chronicle of the author's visit together with written sketches of the artists named in the title. Fournier was an avid collector of any scrap of information he could find about the Barbizon school and the book may have come to his attention. The Barbizon Homes project was, perhaps, further stimulated a few years later by the example of Elbert Hubbard's *Little Journeys*, a series of small books published and beautifully printed and decorated by the Roycroft Press. The series recounted the author's fictional visits to the homes of the great men of the past, a few famous artists among them.

The idea of a pictorial equivalent of the *Little Journeys* would be particularly appealing to an artist who was as fond of painting pictures of houses of historic or personal interest as Fournier was. Such a predilection is evident from Fournier's many examples in this genre, going back as far as 1888 and his painting of *The Old Home of Gen Sibley*, Minnesota's first governor. But it was more than just the homes that Fournier had in mind for the Barbizon series. He also planned a set of landscapes devoted to the countryside familiar to his heroes, the countryside they themselves captured on their canvases. Thus *The River Oise at Auvers*, *In Daubigny's Country*, *In Corot's Country*, *In Cazin's Country*, *In Millet's Country*, and *Daubigny's Neighbors*, were painted as part of a companion series constituting the "haunts" of the Barbizon masters. Apparently, the "haunts" set was never completed, however, and Fournier incorporated the ones he did paint into the series of Homes.

In later reminiscing about the year that he spent sketching his impressions of the Barbizon masters' homes and the countryside celebrated by them, Fournier recalled "making dozens of visits to a certain spot to watch the effects of light and shade under different conditions. Dawn found me in the streets or on the hills and even by moonlight I sketched my impressions." He added that it was all "tremendous work and endless amount of trouble." But he was tenacious in pursuing his goal, for "I had in my mind a fixed purpose, to make this series the great work of my life. I was consumed with the ambition to paint better than I had ever painted before . . . Though the peasants stared at me suspiciously and wondered of what interest their crazy huts could be to a foreigner, I worked on, sure of myself and filled with my subject."[9]

Though Fournier settled in Auvers, in the old house formerly occupied by Charles François Daubigny, he was frequently in Barbizon as well. Here he was the welcome guest of Carl Millet, the son of the famous Jean François Millet. The two men became good friends, spending many leisure hours together, the Frenchman reminiscing about his father and the American devotee hanging on his every word.

Nevertheless, although Fournier steeped himself in the world of the Barbizon masters and absorbed the lessons of their school, his series of Barbizon Homes is far from an imitation of any one of them. Distinguished by Fournier's special sense of color the series of twenty paintings is his individual tribute to them, expressed in terms of the flowing light and subtle atmospheric effects that were peculiarly his own. Ever sensitive to the nuances of nature's moods, he tried moreover to choose a time of day or atmospheric condition appropriate to the personality and style of each of the Barbizon masters. "I studied each home at various hours of the day before I lifted a brush," he later said. "I wanted to catch the mood of the departed owner when it seemed most vibrant. When my pictures were finished, I found to my surprise, that each one had been painted at a different hour, and that I had represented the sky and every change of light and shadow from faint gleams of dawn to the cool silver of moonlight."[10] In this way, *Millet's Birthplace*, for example, reflects the austere and melancholy character of that painter, and *Daubigny's First Studio* evokes the sense of peace, of man in harmony with nature that is so characteristic of Daubigny's work.

The paintings that formed the series dedicated to the memory of the Barbizon masters were; *The Père Gannes Inn, Barye's Studio, Cazin's Studio, Corot's Studio, Daubigny's Home, Daubigny's First Studio (The Charcoal Burner's Hut), The River Oise at Auvers, Daubigny's Studio, Daumier's Studio/Home, Diaz' Studio, Dupré's Studio, View from Dupré's Home, Jacque's Studio, Millet's Studio, Millet's Birthplace, Door to Millet's Studio, Millet's Country*, and *Rousseau's Studio.* To these eighteen original canvases Fournier later added two more when the series was exhibited in the United States. They are *In Cazin's Country*, and *Daubigny's Neighbors.* For each of the finished pictures, which generally measure about 28″ x 39″, numerous smaller studies (and copies) were made by the artist, and all are signed and bear a copyright date of 1907 through 1912.

Fournier put a rather loose interpretation on his definition of the Barbizon masters. Antoine-Louis Barye, for example, is better known as an animal sculptor than as a painter, although, when his sculpture foundry failed, he retreated to the village of Barbizon, devoting himself there to landscape painting before his early death. Honoré Daumier made a name for himself as a newspaper cartoonist, bitingly criticizing contemporary politics and politicians as well as middle class pretensions. His few paintings sympathetically portray the urban poor rather than tranquil scenes of nature and he is not generally included among the "Men of 1830."

The *Père Gannes Inn*, however, was quite appropriately included in the series. The painting today is badly in need of restoration, but it still shows the quaint village hostelry where the Barbizon masters took up temporary abode while sketching and painting near the village or, for some of them, prior to buying a home and settling there. Fournier chose to show the inn at twilight when the artists had returned from their day's work in the forest of Fountainebleau or the nearby farms and meadows, and were gathered for a convivial evening before the inn's hospitable hearth. A welcoming light streams from the windows and open door of the long, low building. In depicting it as the beacon of the artist's refuge in Barbizon, Fournier exploited to the full the dramatic and pictorial possibilities of the warm firelight indoors casting a cheerful glow in the gathering dusk outside.

Daubigny's First Studio (Fig. 1), also called *The Charcoal Burner's Hut*, is painted in a less dramatic vein, indeed in a style that is closer to the school of the Barbizon masters than most of Fournier's other paintings. The small, thatch-roofed stone cottage at Auvers-sur-Oise is seen in a forest glade against a rich background of various shades and permutations of green. The grain shocks surrounding the house and the neighboring woods in their rich summer foilage are resonant with the freshness and fertility of the countryside. The thin curl of blue smoke that spirals upward from the cottage chimney, shimmers in a thin, diaphanous veil against the dark green of the forest trees. It is a sign of human presence in the woods and a suggestion of the immutable bond between man and nature. It is also a characteristic motif in Fournier's work, appearing frequently enough in his landscapes to constitute an artistic signature.

Fournier went rather far afield in his search for the homes of the Barbizon masters. *Millet's Birthplace* at Gruchy, Normandy (Fig. 2) is in a village east of the city of Rouen and nowhere near Barbizon. It is, like *Père Ganne's Inn*, an evening scene in rustic surroundings. A woman sweeps the steps of a cottage, Millet's birthplace, on the village street. A small child watches her as a scattering of geese and chickens peck for crumbs nearby. The crescent moon hangs low behind the trees where tones of dark green and brown predominate. The mood is sombre and subdued, in keeping with Millet's stern and melancholy personality.

The Studio of Antoine-Louis Barye (Fig. 3) is painted in the even more shadowy light of the full moon. Beyond a small courtyard bathed in the pale glow of the moon, Barye's white-washed home with its tiled roof and dormer windows appears half hidden behind the foliage of the encircling trees and a lattice work of grape vines. The mysterious half light and the hush of night evoke a vanished time and a hand that was stilled before its time.

The Studio of Charles Jacque (Fig. 4), one of the last to join the Barbizon group, is a more pastoral scene in which sheep graze contentedly in the foreground. The home itself, improved somewhat after the painter's death, was a long, rambling structure, constructed of timber, cement and stone and painted in warm colors. This studio and the one occupied by Diaz de la Peña were among the most elaborate of the Barbizon studios. In keeping with the more genre quality of Jacque's work, Fournier painted it in the full light of an ordinary day, surrounded by its lawns, flower beds and vines.

Echoing Jules Dupré's gentle scenes of nature generally painted in a low but luminous key, Fournier painted the *View from Dupré's Home* (Fig. 5) at L'Isle Adam in the same sombre but light tinged colors. The title is a misnomer, for the scene is actually the view from the artist's studio toward his house. This is seen at a distance beyond a meadow and beside the narrow stream which flows at the left toward the bridge known as Le Pont du Cabouillet. The house and trees are silhouetted against the glow of the morning sky while a cool, dewey freshness pervades the day before the sun has reached its zenith.

The House of Honoré Daumier (Fig. 6) at Valmondois and *The Studio Home of François Daubigny* at Auvers, are also painted in the light of a bright summer sun. Daumier, having retired to this house and now old and blind, was about to be evicted for unpaid rent when he was rescued by his old friend, Corot, who bought the place for him. Daubigny's studio-home, the Villa des Vallées on the Rue Daubigny, was a much more substantial affair. After the artist's death it was rented during the summer to visiting artists, and it was here that Fournier himself resided while making his studies for the series of Barbizon paintings.

Daubigny's Neighbors (Fig. 7) is one of the paintings originally planned for the Barbizon "Haunts" series and included in the "Homes" set after Fournier's return to the United States. It shows Daubigny's street in Auvers. The modest houses, whose ramshackle variety lend a picturesque quaintness to the scene, huddle along the muddy, rutted street

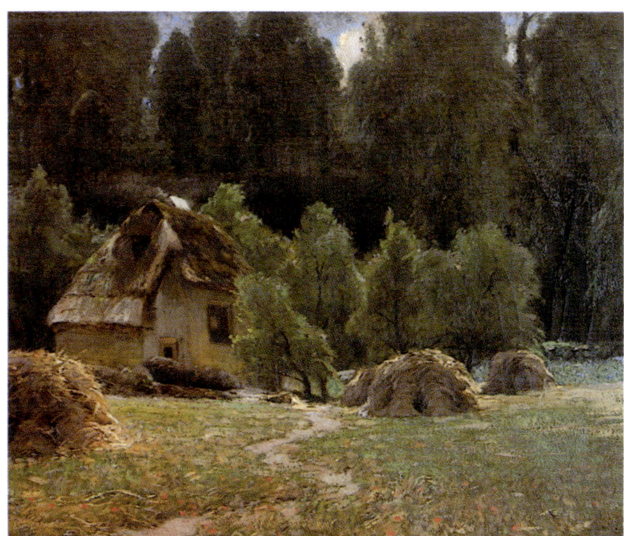

Fig. 1. The Charcoal Burner's Hut.

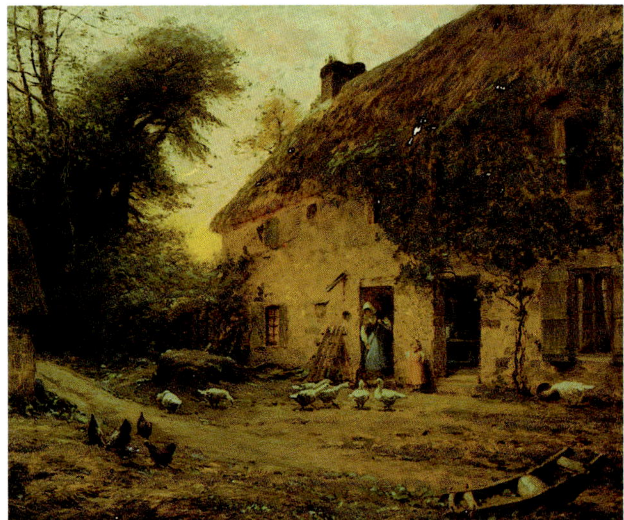

Fig. 2. Millet's Birthplace.

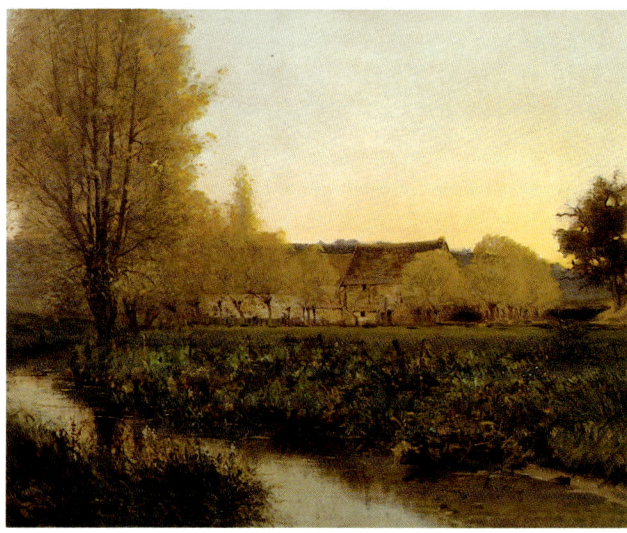

Fig. 5. View from Dupre's Home.

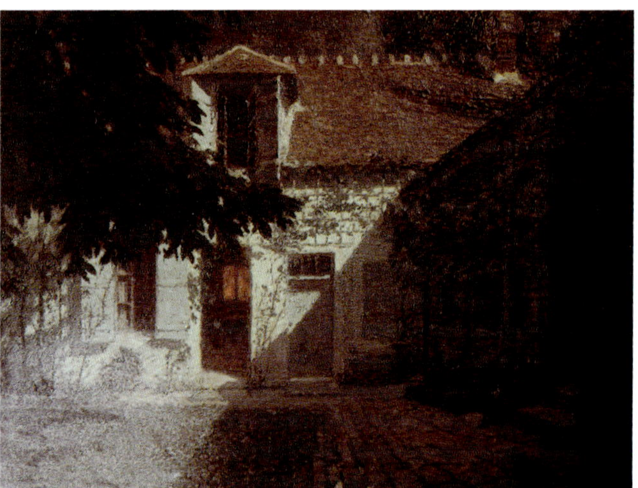

Fig. 3. Studio of Barye.

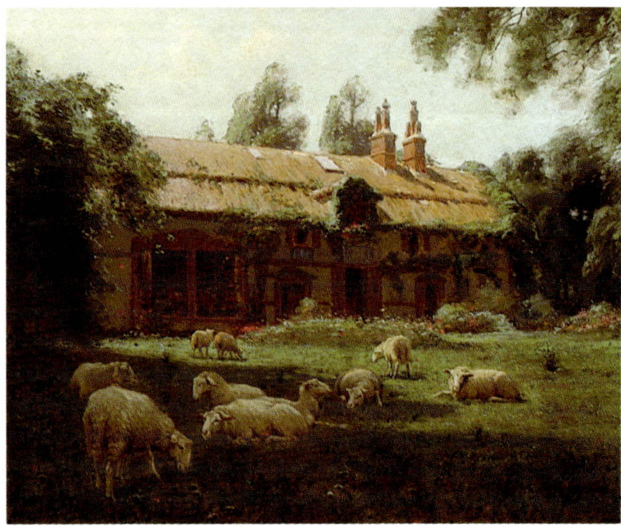

Fig. 4. The Studio of Charles Jacque.

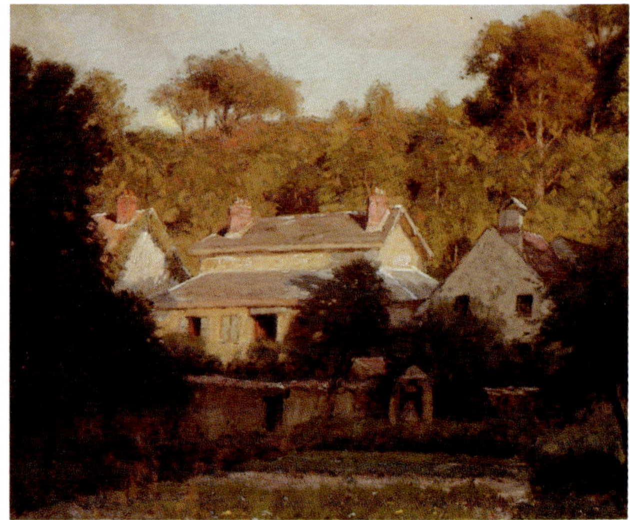

Fig. 6. Home of Daumier.

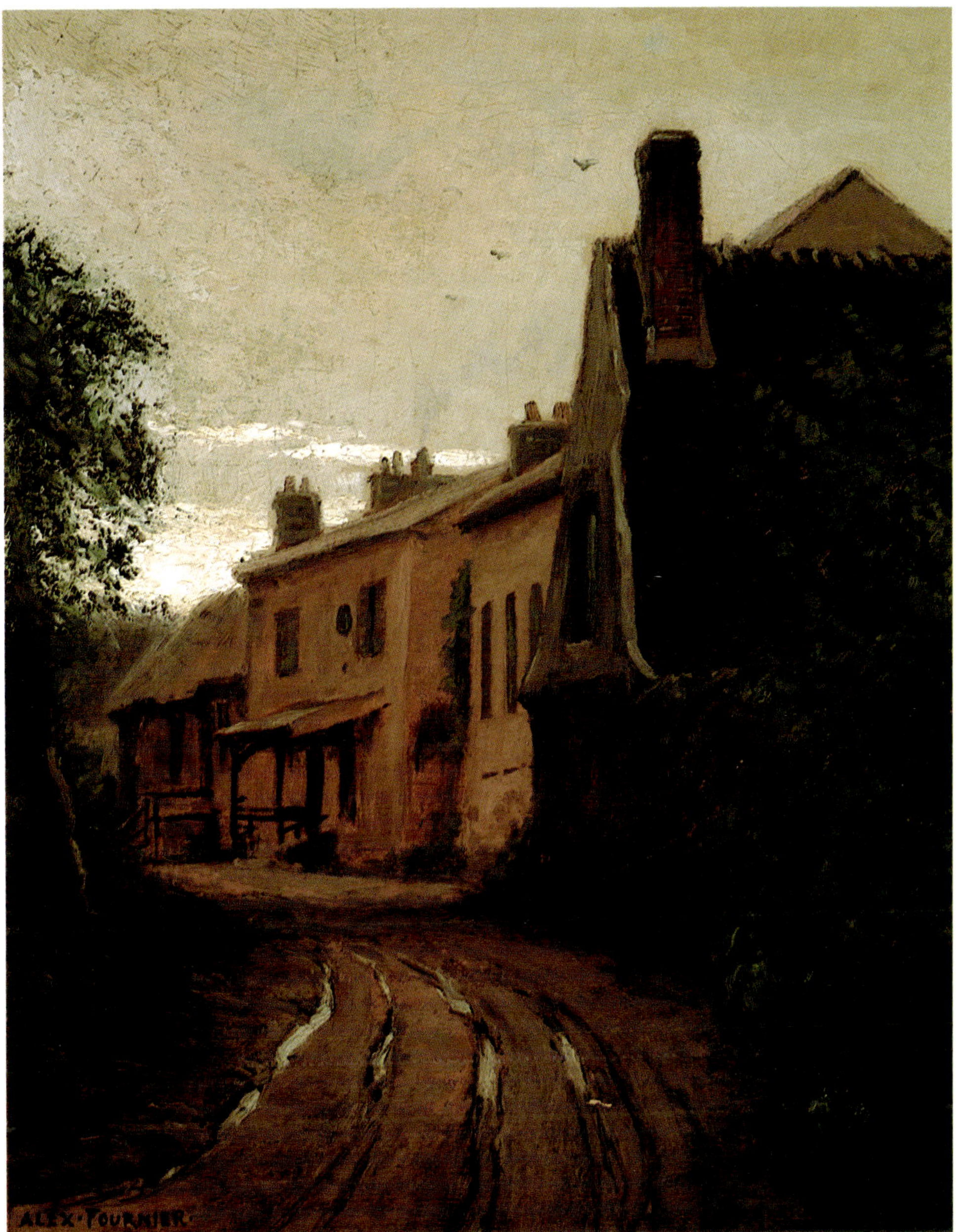

Fig. 7. Daubigny's Neighbors.

of the village. In the treatment of the mass of these buildings, Fournier shows himself to be a master of composition as well as of the atmospheric effects of light and shadow for which he was justly admired.

In addition to his home in Auvers, Daubigny also had a houseboat moored on the Oise nearby. Thirty-five feet long, and equipped with a cabin accommodating four, and a tent on the deck to provide shelter for even more, it was large enough to float down the river, bearing Daubigny and his artist friends on their inland journeys through the waterways of Normandy. Daubigny was so fond of this boat his friends affectionately called him "Captain," and during the Franco-Prussian War, fearing it would fall into the hands of the Prussians, he scuttled it to the bottom of the river, raising it again after the war was over. The boat was the scene of elaborate picnic dinners where conviviality and good fellowship reigned. But at other times, hard work was the order of the day (and night, for these painters were as interested in the effects of moonlight on the landscape as they were in nature's daytime moods). The boat and its journeys recalls, in fact, the similar excursions of Fournier and his friends on the lagoons of Venice in the summer of 1901. Furthermore, as Daubigny was preeminently a painter of river scenes, the choice of subject was especially appropriate to that master.

Narcisse Virgile Diaz de la Peña (known generally as Diaz) was both the wildest and the wealthiest of the Barbizon painters. His home (Fig. 8) reflects the commanding prices that his canvases brought and that were the wonder of the others in the Barbizon coterie. Known for his colorful woodland scenes executed with a quick, paint-laden brush, Diaz was of Spanish descent. Orphaned at a young age, he overcame the poverty and adversity of his childhood to become successful and honored during his own day. His home at Barbizon was an elegant, vine covered stone house in the latest Gothic revival style with picturesque gables, trellises, and a vast, well cared for lawn. Bits of ancient sculpture decorated the grounds and, as an added conceit, a peacock strutted around the grounds. Fournier's painting emphasizes the stylishness of Diaz' country mansion and the refreshing coolness of the surrounding green lawns and gravelled walkways in the dappled shade of the great trees above them.

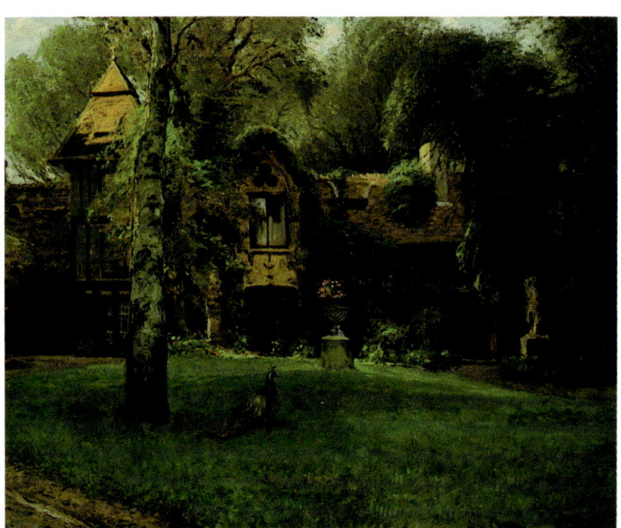

Fig. 8. Home of Diaz.

Fournier returned to the United States after about a year in France, determined to keep his series of Barbizon Homes together as a group, and hoping to sell the entire collection to a museum that would thus honor the Barbizon painters as he had done. The series was first exhibited at the Schaus Art Galleries on Fifth Avenue in New York City from March 16th to April 16th, 1910. In connection with that exhibition William Schaus also published a book by Fournier, *The Homes of the Men of 1830*, reproducing some of the homes and containing the artist's comments on them with an introduction by Fournier's old friend, Herbert Waldron Faulkner.[11] The book is a chatty discussion of the Fournier project with a brief biography of each of the Barbizon masters and an even briefer description of the homes themselves. Calling Fournier "the disciple of masters of the Barbizon school," Faulkner writes that "it is as if he had walked and talked with each and all beneath the shade of Fontainebleau Forest . . . Mr. Fournier has lovingly studied the lives of these, his masters, and has gone to the homes of each, there to live over again in his eager imagination what they lived and saw and did. In each place he has patiently sought out their haunts, living in Daubigny's studio, sailing down the Oise . . . and associating with the peasants of Millet—and has looked at nature through their eyes, thus treading in their footsteps, breathing their artistic atmosphere, dwelling in the very pictures that they painted. In doing so he has acquired a rare insight into the works of the Barbizon painters, and is peculiarly fitted to interpret their meaning."[12]

The series of Barbizon homes was widely exhibited elsewhere in the United States after the initial showing in New York. In the spring of 1911 the collection was displayed in the Detroit Art Museum, after which it travelled to the Chicago Art Institute, where it was seen from July 18th to August 15th, 1911. In October of that year the paintings were exhibited in the Art Gallery of the Minneapolis Public Library and later at the Minneapolis Institute of Arts and the St. Paul Institute's Studio Building. Other exhibitors of the Barbizon Homes included the Buffalo Fine Arts Academy in April, 1914, and, Vose Galleries in Boston which, from March 3rd to March 15th, 1919 showed selections from the exhibition. The Milwaukee Art Society also exhibited nineteen of the canvases at a later date.[13]

The collection was acclaimed as the greatest work yet from the brush of the artist, "full of poetry and charm," as one Chicago critic wrote.[14] After noting that "the paintings were visited by thousands" while in New York, a correspondent for the *Minneapolis Journal* wrote that "In Detroit, at the Art Museum, they created a furor and at the Art Institute in Chicago . . . they captured public and critics as well. During Aviation week in August they were viewed by 151,000 persons." The same correspondent went on to advise his readers that "almost every mood of nature, every hour of the day and night from tenderest, softest twilight to mysterious moonlight, from glaring sunlight to mellow evening glow, and all the subtle nuances that lie between—all these are found in this remarkable series of pictures." And, pointing to the artist's ties to the Barbizon masters, the writer noted that "though he [Fournier] insists on calling Harpignies the last of the Barbizon school, it is not far from right to reserve that distinction for Mr. Fournier himself. He has imbibed the tradition of the Barbizon school, but has added to it his individuality, imparting to each picture a wholesome charm peculiarly his own."[15]

The enthusiastic contemporary response to the Barbizon Homes and Haunts did not, however, translate into a commercial success, nor was Fournier able to keep the collection together as he had hoped. Efforts were made in Minneapolis and St. Paul by some of his admirers to raise the money for the complete set "in a movement," as the same correspondent noted, "to purchase the series and present it to the Art Museum as the most notable work of Minneapolis' most distinguished artist." Fournier himself was more than willing to give talks on his experiences in Barbizon to aid the various fund drives.[16] But nothing came of these attempts and the series was eventually broken up and dispersed. Many of the paintings disappeared, singly, into private collections and not one of them was purchased by a public museum. Unfortunately, several of them were lost over the ensuing years and remain unlocated today.

Though Fournier returned to France only once more, very briefly in 1913, the impressions he had recorded there, bolstered by many notes and drawings, furnished a wealth of material for future use. One of the most important of the later pictures, which may actually have been begun in France, is *The Gleaners* (Fig. 9) painted in 1908. Undoubtedly inspired by Millet's picture of the same theme, it is

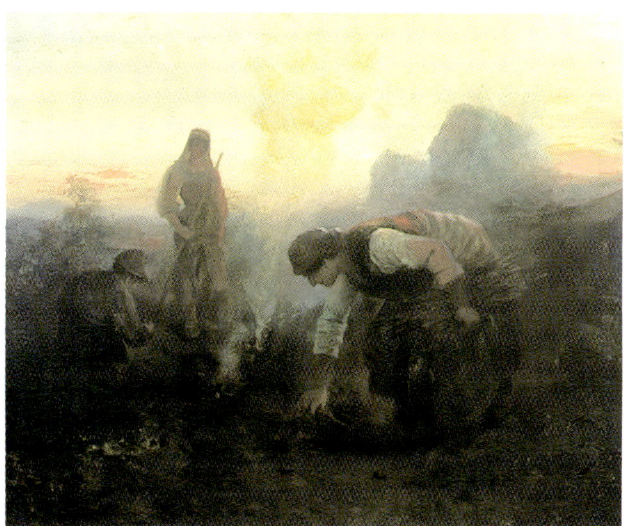

Fig. 9. The Gleaners.

still very different. Where Millet stresses the monumental forms of the gleaners bending to their toil in a tight, almost abstract compositional arrangement, Fournier stresses the coloristic effects of light and atmosphere. In the light of the setting sun, reflected in fiery streaks in the evening sky, three gleaners, dimly seen in the darkening foreground, gather around a small fire to ward off the chill of the evening air. One of these figures still bends to her task, and, of the three, is the closest to Millet's gleaners. But color, not mass, is Fournier's purpose and his brush delicately suggests the gathering shadows about to envelope the gleaners, the field and the distant cottages.

Judging from its 48″ x 59″ size, *The Gleaners* was probably intended as an exhibition piece, but its history is obscure and it has only recently come to light near Lee, Massachusetts, where Fournier had a temporary studio. It was apparently abandoned there, with a number of other Fournier canvases and either neglected or forgotten during the ensuing years. Fournier moved around so much, establishing studios in so many different places, he may have forgotten where he had left even as important a painting as *The Gleaners*.

That Fournier had not abandoned his fondness for the moonlit scene is evident from the many moonlight views which he painted in France and after his return to the United States. As few of them are dated, it is difficult to establish a clear chronology, though, in time, they developed a pattern which became almost a formula. One of them

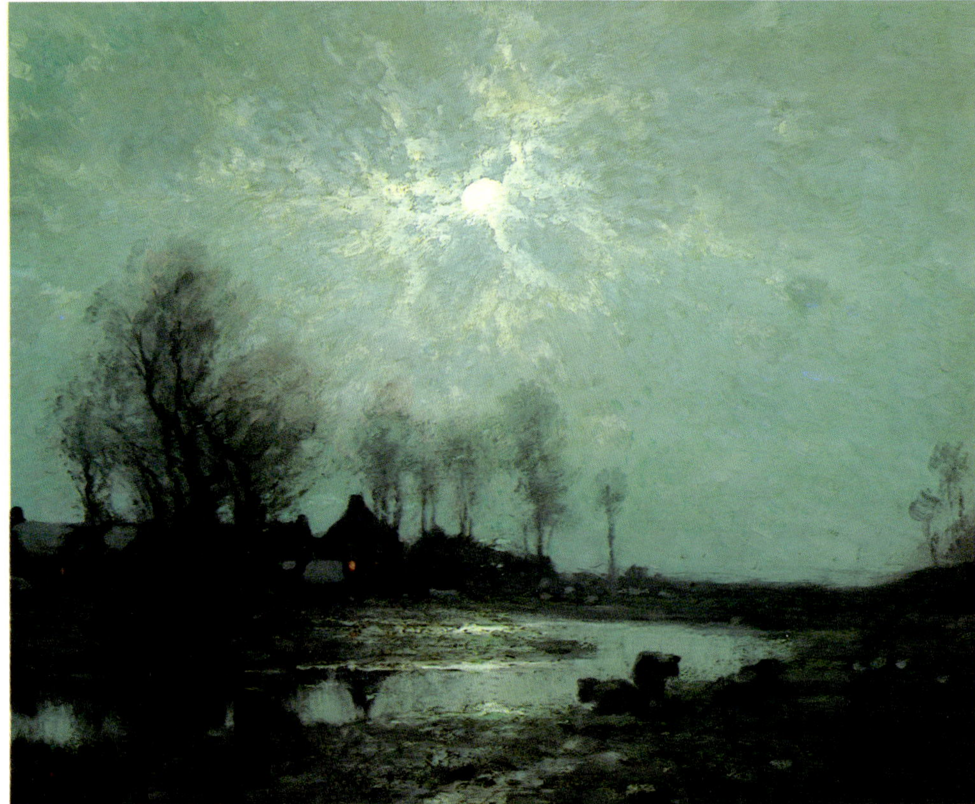

Fig. 10. Peaceful Night: Normandie.

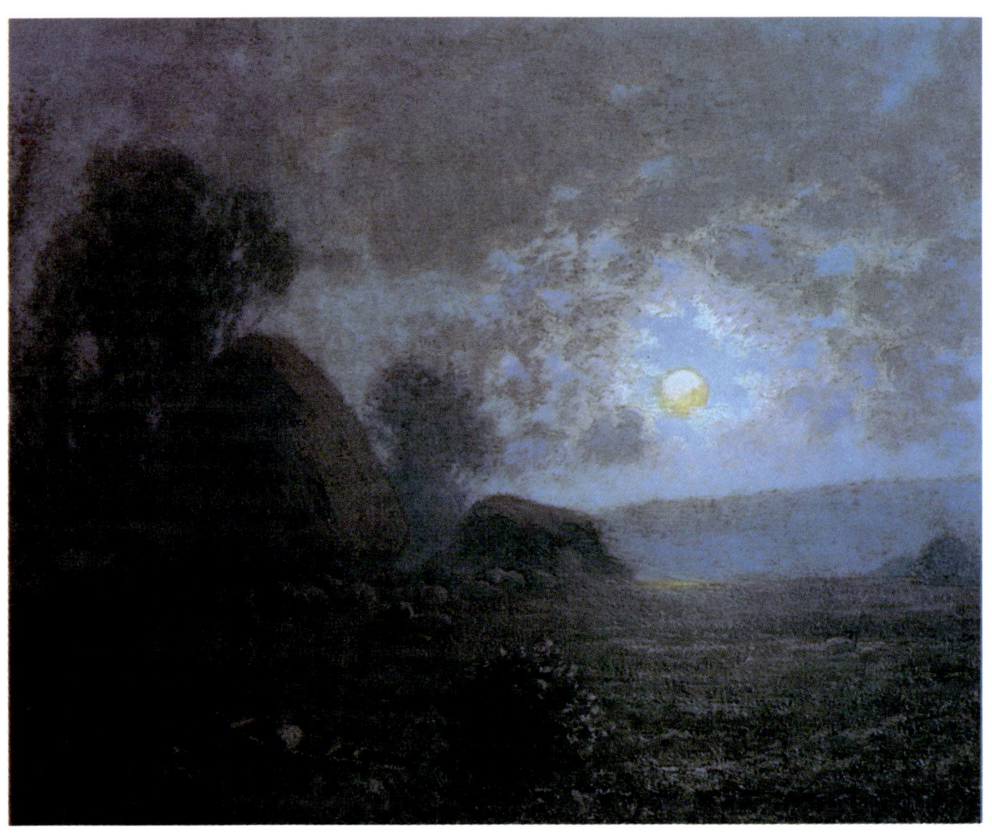

Fig. 11. Moonlight Near Barbizon.

is *Peaceful Night in Normandy* (Fig. 10), painted in 1904 and originally in the collection of the artist's friend, Dr. Soren Rees of Minneapolis. It is typically Fournier in the way that the pale moon glow is reflected in the shallow, winding stream, darkly revealing the shadowy forms of the cattle that graze on its banks. In the distance, behind the thin and whispy trees, the lamplight shines in the window of a cluster of farmhouses, startling in its contrast to the surrounding shadows. Such pictures as this, or the similarly nocturnal scene, *Moonlight Near Barbizon* (Fig. 11), recall George Inness' moonlit scenes in their stillness and tranquility, though Fournier's work retains a clearer sense of object and of specific time and place. It thus avoids, to some extent, the dissolution of form and the moody, intensely private quality of the earlier artist's oeuvre.

Fournier continued, through the next few years, to paint pictures based on sketches made earlier during his search for the Barbizon homes and haunts. *In Daubigny's Country: Chaponval, France* (Fig. 12), was probably intended as one of the "haunts" series, and a small study of the same scene (Fig. 13) was probably painted while the artist was still in France. In translating the sketch to the larger studio piece, Fournier lost none of the freshness and spontaneity of the smaller picture. It captures the immediacy of time and place characteristic of Impressionism, though the fleeting moment is still anchored in permanence, in the furrowed meadow darkened in the shadow of a passing cloud, in the distant, red roofed houses nestling

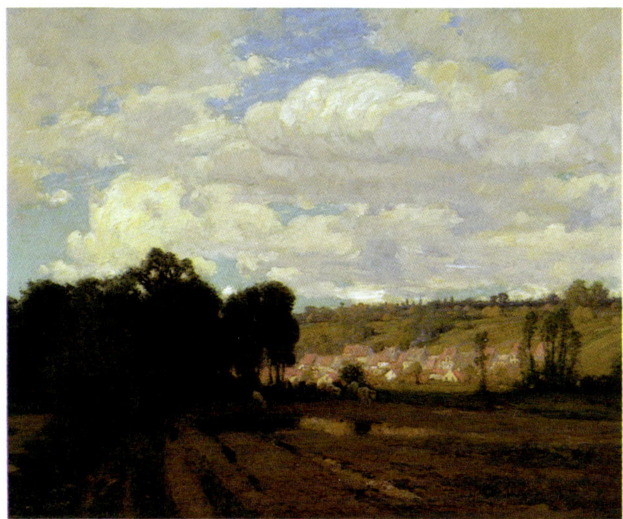

Fig. 12. In Daubigny's Country.

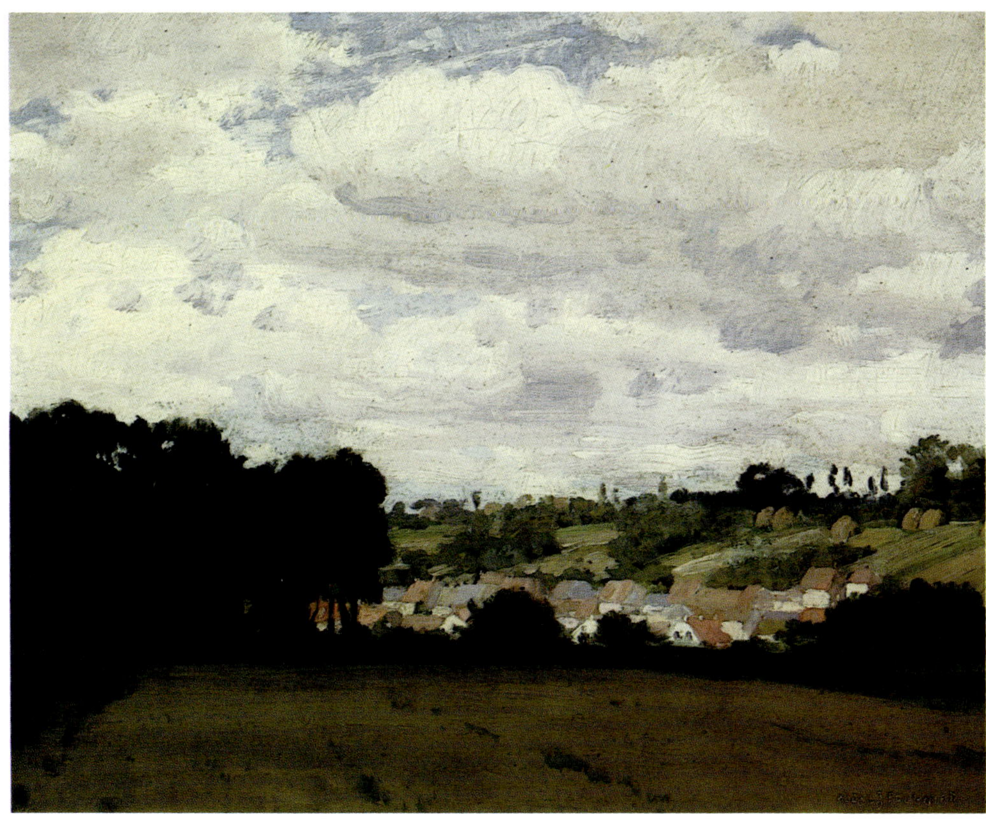

Fig. 13. Sketch for In Daubigny's Country.

in the valley, and in the high cloud formations that sail across the sky.

Fournier returned to France for one final trip in the spring of 1913. For some time during that trip he and Charles Francis Browne of the Chicago Art Institute were guests of Mr. and Mrs. Carl Daubigny, son and daughter-in-law of the Barbizon master, with whom Fournier had established a warm friendship on his earlier trips to France. The Daubigny home had recently been acquired by the French government as a historic house—the sale including four large Corots that hung in the living room—but the Daubigny family had been given the right to continue living there for the remainder of their lives.

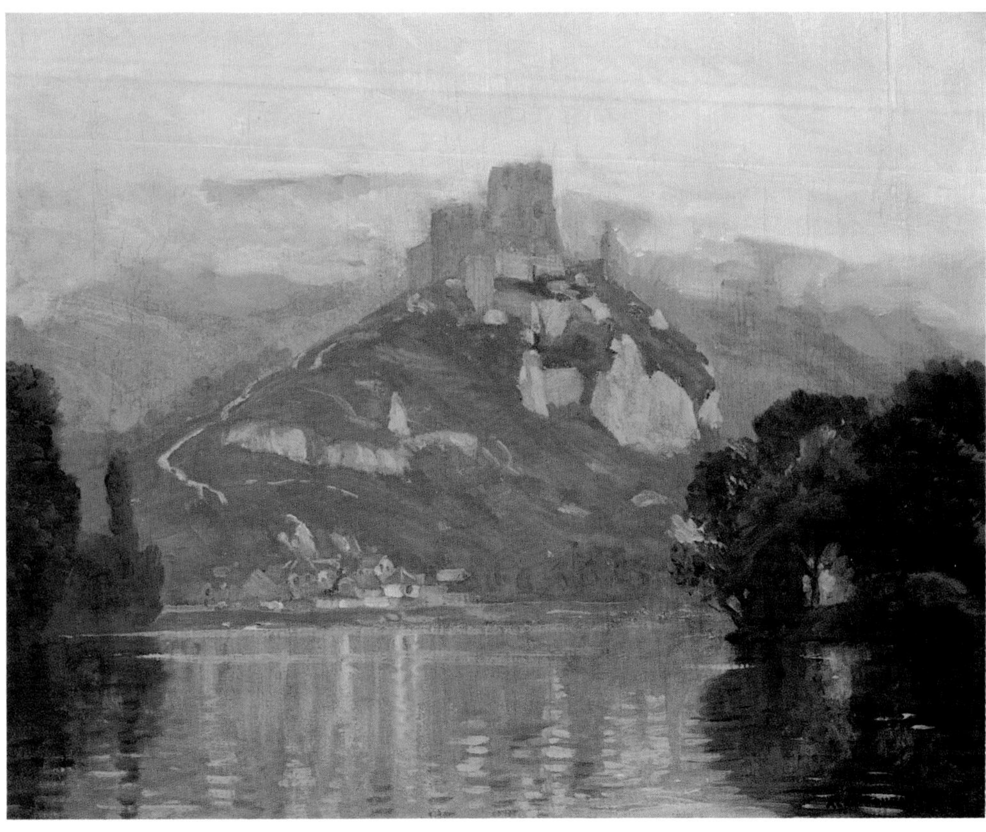

Fig. 14. Château Gaillard in the Mist.

It is not known exactly how long Fournier remained in France during the 1913 visit. He seems to have felt, however, that the pictorial possibilities of the Barbizon Homes and Haunts had been exhausted, and, travelling more widely, other subjects captured his attention and soon engaged his brush. For example, he painted a number of views of the Château Gaillard at Les Andelys on the river Seine south of Rouen. The castle was built in 1196 by King Richard I, the "Lion-Hearted," of England. At the time of its construction it was one of the largest and strongest yet known in France, and its name, "the saucy castle," may have referred to its having been built to deter attacks by the King of France on Richard's Normandy domain.

Fournier painted the castle many times and under a variety of atmospheric conditions. In painting one subject in nature's changing moods he repeated, of course, the Impressionist's fondness for showing the effects of different light and climatic conditions on a single pastoral, or even urban subject, like Monet's series of haystacks at Giverny, for example, or his many views of the Cathedral at Rouen. And, indeed, some of the small studies that Fournier painted of the Chateau Gaillard are quite impressionistic in their broad, loose brushwork and broken color technique. But a more finished piece, *Château Gaillard in the Mist* (Fig. 14) dated 1913, in its restricted color pallette in which one "tone" predominates, is closer to American "Tonalism" than either French Impressionism or the Barbizon school.[17]

As Charles Caffin, the contemporary art critic defined it, Tonalism implied an "even subtle luminosity" which created the effect of "looking at objects through a great gauze veil—the veil in nature being produced by sunlight diffused through atmosphere which 'tones' in a uniform light all the objects seen."[18] This veil of atmosphere, so characteristic of tonalist paintings, evoked a mood of reverie, of nostalgia, "frequently tinged by a pervasive, if understated melancholy."[19] The sources of the style are to be found in the work of George Inness and James Abbott McNeill Whistler with their blurring of recognizable forms behind a thin curtain of atmosphere to suggest a subjective and highly personal view of nature. A younger group of Tonalists led by Henry Ward Ranger included also Dwight W. Tryon, John Francis Murphy, Elliott Daingerfield, Thomas W. Dewing, Bruce Crane and Charles Warren Eaton. Both William Merrit Chase and Theodore Robinson were briefly influenced by tonalist ideas early in their careers, and even the landscapes of such well known American Impressionists as Childe Hassam, John Twachtman and Willard Metcalf are sometimes modified by tonalist values. Contemporary photography revealed a similar tonalist response to nature, for Edward Steichen, Gertrude Käsebier and Clarence White all pursued similarly subjective pictures of mood rather than fact. Indeed, these photographers would sometimes stretch a piece of gauze across the camera lens to achieve the "lost edge" effect of the tonalist landscape and to avoid a distinct contrast of light and shadow.[20]

Because of their bias against objectivity in translating nature on the canvas, the Tonalists, by and large, were hostile to the precise and detailed realism of the Hudson River School. They were equally unsympathetic to French Impressionism with its bright colors and sunny spontaneity. Their admiration for the paintings of the Barbizon school, however, was apparent in their paintings and in what they wrote. It was strong enough, in fact, for Tonalism to have been described as an offshoot of the American Barbizon tradition. But as one perceptive observer has recently pointed out, in spite of the allegiance that almost all of the Tonalists swore to the French Barbizon masters, they were a later group of artists concerned, for the most part, with the American landscape.[21]

In this particular respect, Fournier was an exception, as *Château Gaillard in the Mist* amply demonstrates. Its subject, of course, is thoroughly French, though it is not truly Barbizon in mood and execution. Rather it comes closer in spirit to the art of Puvis de Chavannes and to the simplified backgrounds of that artist's neo-classic allegories decorating, for example, the Boston Public Library. These were executed by the French artist between 1891 and 1896 and were undoubtedly well known to Fournier from his frequent visits to that city. Still, *Château Gaillard in the Mist* clearly participates in the American Tonalist esthetic. Its simplified forms, seen through a veil of mist and its subdued tones of greys, blues and violets, suggest the quiet reverie and subjective contemplation of nature that are the hallmarks of Tonalist paintings. Fournier defines the source of the mistiness in the bank of clouds that hover over the ruins of the castle above the village of Les Andelys. But in spite of its airy curtain, the steep hill crowned by Richard the Lion Hearted's castle, rises dominantly in the center of the picture, framed by the tree lined river banks on either side. The somber tones, evoking a typically tonalist nostalgia, are found in a number of earlier Fournier paintings too, particularly in some of the Barbizon Homes and in the moonlit scenes of Normandy.

Entirely different in tone and atmosphere, and suggesting a note of playfulness that was very much a part of the artist's personality but is seldom evident in his paintings, is a small but delightful picture, possibly painted during the 1913 visit to France. It shows a line of laundry flapping and billowing in a stiff breeze in front of a Normandy cottage. Entitled *A Breezy Day* (Fig. 15) it is a rare example of a genre work by the artist in which he seized upon the pictorial possibilities of the most everyday subject—a family's wash hanging out to dry—and transformed it into a vivid picture of wind and weather.

The 1913 trip to France was a brief one compared to the more purposeful visit of 1907. At some time, probably in the fall, Fournier returned to America to resume his loosely defined duties with the Roycrofters in East Aurora and to continue to divide his time between western New York state and Minnesota. Increasingly, however, he was also identifying himself with another group of artists, those who were beginning to establish a regional school of landscape painting in the scenic countryside of Brown County, Indiana.

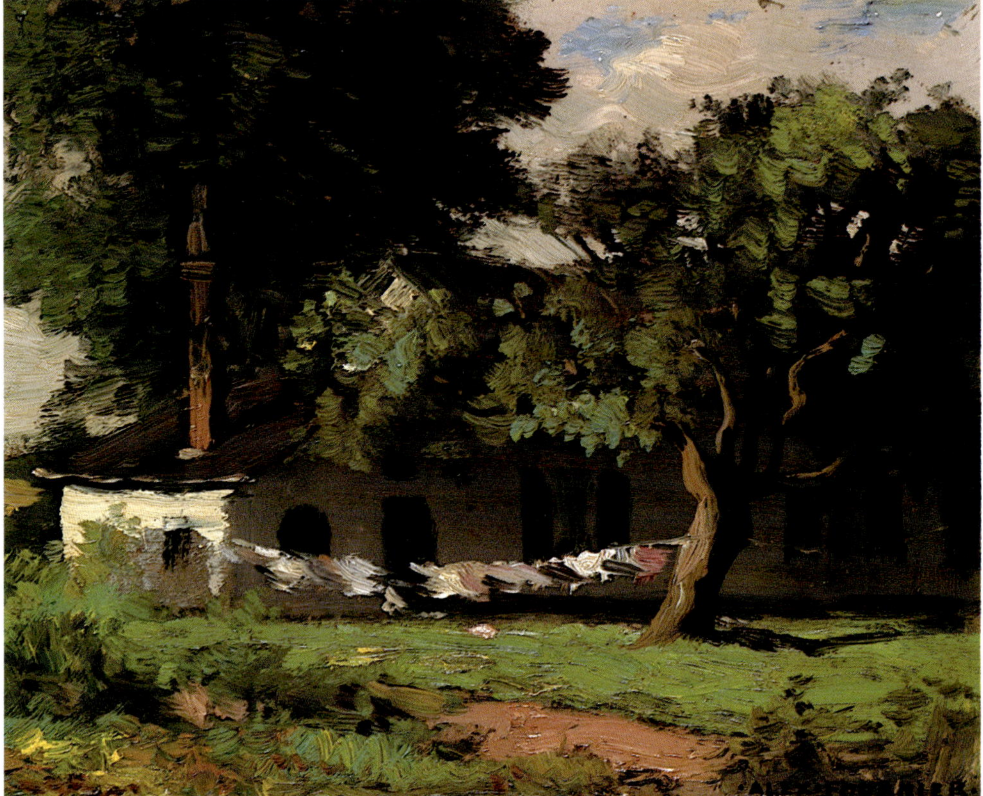

Fig. 15. A Breezy Day.

NOTES: CHAPTER 7. The Homes and Haunts of the Barbizon Masters

1. See Robert L. Herbert, *Barbizon Revisited*, San Francisco, California Palace of the Legion of Honor, 1962, Peter Bermingham, *American Art in a Barbizon Mood*, Washington, D.C., Smithsonian Institution Press, 1975, and Laura Meixner, *An International Episode, Millet, Monet and their North American Counterparts*, Memphis, Tenn. Dixon Gallery, 1983 for discussions of this subject.
2. As described by Bermingham, Op. Cit., Introduction by Joshua Taylor, p. 15.
3. Meixner, Op. Cit., p. 15.
4. Ibid., p. 22.
5. William M. Hunt, *W. M. Hunt's Talks on Art*. Series I, Boston, 1875, p. 33.
6. Bermingham, Op. Cit., p. 26.
7. Quoted in Bermingham, Op. Cit., p. 27 from Nicolai Cikovsky, *The Life and Work of George Inness*, Ph.D. Dissertation Harvard University, p. 173.
8. Charles Sprague Smith, *Barbizon Days: Millet - Corot - Rousseau—Barye*, New York, A. Wessels & Co., 1902.
9. *Minneapolis Journal*, Oct. 8, 1911, p. 6.
10. Unheaded, undated clipping, Fournier's Scrapbook, Collection, Allan Bartlett.
11. Alexis Jean Fournier, *The Homes of the Men of 1830*, New York, William Schaus Galleries. 1910. Introduction by Herbert Waldron Faulkner.
12. Ibid., pp. 3-4.
13. Unheaded, undated clipping, Fournier Scrapbook, Collection, Allan Bartlett.
14. Unheaded, undated clipping, Fournier's Scrapbook, Collection, Allan Bartlett.
15. *Minneapolis Journal*, Oct. 8, 1911, p. 6.
16. On Jan. 4, 1915, for example, Fournier lectured on the Barbizon Homes while the series was on exhibit at the Studio Building of the St. Paul Institute. See *St. Paul Institute Bulletin*, Jan. 1915, Vol. 6, No. 4, p. 6.
17. See William H. Gerdts, Diana Dimodica Sweet and Robert R. Preato, *Tonalism, An American Experience*, New York, Grand Central Galleries, 1982, for the most perceptive and up to date discussion of this subject. Wanda M. Corn's *The Color of Mood: American Tonalism, 1880-1910*, San Francisco, M. H. De Young Museum, 1972, is also an important essay on tonalism and broke new ground in understanding the style.
18. Charles H. Caffin, *American Masters of Painting*, New York, 1902, p. 13.
19. Corn, Op. Cit., p. 4.
20. Ibid., p. 3.
21. William H. Gerdts' essay in Gerdts, Sweet and Preato, Op. Cit., pp. 17-18.

Chapter 8

With the Hoosier Impressionists

In 1894 an exhibition sponsored by the Central Art Association of Chicago was held at the studio of the sculptor, Lorado Taft, in the Chicago Atheneum Building. The exhibition was entitled "Five Hoosier Painters" and it included works by John Otis Adams, William Forsyth, Richard Bruckner Gruelle, Otto Stark and Theodore Clement Steele, all of whom (except Adams) had exhibited together the previous year at the Denison Hotel in Indianapolis. The significance of the exhibition lay not only in the identification of the group as a regional school of American landscape painting but in the enthusiastic praise they received from Hamlin Garland, a writer and promoter of a regional consciousness in American literature. Garland held that "these artists have helped the people of Indiana to see the beauty in their own quiet landscape. They have not only found interesting things to paint near at hand, they have made these chosen scenes interesting to others."[1]

In 1907, Theodore Steele, the dean of the Indiana artists and one of the "Hoosier Five," discovered the quiet, rural beauty of southern Indiana in Brown County and began to paint and sketch there near the small town of Nashville, Indiana. Eventually he built a home in the area, the "House of the Singing Winds."[2] Attracted by the unspoiled hills and meadows, the rural remoteness and the quiet, picturesque surroundings, other artists began to join him there—encouraged by the building of a railway and the opening of hotels in the area. In 1925 the Brown County Art Gallery Association was formed to present the work of the colony's artists in public exhibitions.

One of the important artists of the group was Adolph Robert Shulz who had actually "discovered" Brown County even earlier than Steele and who later became the first chronicler of the artists' colony. Writing of his first encounter with the place in August, 1900, when he and a companion took a horse and buggy tour from Columbus, Indiana, following creek beds for three days to make a trip now made in less than an hour, Shulz described his first reaction to Brown County. "Never before had I been so thrilled by a region; it seemed like a fairyland with its narrow, winding roads leading . . . down into the creek beds, through the water pools and up over the hills. Everywhere there were rail fences almost hidden by Queen Anne's lace, goldenrod and other interesting weeds and bushes. Picturesque cabins here and there seemed to belong to the landscape as did the people who lived in them. I was much impressed by the beautiful and dignified growth of timber. All the country was enveloped in a soft, opalescent haze. A sense of peace and loveliness never before experienced came over me and I felt that at last I had found the ideal sketching ground."[3]

The landscape described by Shulz seemed made to order for Fournier who, in fact, had known Shulz when both of them were studying at the Académie Julian in Paris. As Shulz later recalled, in his first introduction to Fournier, he was "the dark little chap we all admired because he could speak French."[4] Later, when, perhaps at Shulz' suggestion, Fournier came to Brown County to paint, Shulz remembered how Fournier had "gone about in the Barbizon country of France, conversing with the peasants and getting so much more out of his work than we did who were limited to our native tongue."[5]

Fournier also had other connections with the Brown County artists through his contacts in Chicago where the Indiana Art Association's annual Exhibitions of Western Artists were held. He was, throughout his life, an active member of the sponsoring Society of Western Artists which had been formed in Chicago in 1896 to encourage what we would today call midwestern regionalism. The first president of the group was Frank Duveneck, but its most enthusiastic spokesman was, again, Hamlin Garland.

In this connection it is interesting to note that Garland's *Impressions on Impressionism* which appeared in the fall of 1894 in a pamphlet printed for the Central Art Association in Chicago reviewing the Seventh Annual Exhibition of American Paintings at the Chicago Art Institute, lauded the American Impressionists in the show, particularly T. C. Steele. The essay purports to reproduce a free wheeling discussion of the show by a novelist (Garland himself), a sculptor (Lorado Taft), and a "conservative Painter" who was Charles Francis Browne, an American artist in the Barbizon tradition and who, in 1913, was to accompany Fournier on his last visit to Barbizon. Garland maintained that what was missing in the exhibition was "the drama of American life . . . We can't go on doing imitations and taking notes abroad . . . The next step is to do American themes and do it naturally."[6] Then, identifying Impressionism with Modernism, he added, "The public will rise to meet the impressionist half-way; we never will return to the dead black shadow, nor the affected grouping of the old."[7]

Surprisingly, even the "conservative painter" agreed with him. Browne too thought that the American landscapists should give more thought to incorporating an element of native identity into their paintings. "We will never have any home art with the real home flavor unless we are in close touch with what's around us here . . . (we have) educated the public into thinking that a picture isn't good for much unless dated and signed abroad . . . Is a Brittany peasant more to us than everything else? . . . Haven't we out-door subjects in our fields, or our mountains, by our glorious lakes, on the shores of our loud sounding seas? . . . Painting is more than paint, and sunlight is more than orange and purple, and a landscape as well as a figure means more than a symphony of color, a pang of grey or a whoop of violet."[8]

On a different occasion, a year later, Garland made a similar plea: "Monet makes Giverny, Giverny does not make Monet . . . there must be keen sensitiveness to the beautiful and significant in nearby things. The Chicago artist, being denied certain picturesque aspects of seashore and mountainside, has a rare chance to develop unhackneyed themes in sky and plain . . . The light floods the Kankakee marshes as well as the meadows and willows of Giverny. The Muscatatuck has its subtleties of color as well as L'Oise, and a little young haymaker on the banks of the Fox River is certainly as admirable . . . as a clumsy Brittany peasant in wooden shoes."[9]

Though Browne did not join the Hoosier Impressionists as a Brown County artist, a number of Fournier's other Chicago friends did. One was Adam Emory Albright, a fellow member of the Society of Western Artists whom Fournier may have first met at the Chicago World's Columbian Exposition of 1893 where both of them were represented. Their paths crossed occasionally thereafter and they exhibited together in Minneapolis and Chicago. Another was George Ames Aldrich who had been in Paris from 1893 to 1901. Fournier's friendship with him may have started when both were students at the Académie Julian and been strengthened when Aldrich later settled in South Bend and became an established landscapist and a drawing teacher in the Fine Arts Club there. His painting technique, with its shimmering light effects, was influenced by that of the great American Impressionist, John Twachtman, with whom Aldrich had studied at the Art Students' League in New York City before embarking on his studies in Paris. Aldrich, like Fournier, also admired the work of Fritz Thaulow, a popular Norwegian Impressionist working in Paris during the early part of the twentieth century. Indeed, a certain affinity in the artistic manner of Aldrich and Fournier, especially in the mellow warmth of their autumnal landscapes, may be due to the influence of Thaulow on both of the young and impressionable Americans.

One of the attractions of the Brown County landscape, aside from its rural picturesqueness, was the special light and color that its artists found unique. As a South Bend reporter observed in commenting on the area, the still, clear air transformed color with a suddenness in which . . . light blue takes the place of green in trees and grass on the opposite side of the valley. It lends a great deal more distance, and hence delicateness to the view . . . a definite touch which I confess I thought a southern Indiana affectation until I stood upon a hill in Bean Blossom, Ind. and watched the trees a few hundred yards away fade into such a delicate hue . . ."[10]

Though the history of Fournier's early association with the Hoosiers is difficult to trace, it becomes much clearer after 1921. In that year his first wife, Emma, died, and as their two children had married and left home, Fournier was left quite alone. 1921 was a busy year professionally, with exhibitions at the Chicago Art Institute from February to March, at the Beard Art Gallery in Minneapolis in March, in Detroit in April and in Toledo later in the year. But, as his friend, Nicholas Brewer observed, "meeting him in Toledo . . . I noticed that my poor friend seemed all broken up and so low in spirit that his work showed the effect of his grief."[11] Fournier's characteristic optimism, however, soon pulled him out of his depression and he began to pay court to Cora May (Platz) Ball, the widow of his friend, L. Clarence Ball, an Indiana painter of landscapes and still-life subjects, who had died in 1915.

Fournier may have known the Balls through his Chicago connections, for Clarence Ball was a member of the Chicago Society of Artists and frequently exhibited there. Ball's and Fournier's association may even have gone back to 1893 when each had won a measure of success at the Chicago World's Columbian Exposition. In any event, on May 9, 1922, Fournier and Cora Ball were married and the artist moved into the house at 142 Elder Street, South Bend, where Cora had been born and spent her entire life. From 1922 to 1937 when Cora died, the couple divided their time between South Bend where they resided in the winter, and East Aurora where they spent the summer.[12] Fournier, accompanied by his wife, continued his painting treks to Brown County as well as other more far flung artists' colonies, including the one at Woodstock, N.Y. where he was the house guest of Richard Le Gallienne, and the one in Provincetown, Massachusetts where he painted a number of Cape Cod scenes. In 1935 the couple spent some time in Miami and St. Petersburg, Florida, briefly contemplating making their winter home in that state.

A photograph taken in October, 1927 and later published in a newspaper article about Fournier[13] shows the artist on one of his painting trips to Brown County (Fig. 1). Rather formally dressed, even for that era, in a suit, hat, and tie, Fournier is seated on his camp stool, palette and brushes in one hand and his inseparable companion, a homemade pipe, in the other. With his paint box open in front of him, he may have been painting that day, any one of a number of Brown County scenes which form a substantial part of his artistic work.

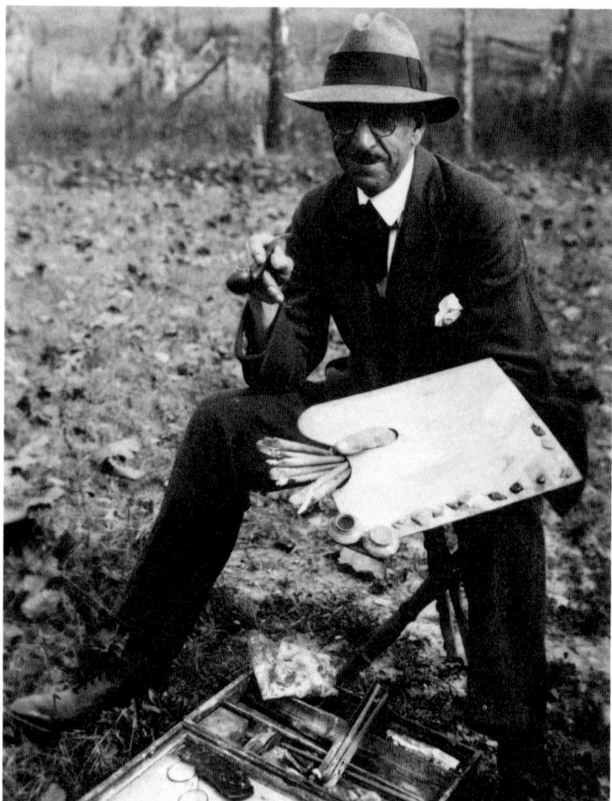

Fig. 1. Photograph: A. J. Fournier with palette, brushes and pipe on camp stool.

Even amidst the scenic beauties of Brown County, however, Fournier occasionally put aside pure landscape in favor of a picture of a house of unusual interest. Fournier was very much a social creature, a joiner and frequent organizer of social activities, and though in love with nature, he also loved the human connection. Perhaps this accounts, in some part, for his interest in homes with a historic or personal association. *The Stinson Homestead*, a log cabin pioneer home in Brown County that Fournier painted in the summer of 1927 is a case in point. Though its present whereabouts is unknown, the picture was described as a "log cabin with the usual log cabin setting."[14] Whatever that setting might mean, the picture attracted much attention when it was exhibited at the Chicago Galleries Association later that year. During its exhibition, the artist, ever one to relish a good story, related that the old Mr. Stinson, still the owner of the property, had engaged him in conversation as he was painting the house. The old log cabin had been painted on canvas by about fifty artists, he told Fournier and now he thought it was about time for one of the artists to give the cabin itself a new coat of paint.[15]

Fournier's landscapes of Brown County appear more impressionistic than his earlier canvases in that they use a thicker impasto and a more flickering brush, increasingly attempting to capture a fleeting moment in time and a transient atmospheric effect. The dramatic light effects of his earlier style have been succeeded by the more natural, if brighter, light of Impressionism. And Impressionism was, in fact the order of the day, at least among those artists who eschewed the avant garde directions of the twentieth century imported from Europe. And though the exuberant style of the French Impressionists and their attempt to capture the transitory phenomena of nature through a new understanding of color and light had led American artists to take a fresh look at their native landscape, their canvases tended to be less radical than their French counterparts. They may have disdained the emphasis on drawing and the smoothly polished surface of the academic tradition in painting, but they still considered themselves part of the mainstream tradition in American art and therefore, unlike the French Impressionists, they were unwilling to allow color and light to completely dissolve form.

Although the close contact that Fournier established with the Hoosier Impressionists was certainly one explanation of his increasingly impressionistic style during the 1920's, his own keen and sensitive observation of nature and his dedicated pursuit of the effects of light and atmosphere in painting made his transition from Barbizon moodiness to Impressionist ebullience all the more likely. Moreover, Fournier was no stranger to the French Impressionists' broken color technique. He had undoubtedly seen their work while in France and was acquainted with one of their leaders, Claude Monet. Indeed, the Impressionists' broad brush techniques and flickering light effects are evident in the innumerable small sketches which served as studies for Fournier's more carefully finished studio pieces and some were even regarded as small, informal pictures complete in themselves. But even in his Indiana years, Fournier never entirely abandoned the characteristic Barbizon sense of a timeless harmony in nature. His canvases still combined a sense of permanence in the natural world with the transient effects of season, climate and atmospheric condition. Through the various permutations of color and light he was able to suggest the ephemeral quality of the outdoor scene while respecting, at the same time, nature's essential immutability.

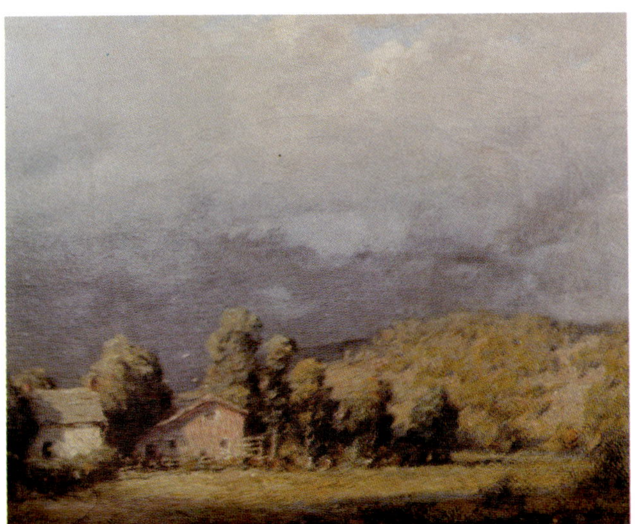

Fig. 2. Clearing After Rain.

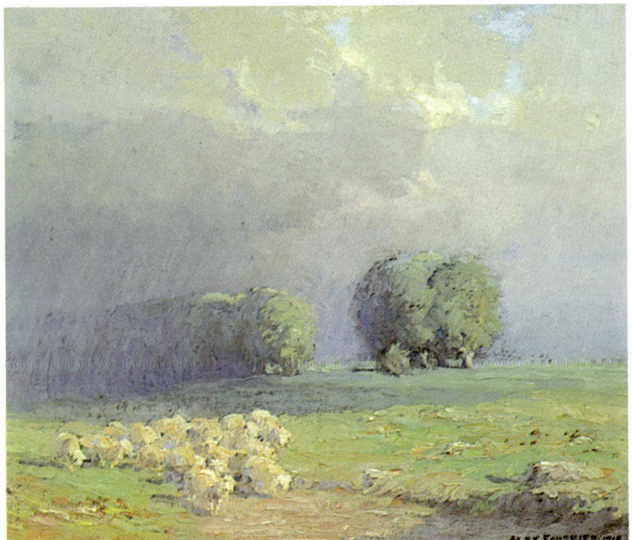

Fig. 3. The Coming Storm.

Clearing After Rain (Fig. 2), vividly suggests such a transitory moment in nature. Sunlight, breaking suddenly through the clouds, illuminates a group of farm buildings and a foreground meadow, while the dark rainshower still hovers over the distant hills. It is as impressionistic in depicting a fleeting moment in time as *The Coming Storm* (Fig. 3), dated 1918, and even more loosely painted. Here, in a grassy field still shining in the sunlight, a flock of sheep flee the threatening storm building up in the background. In this picture the artist's brushstroke is loose and bold, forming a part of the texture of the painting. But though the artist manipulates the transitory effects of color and light, the forms are still solid, creating, even in this small painting, a simple monumentality. It differs from French Impressionism too, in that the French masters seldom painted nature in such a dark and lowering mood.

The impact on Fournier of the Hoosier Impressionists is most clearly evident in an untitled painting of a South Bend scene (Fig. 4). Painted with the loose brush of the Impressionists, and incorporating their dazzling light effects, it shows an autumn landscape with South Bend's Michigan Avenue bridge half hidden by a curtain of golden leaves and shrubbery. The gold of the background colors contrasts strongly with the cooler greens of the trees that still retain their summer foliage, and both green and gold are reflected in the small stream that flows beneath the bridge and trickles over the shallow falls in the foreground. In portraying the effects of intense daylight in strong tonal contrasts, the painting is an example of what Gerdts has called the "glare aesthetic" typical of American Impressionist and Post-Impressionist painting.[16]

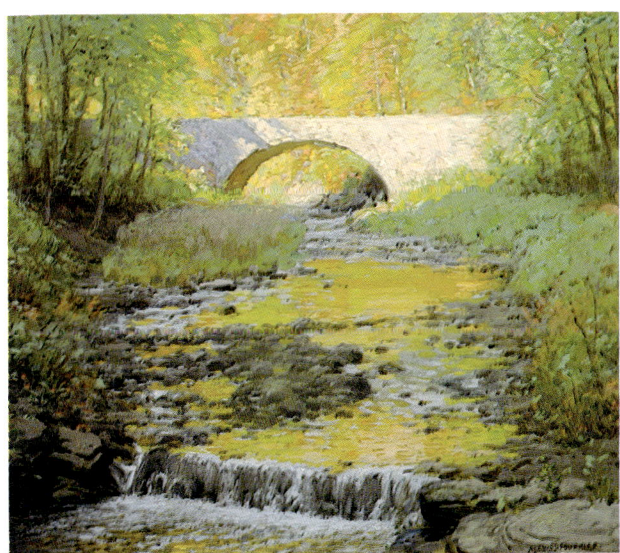

Fig. 4. Untitled: South Bend Scene in Autumn.

The glorious color and transparent light that is unique to a North American autumn began, during the Indiana years, to engage Fournier's major attention, just as the fresh and subtle colors of Spring had been preferred in an earlier period. *Autumn Glory, Golden Harvest, Autumn Woods* and *Purple and Gold*, the latter portraying the copper beeches of southern Indiana, are the titles of some Brown County paintings whose present whereabouts are unknown. We can, however, get

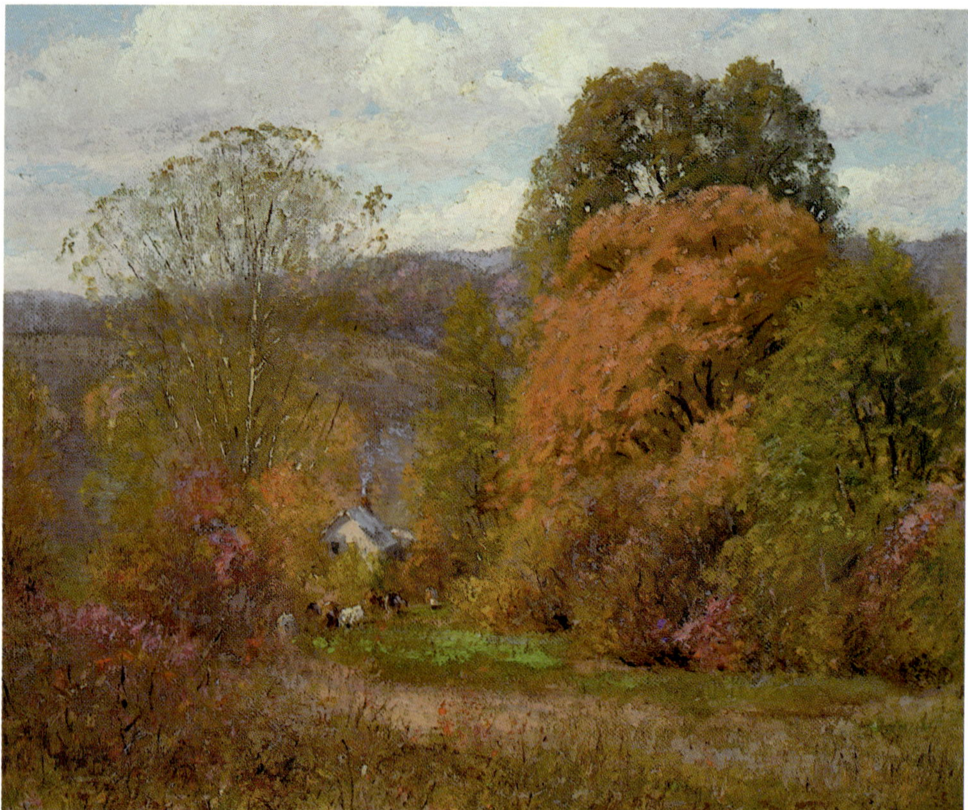

Fig. 5. Autumn in Brown County.

a sense of their mood and atmosphere from *Autumn in Brown County* (Fig. 5), which is typical of Fournier's Brown County paintings, tinged as it is with the rich colors of early Fall. The time is still early in the season, however, for though the silver birches have already shed their leaves, the foliage still clings to the other valley trees. Their green mantles, however, have now been exchanged for the variegated ones of autumn. They, as well as the half hidden farmhouse and the few grazing animals beside it, are revealed in the clear atmosphere and golden light of an Indian summer day.

A similar sense of tranquility pervades *Early Autumn Morning* (Fig. 6), another Brown County scene in which cows graze on the banks of a shallow stream winding into the distance. A cottage or cottages, hidden in the distance, emit thin curls of blue smoke which rise above the trees into the thin air. The smoke is all that attests to the presence of human habitation, but it is enough. Like *Autumn in Brown County*, this painting reflects a sense of peace and of the harmony in nature of all aspects of life. In this sense both paintings reflect the subjective poetry of the Barbizon aesthetic though the brushwork is looser, the colors more vivid and the atmosphere brighter and clearer.

Though he apparently preferred them, Fournier did not limit himself only to autumnal scenes during his Indiana years. A South Bend winter landscape painted in 1930, called *Winter Oak* (Fig. 7), is painted with the loose brush of the Impressionists and even with their characteristic high horizon line and natural light. The single oak, standing sentinel in a snowy meadow and still clinging to its dead leaves, injects a note of drama, of survival, not usually present in the canvases of the French Impressionists. Moreover, in its solid form, undissolved in the haze of atmosphere, it clearly reveals its American locale. Less dramatic, perhaps, though equally impressionistic in its suggestion of a transient moment in nature is *Springtime in Brown County* (Fig. 8). The painting captures an early spring day when the trees are in blossom and the waters run swift and cold in the shallow creek beds. Even the rustic cabins absorb the greens and blues of the landscape around them as those colors reflect and distill the cool light of the day.

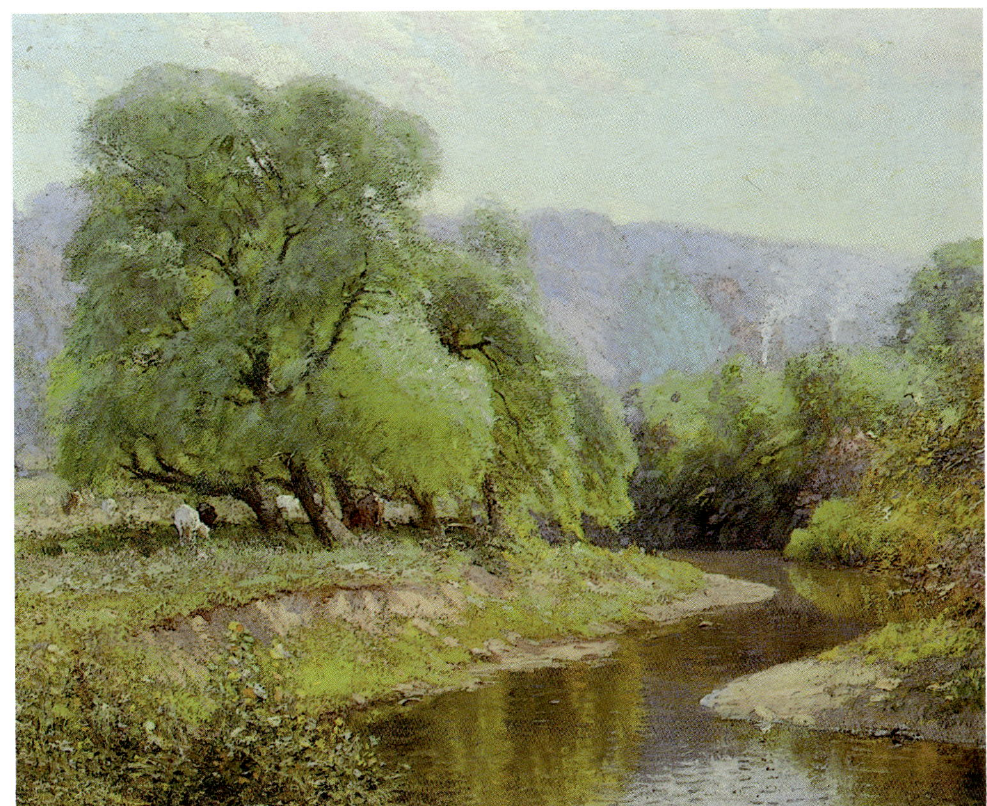

Fig. 6. Early Autumn Morning.

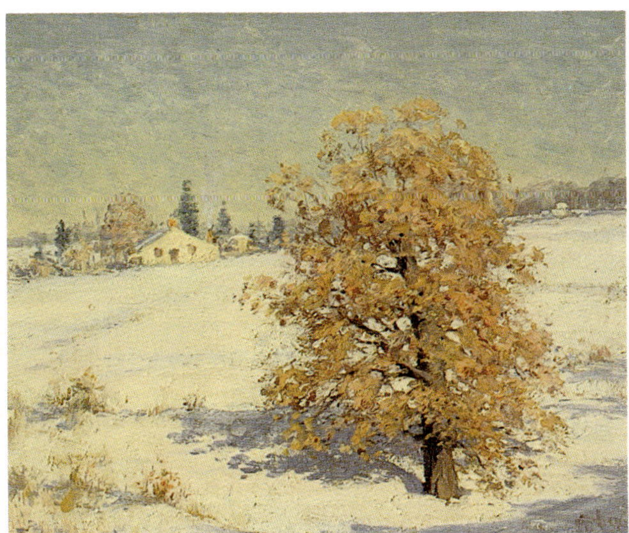

Fig. 7. Winter Oak.

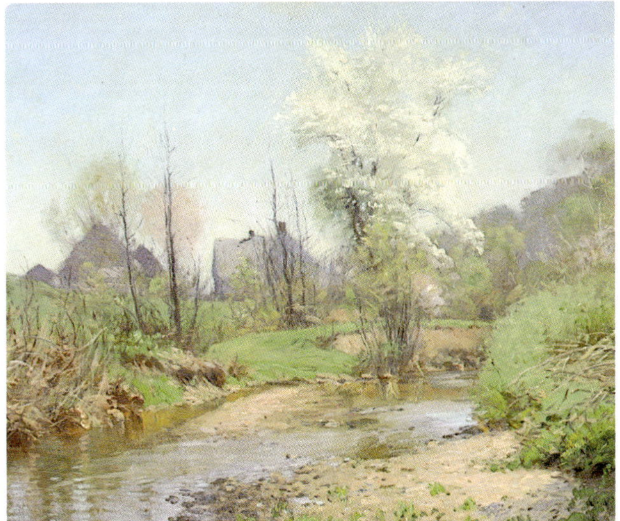

Fig. 8. Springtime in Brown County.

Fournier's Indiana paintings were much admired by public and critics alike and by the early 1930's he had established himself as an important member of the Brown County group. In 1934 he was awarded the Meek Memorial Prize for his landscape *Between Showers*, exhibited in the Tenth Annual Hoosier Salon in the Marshall Field Galleries in Chicago, and in 1940 *Wet and Windy* won the Vance Memorial Award, established by the Brown County Art Galleries Association in memory of Frederick Nelson Vance, a Brown County artist who had died young.

Fournier and his colleagues in the Hoosier school of landscape painting differ from the American landscapists of the nineteenth century, particularly the Hudson River School, in that, though both sought to memorialize the American scene, the Indiana artists did so in a more direct, less dramatic vein, than the earlier painters. They chose serenity above excitement and a sense of the tranquility of nature as opposed to its awesome and theatrical aspects. Perhaps in this way they reflected a transition from the earlier view of rural America as an uncorrupted wilderness offering a moral and redemptive haven for those who sought escape from urban evil and corruption, to a more secular view in which the countryside offered merely repose and peace. In this respect the pastoral but domesticated scenery in Brown County, Indiana, resembled the picturesque and rustic landscape that attracted the "Men of 1830" to the Forest of Fontainbleau and the village of Barbizon. With their technique further refined and influenced by the French artists who found in Etretat and Giverny the essence of the rural scene, the Brown County painters, as was said of Theodore C. Steele, "learned in Europe only a better way of expressing Indiana."[17]

On January 27, 1937 Cora Fournier died at her home in South Bend. A woman of forceful and determined character as well as of some social standing in her community, she had actively promoted her husband's work. She had also followed him happily to the art colonies of Brown County, East Aurora, Provincetown, Massachusetts, and on the many painting trips the restless Fournier was always undertaking. Though he moved to East Aurora on a year-round basis in 1938, Fournier maintained the family residence in South Bend until 1941, after which the City Directories no longer list him as a resident.

Fournier took with him from his Indiana experience, a lightened palette, an appreciation for the texture of brush stroke and paint on the canvas, even in a finished "studio piece," and the memory of the Indiana communities—South Bend and Brown County—that had honored and rewarded his work. Except for excursions of gradually decreasing frequency, the small bungalow in East Aurora with the apple trees growing through the roof, now became his permanent home until his own death some ten years later.

NOTES TO CHAPTER 8: With the Hoosier Impressionists

1. Quoted in Judy Oberhausen, *Impressionist Trends in Hoosier Painting,* South Bend Art Center, South Bend, Ind., 1979, p. 10.
2. See Selma N. Steele, *The House of the Singing Winds; The Life and Work of T. C. Steele*, Indianapolis, Indiana Historical Society, 1966.
3. Adolph Robert Shulz, "The Story of the Brown County Art Colony," *Indiana Magazine of History*, Vol. 31, No. 4, December 1935, p. 282-289.
4. South Bend *News-Times*, July 29, 1934.
5. Ibid.
6. The quotations are from William H. Gerdts, *American Impressionism*, Henry Art Gallery, University of Washington, Seattle, 1980, p. 104. Chapter 15, "Regional Impressionism," contains an excellent discussion of the Hoosier Impressionists. See also Gerdts' essay, *Indiana Influence, The Golden Age of Indiana Landscape Painting*, Fort Wayne Museum of Art, April 8 - June 24, 1984.
7. Gerdts, *American Impressionism*, p. 104.
8. Ibid.
9. Ibid.
10. George Scheuer, "Artists in Brown Colony Approach 'School' Ideal," *South Bend News-Times*, July 29, 1934.
11. Nicholas Brewer, *Trails of a Paintbrush*, Boston, Christopher Publishing House, 1938, p. 172.
12. The South Bend City Directories list Fournier as a resident from 1923 to 1941.
13. *South Bend Tribune*, November 20, 1927.
14. Ibid. December 25, 1927.
15. Ibid.
16. Gerdts, *American Impressionism*, p. 17.
17. Ibid., p. 106.

Chapter 9 Later Years

Fournier was in his early seventies when he moved back to East Aurora and his most productive years were now behind him. Though Elbert and Alice Hubbard were long since gone—twenty-three years had passed since their tragic deaths—and the Roycroft enterprises about to be sold, old friends still lived in East Aurora and the environs of the pleasant village were still as scenic and unspoiled as ever. Moreover, though Fournier had genuinely admired Hubbard for his energy and vision, perhaps he welcomed the slower pace and quieter atmosphere that now prevailed in East Aurora.

He was ready for that slower pace, for though still vigorous, the years were beginning to tell. For many decades he had worked hard in his profession, producing on the average more than forty finished oils a year, in addition to innumerable drawings and sketches, and many monotypes. Though gregarious and full of fun, he was essentially a modest man who shied from the sort of competition major public exhibitions frequently entailed. His paintings were, of course, exhibited but Fournier seldom initiated their showing, preferring to wait for the invitations to come to him. As his friend, Nicholas Brewer, commented, "Fournier seldom sent anything to art exhibitions. Why, I do not know; nor did he court the acquaintance of prominent artists, men who could place him in the front ranks—a thing which I urged him to do."[1] Fournier realized too that his canvases represented a style very much out of official favor by the late 1930's. European avant garde trends such as Cubism, Futurism, Expressionism, Surrealism and other abstract and semi-abstract ways of painting were admired by the cognoscenti, and lyrical paintings of nature were considered a relic of the past. Indeed, America's own contribution to twentieth century art, Abstract Expressionism, was hovering in the wings, about to emerge in the 1940's and to dominate American painting for at least the next generation.

Nevertheless, Fournier did continue to exhibit, generally in a few galleries where he knew he would reach a receptive audience, and where, frequently, he would speak. At one of them he delivered himself of his personal opinion about the "latter day fantastics," as he called the currently fashionable abstract trends. "A wealthy American had the portrait of his very handsome wife painted by a . . . futurist in Paris," he recounted. The canvas was rolled up and placed in their luggage, but when they left (France) they were stopped at the frontier and the painting removed for examination by Customs officers. The next day they were permitted to continue their journey with the comment, "we have had the thing examined by our experts. They know that it is a plan for a new American motor,

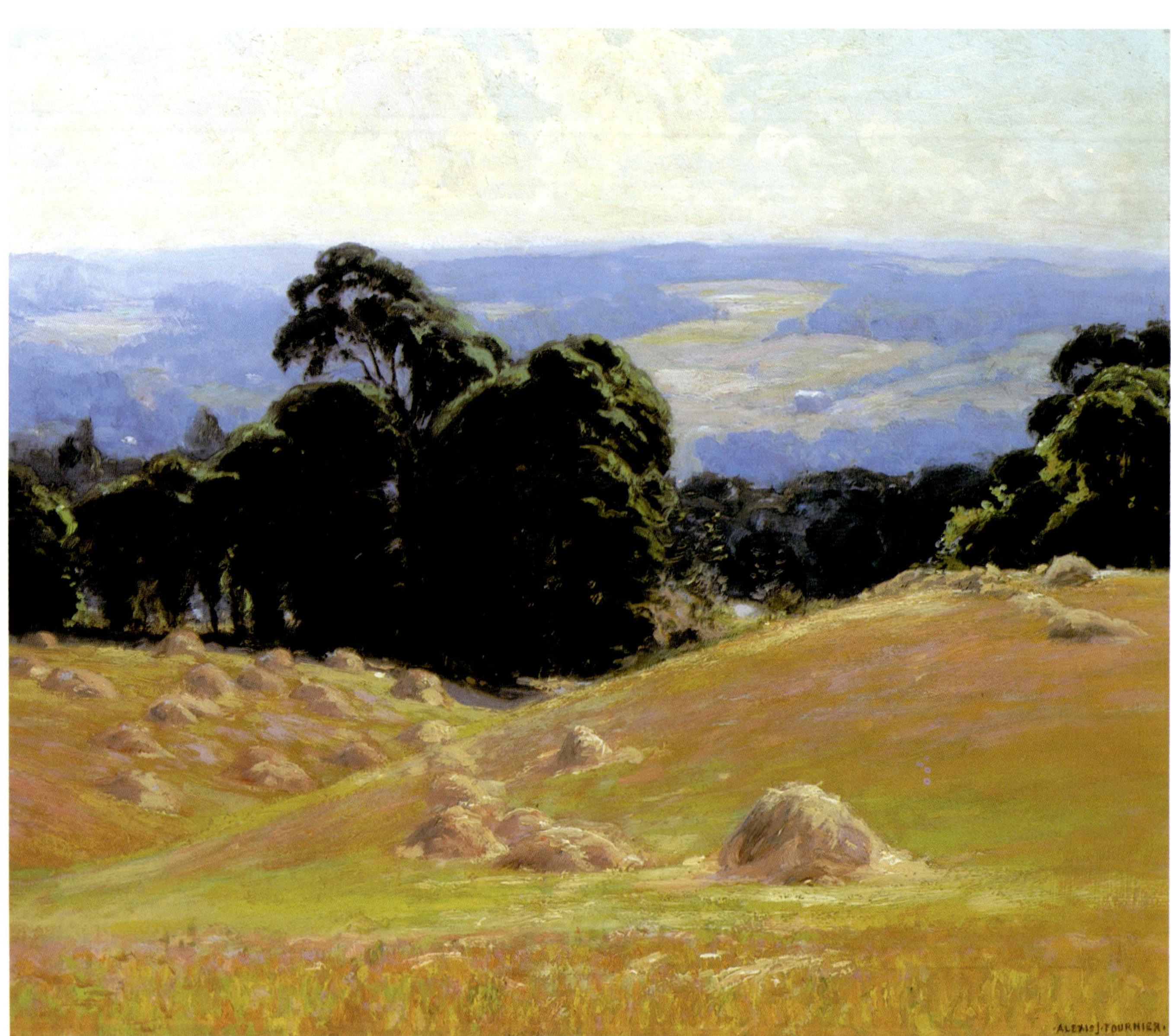

Fig. 1. Over the Hills at Harvest Time.

all right, but they also know the darn thing will never work."[2]

In the spring of 1937, shortly after the death of his wife, Cora, Fournier showed, at the Chicago Art Galleries, a painting entitled *Over the Hills at Harvest Time* (Fig. 1) which is a prime example of the artist's mature work. It is a September scene, where we look down past a golden harvest field into a broad valley stretching into the blue and hazy distance. A row of trees in the center of the composition divides the picture in a loose, informal way, into foreground and background space, into the easily comprehensible reality of the here and now, and the mystery of the infinite space beyond. The color is typically Fournier, with the edges of the dark green trees tipped by the gentle glow of sunlight. The painting is a distillation of the visual experience of nature, rich, bountiful and peaceful, transformed by the artist's brush into a symphony of green, gold and blue.

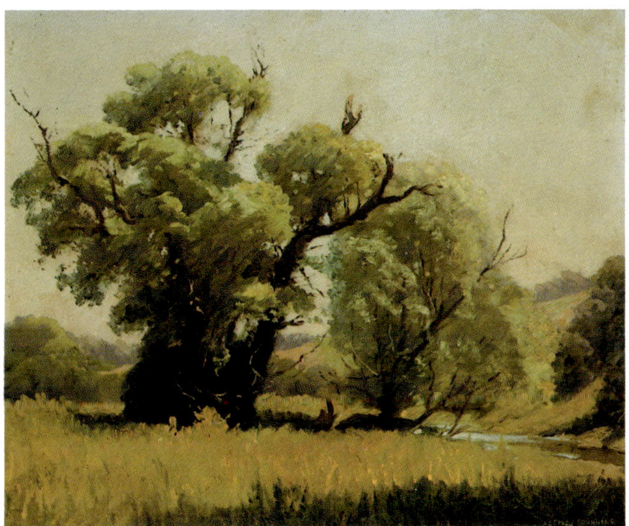
Fig. 2. Willows.

The same almost mystic sense of nature's presence as a force larger than the individual experience is evoked in *Willows* (Fig. 2), undated, but probably painted about the same time as *Over the Hills at Harvest Time*. Again, an infinite variety of greens, in all shades and combinations, is used to portray two willow trees, one ancient and half denuded, raising a few bare branches to the sky. The trees cling to a shallow, barely visible stream that borders the grassy field from which they rise. Ascending high above the horizon and the distant, rolling hills, the willows assume heroic proportions as they stand, like nature's own monuments, beneath the blue dome of heaven.

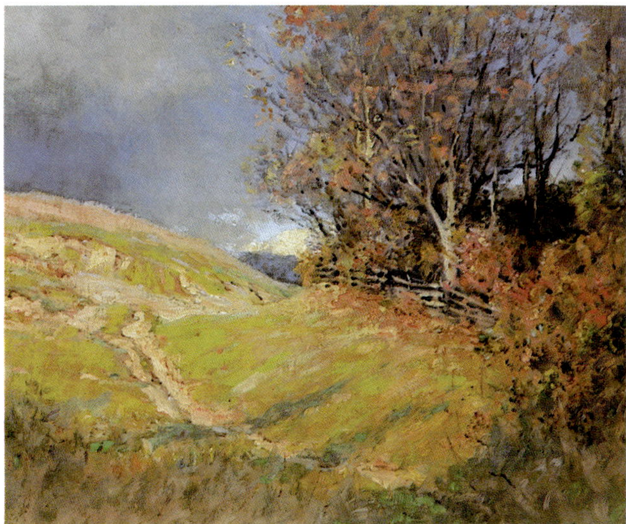
Fig. 3. November Arrives.

Though it is difficult to arrange chronologically the paintings Fournier himself left undated (and from the 1920's until his death he rarely dated a canvas), one can still place the pictures in certain broad categories. *November Arrives* (Fig. 3), though quite different in mood from the two paintings just discussed, was probably painted during the 1930's either in East Aurora or Brown County, Indiana. Like many of his pictures of this period, the painting depicts nature in less than a kind and pleasing mood. Sunlight fitfully illuminates an unkempt field, and shadows of unseen shrubs and trees darken the foreground space. Behind a low rail fence, bare trees cling to a few rusty leaves, as a chill wind rustles their branches. The storm clouds that rise in the distance threaten to engulf the small clear patch of sky on the horizon and to shower the sad, half naked trees and untidy meadow. We are aware here not so much of nature's smiling charity as of its chill and awesome power.

One of the few paintings of this period that *is* dated is *The Garden at Evening* (Fig. 4), the only picture that the artist painted in the summer of 1938. He was still lonely following Cora's death, and perhaps the just completed sale of the Roycroft enterprises to a religious organization further dampened his spirits, terminating, as it so definitely did, a happy and productive period in his life. Moreover, he rationalized, he didn't like painting in the summer, "particularly this summer.

Everything's a dirty green and furnishes little imagination for painting."[3] Nevertheless the painting is full of soft and subtle color, revealing little of the artist's melancholy mood at this time. Beyond the colorful hollyhocks and climbing roses in the

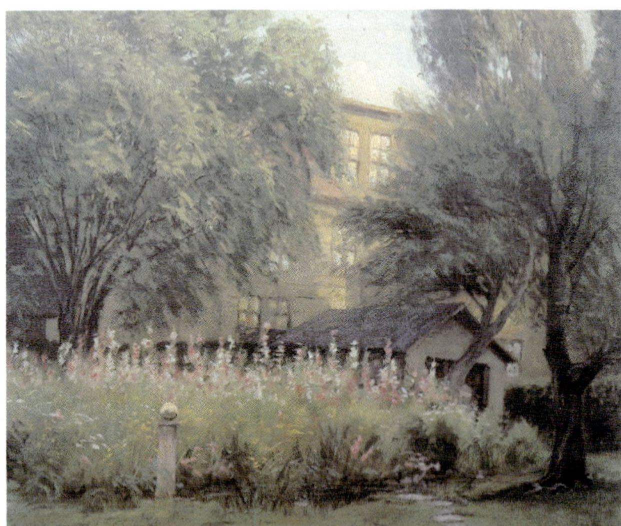

Fig. 4. The Garden at Evening.

garden beside the "bungle house," a garden Fournier himself carefully tended, the building housing the Roycroft book bindery is bathed in the mellowness of vanishing sunlight, a tone and mood the artist specially favored.

On October 1, 1944, at the age of seventy-nine, Fournier married for the third time. The new Mrs. Fournier was Coral T. Lawrence, a widow whom Fournier had known for many years. She had come to East Aurora in 1903, the same year as Fournier himself, and had been employed as a writer for the Hubbard publications. She survived him at his death a little over three years later.

In the final years of his life Fournier continued to paint in and around East Aurora, particularly near Cazenovia Creek. Generally, however, he was content enough to putter about the "bungle house" and to entertain the large circle of friends, acquaintances and newspaper reporters who increasingly dropped in for a friendly chat or for the reminiscences he brought forth between long puffs on his pipe. He was playing elder statesman of the art world and enjoying the role thoroughly. Ever as ready to laugh at himself as at the vagaries of the world, he regaled his visitors with anecdotes, opinions and memories.

His memories went back, indeed, halfway into our national history. A covered wagon had sheltered him in his infancy but the atomic age had become a reality before his death. Andrew Johnson, who had been Lincoln's vice president, was in the White House when he was born and Harry Truman lived there when he died. The western frontier had vanished and in its place was a new frontier of scientific and technological discoveries. Though the United States had emerged from mid-nineteenth century provincialism to twentieth century superpower, confidence in its national destiny had been replaced by anxiety and the shadow of the mushroom cloud darkened the imagination.

Fournier's art reflected none of this however. Deliberately clinging to an earlier vision of America as a pastoral paradise, he represented a deep and continuing current in American art, namely a reverence for the world of nature as translated through the hand and eye of a poet. He believed passionately in the validity of the visual experience, and though keenly aware of the importance of balanced form, composition, texture and color, he did not believe that in and of themselves they should be the subject of a painter's canvas. Responding at one time to a visitor's query as to whether he had ever had an experience similar to that of a modern artist, who had received $999 for a painting rather than $666, from the accident of having the painting exhibited upside down, Fournier, his dark eyes twinkling, replied that he had received as much as $3,000 for a painting by having it hung right side up.[4]

Meanwhile, he continued to show his paintings, "selling his papers" as he called it, at the annual Hoosier Salons, at the John Herron Art Institute in Indianapolis, in Chicago, South Bend, East Aurora and Buffalo. By 1942 his paintings had also been exhibited in England, Australia, Belgium, Germany, and, of course, in France.[5]

On the morning of January 16, 1948, on his way to the corner mailbox, Fournier apparently suffered a stroke and fell on the icy sidewalk in front of his house in East Aurora. He became unconscious late that night and was taken to Our Lady of Victory Hospital in Lackawanna, N.Y. He died four days later, on January 20, 1948, at the age of 82.

The obituaries that appeared in the Minneapolis, St. Paul, South Bend, Buffalo and East Aurora newspapers, as well as the *New York Times*, mentioned Fournier's representation at the Paris Salons of 1894-95, 1899-1900 and 1901, and the public institutions in the United States that held examples of his work. They also listed him as a member in the American Art Association of Paris; founding member of the Minneapolis Art League; member of the Chicago Art Galleries Association, the Society of Western Artists, the National Arts Club of New York, the Cliff Dweller's Club of Chicago, the Buffalo Society of Artists, the Art Klan of Toledo, Ohio, and the Attic Club of Minneapolis. All of the newspaper accounts took special note of Fournier's major work, the series of Homes and Haunts of the Barbizon Masters. They called Alexis Fournier himself "the last of the Barbizon painters." It was an epitaph that would no doubt have pleased him well.

NOTES TO CHAPTER 9: Later Years

1. Nicholas R. Brewer, *Trails of a Paintbrush*, Boston, Christopher Publishing House, 1938, p. 169.
2. *East Aurora Advertiser*, January 1, 1942.
3. *East Aurora Advertiser*, August 8, 1938.
4. *East Aurora Advertiser*, January 1, 1942.
5. Ibid. A photograph in the artist's photo album shows a beach in Samoa, behind which, half hidden in the shrubbery, is a house that is labeled, in the artist's handwriting, "My studio in Samoa." Perhaps he attended the exhibition in Australia where his paintings were shown and stopped in Samoa for a few weeks on the way. No date is mentioned for either the trip to Australia, or the place of exhibition there, or for the visit to Samoa.

Selected Bibliography

Baldwin, Laura, "Minneapolis Artists at the World's Fair," *Literary Northwest*, Vol. 2, no. 4, January, 1893, pp. 152-153.

Bermingham, Peter, *American Art in a Barbizon Mood*, Washington, D.C.: Smithsonian Institution Press, 1975.

Blegen, Theodore, *Minnesota, A History of the State*. Minneapolis: University of Minnesota Press, 1975.

Boe, Roy A., *The Development of Art Consciousness in Minneapolis of the Problems of the Indigenous Artist*, M.A. Thesis, University of Minnesota, March, 1974.

Brewer, Nicholas R., *Trails of a Paintbrush*. Boston: Christopher Publishing House, 1938.

Buffalo Evening News.

Burnet, Mary O., *Art and Artists of Indiana*. New York: The Century Company, 1921.

Caffin, Charles H., *American Masters of Painting*. New York: Doubleday, Page & Company, 1902.

Cathers, David M., *Furniture of the American Arts and Crafts Movement: Stickley and Roycroft Mission Oak*. New York: New American Library, 1981.

Clark, Robert Hudson, et al., *The Arts and Crafts Movement in America*. Princeton, N.J.: Princeton University Press, 1972.

Coen, Rena Neumann, *Painting and Sculpture in Minnesota 1820-1914*, Minneapolis: University of Minnesota Press, 1976.

Corn, Wanda M., *The Color of Mood: American Tonalism, 1880-1910*. San Francisco: M. H. De Young and Memorial Museum, 1972.

Crumrine, Janice C., "Elbert Hubbard: Pragmatic Romanticist," *The Roycroft Movement: A Spirit for Today*. Buffalo: Burchfield Center, State University of New York at Buffalo, 1979.

East Aurora Advertiser.

Eldredge, Charles C., *The Arcadian Landscape: Nineteenth Century American Painters in Italy*. Lawrence, Kansas: University of Kansas Museum of Art, 1972.

Flagg, Maurice I., ed., "Who is Who in Minnesota Art Annals, A Little Journey to the Home of a Well Known

Artist in East Aurora, N.Y.," *The Minnesotan*, Vol. 1, No. 6, Jan. 1916, pp. 15-18.

Fournier, Alexis J., *The Homes of the Men of 1830*. New York: William Schaus, 1910. With an Introduction by Herbert Waldron Faulkner.

Fox, Austin M., and Roelofs, Miriam Hubbard, *Alexis Jean Fournier, A Barbizon in East Aurora*, Burchfield Center, State University of New York at Buffalo, 1979.

Gerdts, William H., *American Impressionism*, Seattle, Washington: Henry Art Gallery, University of Washington, 1980.

Gerdts, William H., "Post-Impressionist Landscape Painting in America," *Art and Antiques*, Vol. 6, no. 4 (July-August, 1983).

Gerdts, William H.; Sweet, Diana Dimodica; and Preato, Robert R., *Tonalism, an American Experience*, New York: Grand Central Galleries, 1982.

Goodrich, Lloyd, *Albert P. Ryder*, N.Y.: George Braziller, Inc., 1959.

Hamilton, Charles F., *As Bees in Honey Drown: Elbert Hubbard and the Roycrofters*. South Brunswick, N.J.: A. S. Barnes, 1973.

Harris, Neil, *The Artist in American Society: The Formative Years*, 1790-1860. New York: George Braziller, 1966.

Heilbron, Bertha L., "Making a Motion Picture in 1848," *Minnesota History*, Vol. 17, Nos. 2, 3 and 4 (June, September, December, 1936).

Heilbron, Bertha L., *The Valley of the Mississippi, Illustrated by Henry Lewis*. St. Paul: Minnesota Historical Society, 1967.

Herbert, Robert L., *Barbizon Revisited*. San Francisco: California Palace of the Legion of Honor, 1962.

Heacock, Lee F., editor, *The Buffalo Artists' Register*. Vol. 1, 1926. "A Monotype Party at Alexis Fournier's," pp. 105-108.

Hunt, William Morris, *W. M. Hunt's Talks on Art*. Boston: Series 1, H. O. Houghton & Company, 1875.

Le Gallienne, Richard, *October Vagabonds*. New York: Mitchell Kennerley, 1910.

Lane, Albert, *Elbert Hubbard and His Work*. Worcester, Massachusetts: Blanchard Press, 1901.

Ludwig, Coy L. *The Arts & Crafts Movement in New York State 1890's-1920's*, Hamilton, N.Y.: The Gallery Association of New York State, Inc., 1983.

Meixner, Laura L., *An International Episode: Millet, Monet and Their North American Counterparts*. Memphis, Tennessee: The Dixon Gallery and Gardens, 1982.

Minneapolis Journal.

Minor, Petronius, "The Work of Alexis Jean Fournier," *The Buffalo Art Journal*, VII, 7, October, 1925, pp. 32-37.

The Minnesotan, "Who is Who in Minnesota Art Annals: A Little Journey to the Home of a Well Known Artist in East Aurora, N.Y." January 1916, pp. 15-18.

Novak, Barbara, *American Painting of the Nineteenth Century*. New York: Praeger, 1969.

Novotny, Fritz, *Painting and Sculpture in Europe, 1780 to 1880*. New York: Penguin Books, 1978.

Oberhausen, Judy, *Impressionistic Trends in Hoosier Painting*. South Bend, Indiana: Art Center, Inc., South Bend, Indiana, 1979.

Oberhausen, Judy, *The Work of George Ames Aldrich, L. Clarence Ball and Alexis Jean Fournier in South Bend Collections*. South Bend, Indiana: Art Center, Inc., South Bend, Indiana, 1982.

Parkhurst, Thomas Shrewsbury, "The Art of Alexis Jean Fournier," *Fine Arts Journal* (March, 1916). Vol. 34, pp. 128-133.

Ramsey, Ronald, L. M., "John Scott Bradstreet and the Minneapolis Crafthouse," *The Tiller*, Vol. 1, no. 4 (March-April, 1983).

Richardson, Edgar Preston, *Painting in America, From 1502 to the Present*. New York: Thomas Crowell Co., 1965.

Rose, E. J. "Alexis J. Fournier," *Brush and Pencil*, Vol. 4, August 1899, pp. 243-247.

Scheuer, George, "Artists in Brown County Approach 'School' Ideal," *South Bend News-Times*. July 29, 1934.

Sellin, David, *Americans in Brittany and Normandy, 1860-1910*. Phoenix, Arizona: Phoenix Art Museum, 1983.

Shulz, Adolph Robert, "The Story of the Brown County Art Colony," *Indiana Magazine of History*, Vol. 31, no. 4 (December 1935).

Shutter, M.D. (ed.), *Progressive Men of Minnesota*. Minneapolis: The Minneapolis Journal, 1879.

Smith, Charles Sprague, *Barbizon Days: Millet-Corot-Rousseau-Barye*. New York: A Wessels Company, 1902.

Steele, Selma N., et al., *The House of the Singing Winds: The Life and Work of T. C. Steele*. Indianapolis: Indiana Historical Society, 1966.

South Bend News-Times.

South Bend Tribune.

Sweeney, J. Gray, *American Paintings at the Tweed Museum of Art*. Duluth, Minnesota: Tweed Museum of Art and Glensheen, University of Minnesota, Duluth, 1982.

Whittington-Eagan, Richard and Smerdon, Geoffrey. *In Quest of the Golden Boy: The Life and Letters of Richard LeGallienne*. Barre, Massachusetts: Barre Publishing Company, 1962.

Selected Exhibitions

1892 Minneapolis Industrial Exposition: Fournier Gallery

1893 Chicago Columbian Exposition: Cliff Dwellers' Panorama

1894 Paris Salon

1895 London, Crystal Palace

New York, National Academy of Design

Paris Salon

1896 New York, National Academy of Design

Minneapolis: Beard's Art House

1897 Minneapolis Art League, May 8 - 23.

New York, National Academy of Design

Chicago Art Institute, Annual Exhibition of Western Artists, Nov. 2 - Dec. 12.

1898 Minneapolis Art League, April 27 - May 11.

Boston, J. Eastman Chase Gallery, Spring, One-man exhibition

Omaha, Trans-Mississippi and International Exposition, June 1 - Nov. 1

Detroit Art Museum, Dec. 20, 1898 - Jan. 15, 1899

1899 Paris Salon

Minneapolis Society of Fine Arts

Boston Art Club, February

Minneapolis Crafthouse, March 23 - 31

1900 Paris Salon

Minneapolis Society of Fine Arts, March

Cincinnati Art Museum: Special Fournier Exhibition, April 12 - May 13

Pennsylvania Academy of Art

1901 Paris Salon

London Crystal Palace

Paris, American Art Association, January

Minneapolis, Beard Art Gallery, January

Pittsburgh, Carnegie Institute, Nov. - Dec.

1902 Chicago Art Institute: Special Fournier Exhibition, Oct. 3 - 19

Chicago Art Institute: Chicago Ceramics Association Exhibition, with A. E. Albright, Oct. 5 - 31

Minneapolis Society of Fine Arts, Sept. 20 - Oct. 12

Detroit Museum of Art, November

1903 New York, National Academy of Design

Toledo Museum of Art, Annual Exhibition of Western Artists, March 7 - 27

Toledo Museum of Art, with A. E. Albright, Oct. 5 - 31

1904 Minneapolis, Louis Sweet's Photographic Studio, January

St. Louis World's Fair Exposition, April 30 - Dec. 1

Buffalo, Albright Art Gallery, 11th Annual Exhibition, Buffalo Society of Artists, May 2 - 14

1905 Detroit Museum of Art, March

Minneapolis Society of Fine Arts, November

Minneapolis, J. A. Clow Gallery, November 15 - December 15

Albany, N.Y. Art Museum Association Exhibition, State Capitol, Dec. 18 - 30

1906 Chicago, Anderson Art Company Galleries, January

Minneapolis, Louis Sweet's Photographic Studio, January

New York, National Academy of Design

Detroit Museum of Art: One Artist Exhibition, March 8 - April 5

1907 Minneapolis, J. A. Clow Gallery, February - March

Buffalo, Albright Art Gallery, Thumb Box Exhibition, Buffalo Society of Artists, Nov. 15

Brown County, Indiana, Indiana Art Association Exhibition of Western Artists

1909 Washington, D.C., Corcoran Gallery of Art, Winter

Minneapolis Handicraft Guild, February 1 - 15

Buffalo, Albright Art Gallery, Spring Exhibition of Buffalo Society of Artists, April

Boston Art Club, January

1910 New York, Schaus Art Galleries: Homes of the Men of 1830, March 16 - April 16

1911 Detroit Art Museum, Homes of the Men of 1830, Jan. 10 - Feb. 1

Chicago Art Institute, Homes of the Men of 1830, July 18 - Aug. 15

Minneapolis Society of Fine Arts, Homes of the Men of 1830, October

St. Paul Institute, Homes of the Men of 1830, November

1912 Toledo Art Museum, Homes of the Men of 1830, May

1913 Toledo Art Museum, Exhibition of Society of Western Artists, Jan. 4 - 29

Buffalo, Albright Art Gallery, 19th Annual Exhibition, Buffalo Society of Artists, April 9 - 30

1914 Buffalo, Albright Art Gallery, Homes of the Men of 1830, Shown at 20th Annual Exhibition of Buffalo Society of Artists, April 15

1915 San Francisco, Panama Pacific International Exposition, Feb. 20 - Dec. 4

Toledo Art Museum, Two Person Exhibition with Paul Manship, December

1916 Buffalo, Broderick Galleries, Feb. 10 - March 1

Buffalo, Albright Art Gallery, 22nd Annual Exhibition, Buffalo Society of Artists, April 15

1917 Chicago Art Galleries, Artists' Guild Prize

Buffalo, Albright Art Gallery, 23rd Annual Exhibition, Buffalo Society of Artists, April 21

1918 Buffalo, Albright Art Gallery, 24th Annual Exhibition, Buffalo Society of Artists, April 10 - May 1

1919 Boston, Vose Gallery, March 3 - 15

Buffalo, Albright Art Gallery, 25th Annual Exhibition, Buffalo Society of Artists, March 10 - April 1

Minneapolis, Beard Art Gallery, April 13 - May 1

1920 Chicago Art Institute, One Artist Exhibition, Oct. 1920 - Jan. 1921

1921 Minneapolis, Beard Art Gallery, March

Minneapolis Institute of Arts

1922 Minneapolis, Beard Art Gallery, March 13 - 31

1923 South Bend, Progress Club, Spring

1924 Minneapolis, Beard Art Gallery, March

1926 Buffalo, Albright Art Gallery, 32nd Annual Exhibition, Buffalo Society of Artists, Jan. 30 - Feb. 17

1927 Buffalo, Albright Art Gallery, 33rd Annual Exhibition, Buffalo Society of Artists, Jan. 29 - Feb. 14

Chicago Art Galleries, October

South Bend, First National Bank, Dec. 1927 - Jan. 1928

1928 South Bend, Progress Club, Sept. - Oct.

1930 Minneapolis, Moore and Scriver Art Galleries, April 1 - 8

Minneapolis, Beard Art Gallery, April

South Bend, National and Union Bank, December

1932 Buffalo, Albright Art Gallery, 38th Annual Exhibition, Buffalo Society of Artists, Feb. 28 - March 21

1934 Chicago, Marshall Field Galleries, Annual Hoosier Salon, Meek Memorial Prize, January

Buffalo, Hotel Statler, 40th Annual Exhibition, Buffalo Society of Artists, April 3 - 15

1937 Chicago Art Galleries, May 2 - 15

1939 East Aurora, East Aurora Artists Association Exhibition, June

1940 Nashville, Indiana, Brown County Artists Association, Frederick Nelson Vance Award, September

1941 East Aurora Free Library, Oct. 26 - Nov. 1

1941-8 Annual Hoosier Salons

1942 Indianapolis, John Herron Art Museum, Indiana Artists' Annual Exhibition, Also 1946, 1947, 1948

1943 Buffalo, Arthur Kowalski Galleries, Fifty Year Retrospective Exhibition, Feb. 14 - 28

South Bend, Progress Club, One Artist Exhibition

1944 Youngstown, Ohio, Butler Art Institute, New Year's Show, January

Chicago Art Galleries Exhibition

1945 Buffalo, Statler Hotel, Exhibition of Buffalo Society of Artists, March 31 - April 8

1946 Indianapolis, John Herron Art Museum, Indiana Artists Annual

1947 Buffalo, Statler Hotel, Exhibition of Buffalo Society of Artists, April 5 - 13

Indianapolis, John Herron Art Museum, Indiana Artists Annual

1948 Indianapolis, John Herron Art Museum, Indiana Artists Annual

South Bend, Progress Club, One Artist Exhibition

Chicago Art Galleries Association

1959 Buffalo, Sisti Gallery, Memorial Exhibition, Sept. 27 - Oct. 10

1979 Buffalo, Burchfield Center: Western New York Forum for American Art, State University College at Buffalo; *A Barbizon in East Aurora*, Jan. 24 - Mar. 11

South Bend, Art Center Inc. *Impressionist Trends in Hoosier Painting*, Nov. 10 - Dec. 30

1982 South Bend, Art Center Inc., *The Work of George Ames Aldrich, L. Clarence Ball and Alexis Jean Fournier in South Bend Collections*, Sept. 19 - Oct. 24

Chronology

1865	July 4. Alexis Jean Joseph Fournier born in St. Paul, Minnesota. First child of Isaie and Annie Marie Mathilde Fournier, recently arrived from Longueiul, near Montreal, Canada.
1866	January. Fournier family leaves St. Paul in covered wagon to live temporarily in Fond-du-Lac, Wisconsin.
1877-78	Alexis goes to school at a religious academy in Milwaukee.
1878-79	Odd jobs in Milwaukee.
1879	Returns to Minneapolis. Works in Chicago on mural decorations for Potter Palmer home.
c.1880-83	Works as a sign painter in Minneapolis.
c.1885	Employed as stage scenery painter in Minneapolis.
1885-87	Early work as landscape painter.
1886	Instruction in art under Douglas Volk, first director of Minneapolis School of Art.
1887	April 26. Marries Emma Fricke of Pine Island, Minnesota.
1888	Birth of daughter, Grace.
1889	Birth of son, Paul.
1891	Joins H. Jay Smith's exploring expedition to Indian Cliff Dwellers country of Colorado and New Mexico as official artist of party.
1893	Exhibits Cliff Dwellers panorama at Chicago World's Columbian Exposition. Fall. First trip to France. Enrolls at Académie Julian, Paris, under Jean Paul Laurens and Benjamin Constant.
1894	First Paris Salon Exhibition.
1895	Second Paris Salon Exhibition. Fall. Returns to Minneapolis.
1896	Fall. Leaves for second trip to France.
1897	Spring. Returns to Minneapolis.

1898	April 10. Sets out for Boston, then leaves for third trip to France. Fall. Returns to Minneapolis.
1899	May. Leaves on fourth trip to France, this time with wife and children. Family settles at Auvers-sur-Oise. Third Paris Salon exhibition.
1900	Fourth Paris Salon exhibition. Fall. Rents studio at 18 Impasse du Maine, Paris. December. Emma Fournier and children return to Minneapolis. It is likely that Fournier either accompanied them home or visited them in early 1901, leaving shortly thereafter for his fifth trip to France.
1901	January 27. Fire at Minneapolis home. Many studies and sketches lost. May. Fifth Paris Salon exhibition. May. Arrives in Venice for visit of several months with the artist Herbert Waldron Faulkner as his companion. July. Travels to Rome. August. Returns to Paris after leisurely trip through Switzerland. November 17. Returns to Minneapolis.
1902	Studio at 719 Hennepin Avenue, Minneapolis. Association with John Scott Bradstreet and Minneapolis Crafthouse. Active in Minneapolis Art League. October 3 - 19. At special exhibition at Chicago Art Institute, renews acquaintanceship with Elbert Hubbard, founder of Roycroft Arts and Crafts community in East Aurora, N.Y. December. In East Aurora to supervise reinstallation of art gallery.
1903	April. Meets Hubbard again at Chicago Art Institute. June 1. Moves to East Aurora on part-time basis. Until 1921 Fournier divides his time between Minneapolis in winter and East Aurora in summer. Becomes "artist-in-residence" at Roycroft community. November. Working in Minneapolis studio.
1904	Builds house at 54 Walnut Street, East Aurora.
c.1906	Rents small studio near Lee, Massachusetts.
1907	June. Leaves on sixth trip to France to sketch the Homes and Haunts of the Barbizon masters. Settles again at Auvers-sur-Oise but makes frequent trips to Barbizon where he is the guest of Carl Daubigny, son of the artist Charles François Daubigny.
1908	Spring. Returns to United States. October. Walking tour from East Aurora to New York City with Richard LeGallienne. Trip commemorated in Le Gallienne's book, *October Vagabonds*.
c.1909-10	Moves to small bungalow in East Aurora next door to first house but retains third floor studio in the latter.
1913	Spring. Seventh and last trip to France, accompanied by artist, Charles Francis Brown. Again guest of Carl Daubigny. End of year. Returns to United States.
1915	May 7. Elbert Hubbard and wife, Alice, die on torpedoed liner, Lusitania.
1921	Emma Fricke Fournier dies.
1922	May 9. Marries Cora May Ball of South Bend, Indiana, widow of L. Clarence Ball, Indiana landscape and still life painter. Moves to South Bend.
1922-30's	Spends winters in South Bend, summers in East Aurora. Travels also to artists colonies in Woodstock, N.Y., Provincetown, Mass. and Brown County, Ind.
1934	Wins Meek Memorial Prize in 10th Annual Hoosier Salon, Chicago.
1935	Paints in and near St. Petersburg, Florida.
1937	January 27. Cora May Ball Fournier dies in South Bend.
1938	Moves to East Aurora on year-round basis.
1940	Wins Frederick Nelson Vance Memorial Award of Brown County Art Gallery Association.
1944	October 1. Marries Coral T. Lawrence of East Aurora. A widow, she had been employed as a writer for the Hubbard publications.
1948	January 16. Suffers stroke and falls on icy pavement near home in East Aurora. January 20. Dies at Our Lady of Victory Hospital, Lackawanna, N.Y. at age 82.

Index

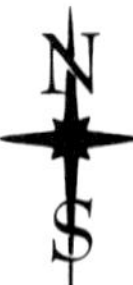

PUBLISHER'S NOTE

The text of this book was set in Century Expanded, a book face which belongs to the type faces called Modern. The book was composed by Media + Materials, St. Cloud, Minnesota, and printed by Park Press, Waite Park, Minnesota, using color separations by Northwoods Color, Minneapolis, Minnesota. This edition was bound in Holliston natural sailcloth book fabric by Midwest Editions, Minneapolis, Minnesota. The Midtec Lithofect Suede text paper was printed by full-color offset lithography. The book was designed by John Nevins and the book jacket was designed by Don Bruno.

In the Mainstream: The Art of Alexis Jean Fournier (1865-1948) was published on August 15, 1985, by North Star Press, St. Cloud, Minnesota.